Representation
and Redistricting
Issues

KF
4905
.A75
R43
1982

epresentation and Redistricting Issues

Edited by
Bernard Grofman
University of California, Irvine

Arend Lijphart
University of California,
    San Diego

Robert B. McKay
Aspen Institute for Humanistic
    Studies and Institute of
    Judicial Administration

Howard A. Scarrow
State University of New York
    at Stony Brook

Afterword by
Heinz Eulau

LexingtonBooks
D.C. Heath and Company
Lexington, Massachusetts
Toronto

321662

Tennessee Tech. Library
Cookeville. Tenn.

Library of Congress Cataloging in Publication Data

Main entry under title:
Representation and redistricting issues.

"The essays in this volume were initially presented at the 'Conference on Representation and Reapportionment Issues of the 1980s,' San Diego, California, June 11-15, 1980" —Pref.
Includes index.
1. Apportionment (Election law)—United States—Congresses.
2. Election districts—United States—Congresses. I. Grofman, Bernard.
II. Conference on Representation and Reapportionment Issues of the 1980s (1980: San Diego, Calif.)

KF4905.A75R43	342.73'053	81-47689
ISBN 0-669-04718-x	347.30253	AACR2

Copyright © 1982 by D.C. Heath and Company

All rights reserved. No part of this publication may be reproduced or transmitted in any form or by any means, electronic or mechanical, including photocopy, recording, or any information storage or retrieval system, without permission in writing from the publisher.

Published simultaneously in Canada

Printed in the United States of America

International Standard Book Number: 0-669-04718-x

Library of Congress Catalog Card Number: 81-47689

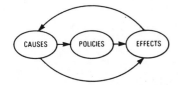

Policy Studies Organization Series

General Approaches to Policy Studies

vi

Specific Policy Problems

We wish to dedicate this book to the memory of Robert Dixon, Jr., 1920-1980, whose research on reapportionment offers a model of excellence for work in the field. This book includes the last essay written by Professor Dixon on methods and standards of districting.

Contents

Preface and Acknowledgments

Bernard Grofman

Earl Warren stated that "the most important Supreme Court rulings of [his] sixteen years as Chief Justice of the United States were those declaring that one man's vote should mean as much as any other man's." Early reapportionment decisions focused on the issue of standards of district population equality. In the 1980s and thereafter, U.S. legislative and judicial organs must come to grips with the thorniest questions of districting:

> Trade-offs among formal and substantive criteria for single-member district apportionments (for example, compactness, contiguity, population equality, preservation of political boundaries, preservation of partisan competitiveness, avoidance of partisan bias, preservation of electoral responsiveness) and the design of appropriate mechanisms to assure equitable apportionment decision making.

> Affirmative action gerrymandering—the constitutionality and desirability of apportionments that are intended to provide more nearly proportional or guaranteed representation to specific racial/linguistic/ethnic groupings.

> The desirability and constitutionality of forms of apportionment other than single-member districting (for example, mixed single-member and multimember districting, at-large districting, weighted voting and modified weighted voting, and various forms of proportional representation).

Those three interrelated sets of issues provide the principal themes of this book. The book also includes essays on related topics, such as evaluation of the policy impacts of previous rounds of reapportionment and discussion of representation issues in the context of internal political party organization.

The essays in this book were initially presented at the "Conference on Representation and Reapportionment Issues of the 1980s," San Diego, California, June 11-15, 1980. The conference was funded by the National Science Foundation Program in Political Science (NSF Grant SES #79-26813) and by the American Bar Association (ABA) Special Committee on Election Law and Voter Participation. (This book has not been approved by the ABA House of Delegates or the Board of Governors and does not constitute the policy of the American Bar Association.) This book and an earlier special issue of the *Policy Studies Journal*, which included the major conference essays, were made possible through support provided by the American Bar Association Committee on Election Law.

We wish to acknowledge our appreciation to Mr. John Feerick and Mr. Steve Uhlfelder, respectively past and present chairmen of the ABA committee, and to Elissa Lichtenstein of the ABA staff for their help. We would also like to acknowledge our special thanks to Sue Pursche, Gillian Cannon, Kathy Alberti, Lillian White, Helen Wildman, Yvonne Maldonado, Kathy Girvin, George Error, Jackie Shea, Laurel Eaton, and other staff of the School of Social Sciences, University of California, Irvine, for their invaluable assistance in conference planning and logistics; to the staff of the Half-Moon Inn, Shelter Island, San Diego, for facilitating on-site arrangements that were ideal; to Linton Freeman, dean of the School of Social Sciences, University of California, Irvine, for providing seed money for conference planning; to Stuart Nagel for his encouragement and assistance in preparing this book; and to Nelson Polsby, whose book, *Reapportionment Issues in the 1970s*, provided the direct inspiration for the conference.

The chapters in this book are intended to serve as a major assessment of research on representation and redistricting issues to assist reapportionment decision making in the 1980s and to put into historical, constitutional, and philosophical perspective the long-run question of how to develop appropriate representation mechanisms for a pluralist society.

Part I
Criteria for Single-Member Districting

Introduction to Part I

Robert B. McKay

The so-called reapportionment revolution of the 1960s was oversold by its detractors and by its supporters. When Justice Frankfurter deplored the Court's entry into the "political thicket," he expressed support for a view of judicial nonintervention that was on the wane. In this instance there was available to the Court—indeed, imperatively present—the requirement that no person be denied the equal protection of the laws. Justice Frankfurter was surely right that there is no easy way to separate the legal from the political aspects of legislative apportionment and districting. But he was in error in suggesting that the matter was outside the authority of federal courts because it was "nonjustifiable." Now it is agreed generally that the courts can act to correct egregious malapportionment. The proof lies in the fact that the courts have done just that. There *is* a revolution in apportionment and districting practices. Equality (at least relative equality) among legislative districts has become more the rule than the exception, and courts, both federal and state, are quick to respond to claims of substantial divergence from the equality standard.

Even as the fears of those who opposed judicial intervention were exaggerated, so were the claims of the advocates of the equal representation principle. Their claims that all legislative ills would be cured by the equality principle promised too much. If legislative authority had been unjustly retained by rural interests, the shift of power was not in all cases to the presumably slighted cities—but often to the suburbs that surrounded the once powerful urban areas. Legislators, wherever located, were not miraculously transformed into superhumans likely to cast aside parochial, even venal, interests for the greater good of the reapportioned polity. In short, life went on much as before, but with the important advantage that legislative bodies were truly more representative of their constituencies; and there was probably even a marginal increase in competence and concern on the part of the new post-*Reynolds* generation of legislators.

It is important to recall, as do the chapters in this part, the practical consequences of the reapportionment revolution and the theories of constitutional law that made possible some developments and made impossible other developments. The chapters that follow remind us of some of the most significant of those consequences.

Egregious malapportionment, often more than ten to one in terms of population among comparable legislative districts, was ended within a few years. Despite extravagant predictions of resistance and noncompliance, the "numbers" were put nearly right before the reapportionment required following the 1970 census. New issues quickly emerged, but the so-called numbers game subsided quickly.

The equality principle promptly accommodated to the various levels of government. The most rigorous equality standards were applied to congressional districts where the interest in the local state government units was less important. More latitude was allowed to state legislative districts, presumably to accommodate to the desirability of conforming to the boundaries of local government units. Within those same local government units the answer was a cautious "It depends."

The pragmatic response to the widespread fear that the cities would submerge the rural areas (which had often submerged the cities) was that the answer was ambiguous. New centers of power emerged in the suburbs of many urban areas, where the power of the ballot was often newly located. Unexpectedly, the interests of the suburbs coincided with those of the rural areas as often as with those of the cities. Once more the result in practice was essentially a standoff between those who hoped for urban dominance and those who feared the same.

Debate continues as to changes in the quality of the affected legislatures, both in terms of the legislatures themselves and the quality of their work product. There are few, if any, objective standards by which to measure; so there are many speculations both ways. The only things that can be said with certainty are the number of lawyers in Congress and in state legislatures has declined and legislative sessions are in general longer. But the two facts may themselves be related. As sessions become longer (for reasons unrelated to reapportionment), lawyers find less advantage in remaining in the legislatures. On the other hand, lawyers in rural constituencies are more likely to seek legislative office than lawyers in urban and suburban settings. While we do not entirely know the reasons, we are at least aware of the consequences.

It is also entirely apparent that political considerations have not been removed from the factors taken into account by legislatures as they make their decisions on apportionment and districting. The desire to preserve the seats of incumbents, even across party lines, remains very strong. And there is absolutely no evidence that parties in power will do anything less than everything possible to maximize the political power of that party and to minimize power of the opposition.

Less clear is the willingness to manipulate the process for the advantage or (more often) the disadvantage of minority racial or ethnic groups. The *Williamsburg* case teaches that an affirmative action gerrymander may be justified, at least with the support of the Voting Rights Act. But *Mobile* v. *Bolden* also discloses that multimember districts are permissible as a device to reduce representation of a disfavored racial group. The result is still a constitutional standoff, but most of the cards are held by those who might from time to time favor discrimination (ever so gently) on racial grounds.

One of the most interesting developments involves the contribution of science. The computer has revolutionized the methodology of reapportionment and redistricting. Infinite variations for legislative districting are now available at the push of a button. Neither legislatures nor courts are sure how to respond to this infinity of choice.

Meanwhile, political scientists and constitutional lawyers debate the standards appropriate for determination of legislative districts. The question is not easily answered, as indicated by the twenty-seven suggested standards offered for consideration at the Conference on Representation and Reapportionment Issues of the 1980s.

Perhaps most important of all, though its significance is difficult to assess, is the assertion in 1980 that the decennial census count is substantially inaccurate, particularly in certain urban areas, because it fails to include many members of minority groups. To the extent there is such a problem, it is obviously a matter of considerable seriousness for legislative districting. But until the dimensions are known, there is no readily agreed-upon solution.

The districting techniques suggested here and in subsequent chapters of this book offer some conventional answers to the methodology question and some quite innovative techniques. Thus, there is reference to such old proposals as proportional representation (still not enthusiastically endorsed) and truly blind (or computer-programmed) districting and to such modern innovations as compromise voting (with differences to be resolved by an arbitrator) and approval voting.

Whatever the results, the 1980s are at the very least benefited by the notion of fairness and equality, now ineradicably rooted in the democratic process of equal representation.

1 Fair Criteria and Procedures for Establishing Legislative Districts

Robert G. Dixon, Jr.

Some Introductory Realities

When the districting of legislative seats was first opened up to judicial scrutiny in 1962 in *Baker* v. *Carr*[1] under the federal Constitution's equal protection of the laws principle, thus signaling the beginning of the "one man-one vote" revolution, Justice Felix Frankfurter made the following observation on the guidance the Supreme Court in *Baker* gave to the lower courts:

> Room continues to be allowed for weighting. This of course implies that geography, economics, urban-rural conflict, and all the other non-legal factors which have throughout our history entered into political districting are to some extent not to be ruled out in the undefined vista now opened up by review in the federal courts of state reapportionments. To some extent—aye, there's the rub.[2]

The extent to which anything other than equality of district population can be or must be taken into account in political districting is still the rub. We approach the next round of reshaping legislative districts, national, state, and local, that will be triggered by the 1980 census, without clear judicial guidance on constitutional ground rules or an informed consensus on proper method.

Indeed, the rub is even worse than this Frankfurter comment signaled. The first key fact is that whether or not nonpopulation factors are expressly taken into account in shaping political districts, they are inevitably ever-present and operative. They influence all election outcomes in all sets of districts. The key concept to grasp is that there are no neutral lines for legislative districts. Whether the lines are drawn by a ninth-grade civics class, a board of Ph.D's, or a computer, every line drawn aligns partisans and interest blocs in a particular way different from the alignment that

This chapter draws upon Dixon (1968, 1969, 1971) and Dixon and Hatheway (1969). It was initially presented as testimony on S. 596, "A Bill to Provide a Fair Procedure for Establishing Congressional Districts," before the Committee on Governmental Affairs, U.S. Senate, June 20, 1979. After Professor Dixon's death, with the consent of his wife, Claire Dixon, this testimony was edited for inclusion in this book.

would result from putting the line in some other place. And (bear in mind that the gross majority in each district captures the seat or seats assigned to that district), the electoral result will be different in each case.

A second key fact is that at any level of equal population stringency—10 percent maximum deviation of a district from ideal district, or 5 percent, or 2 percent, or 1 percent, or less—a computer can churn out not one but hundreds of equally "equal" districting plans. But each plan, because of its somewhat different grouping of partisans and interests, will have a different—and of course nonneutral—impact on the electoral outcomes. We must consider electoral outcomes in two senses. First, there is the outcome in a given district, where the winner-take-all principle operates. Second, there is the outcome for the legislature as a whole where an important part of the power equation, and the reality of effective representation, depend on capturing enough district seats to win a legislative majority and be able to control the key committee chairmanships.

A third key fact is that even with equal population stringency in the drawing of district lines, the manner in which the winner-take-all majorities and minorities in each district add up across all the districts in a state can produce gross inequalities, even a minority election. In Connecticut in 1970 under a one-man-one-vote plan the Republicans polled a statewide popular majority in the legislative seat voting for both houses yet captured a majority of seats in neither house. In Iowa in 1966, although it was not a minority election, the Republicans captured the congressional delegation, five to two, with only a hairline majority of the statewide vote polled for congressional seats. In California in 1966, in the first election after an equal population revision of the district lines, the Democrats won a majority of the seats in each house of the state legislature, although the Republicans polled a statewide majority of the legislative vote for each house.

A fourth key fact, and the saddest of all because seventeen years have passed since *Baker* v. *Carr*, is that the first three key facts are not understood by judges who rule on these matters, many journalists who report these matters, and many members of the general public. There is a sort of vague impression in many quarters that equality in census numbers alone produces basic fairness, that legislative district lines can be politically neutral, that something called nonpartisanship can be built into the districting process. My own experience tells me that although I may find nonpartisanship in heaven, in the real world, and especially in academia, there are no nonpartisans, although there may be noncombatants.

Goals and Difficulties in Legislative Districting

The core problem can be stated somewhat simply: our *ideals* about political representation and our implementing *election system* do not fit together neatly. One of the major ideals, here as well as in Europe, is to have the political parties, who after all still organize and run our legislatures, win seats in legislatures roughly proportional to their share of the popular vote. That ideal is the very core of the term *fair representation*. To the extent that other interests can be factored in, we probably would like that also. Such an effort would be a highly speculative process, however, and probably could not be carried beyond recognition of the fact that the support for any candidate is in itself a collection of interest factions with varying degrees of internal organization, cohesiveness, and visibility. A key stumbling block to formal attempts to factor in subinterests is that district representation is a zero-sum game. Explicit favoring of one subgroup adversely affects another group (and the political party with which it is aligned). That fact is the lesson of *United Jewish Organizations* v. *Carey*[3] and is a background issue in *Whitcomb* v. *Chavis*.[4]

This fair representation ideal, which might be called the ideal of *proportionate representation* of parties (and the interests subsumed within them), does not dovetail well with an election system based on the use of geographic legislative districts and the plurality rule (or the winner-take-all rule) within each district. Obviously, if there are ten congressional districts in a state and the Democratic party polls 55 percent of the vote in each district while the Republicans are polling 45 percent in each district, the Democrats will have a disproportionate 100 percent of the representation in the congressional delegation and the Republicans will have a disproportionate 0 percent of the representation. Indeed, as is well recognized in political science, even under ideal circumstances a district system of electing legislative representatives always tends to overrepresent the dominant party in a given election year. That party's dominance tends to be reflected across many districts—certainly across all of the so-called balanced or swing districts.

But we live with this system because we are used to it and because it accomplishes certain other ideals, or at least beneficial results. It accomplishes the idea (or strongly tends to) of preserving a two-party system. A two-party system operates to produce such coordinate goals as a clear governing majority, governmental stability, and pinpointing of governing responsibility. The Europeans do not use our kind of district system but use proportional representation systems whereby parties are guaranteed seats in proportion to their percent of the popular vote. However, a proportional representation system strongly tends to invite the formation of a multiparty system; even a small party can get some kind of a win in terms of seats in parliament. The result usually is that no party wins a majority of the seats, thus necessitating government by unstable coalitions of minority parties. In short, proportional representation election systems yield more proportionate representation than do district systems, but they sacrifice the coordinate goals of a governing majority, governmental stability, and clear lines of responsibility.

There is no possibility, of course, nor do I now recommend it, of our moving from our present district system of electing legislators, with its combination of stability and inexact representation, to a formal system of proportional representation with its more precise representation of ideology and emotion but greater instability. Nevertheless, to appreciate what we have—its virtues and its problems—it is helpful to note in passing this alternative system, which dominates Europe and perhaps is more easily copied than our own. It substantially avoids the very difficult process of districting, avoids gerrymandering, and produces significant fairness in representation.

The Bipartisan Commission Proposal

There is a possibility, however, of improving our procedure for redistricting. Our experience with almost two decades of the reapportionment and redistricting revolution shows that the device of *bipartisan commission with tie breaker* not only has logical appeal but is better than any other available device. It also can work in practice, as in Connecticut in 1972. (See *Gaffney* v. *Cummings*.[5]) The bipartisan commission with tie breaker device allows combining the population equality principle with political realities and a better informed public scrutiny.

The bipartisanship is an essential built-in check on both conscious and unconscious unfairness in the resulting districts. Although it is never possible to guarantee fairness in a district system of election (any more than the Federal Trade Commission (FTC) can guarantee fairness in competition), it is possible for a bipartisan commission to discard plans that are predictably unfair in the light of all that is known about the political behavior of the area in question. Indeed, this mode is the way the FTC is designed to operate—to negate, case-by-case, unfair methods of competition. Obviously, to accomplish the unfairness policing mission either of the FTC or of a bipartisan districting commission, a broad intake of all relevant data is necessary. For the FTC this means data bearing on all aspects of competition. For a bipartisan commission it means data bearing on all aspects of political and electoral behavior, because the bipartisan commission simply deals with competition in another form—political competition for political seats in the political assembly.

The need to give balanced consideration to political data if avoidance of disproportionate electoral outcomes is the goal in legislative districting is the basis for a recent districting procedure article by two political scientists. They write: "If we accept the premise that seats in a representative body should change in some specified way as vote totals change, then it is apparent that there is a need to incorporate the partisan division of the vote into the criteria for fair districting" (Niemi and Deegan, 1978:1304).

Given the districting realities just sketched and the potential for improvement offered by the bipartisan commission device, it necessarily follows that care must be taken not to tie the hands of the bipartisan commission unduly in the course of specifying standards to guide their discretion. A bipartisan commission with blinders, which can consider only census population equality among districts, would be as useless as a Federal Trade Commission that could look only at market price. The most important injunction is that in its necessary consideration of data on electoral behavior the redistricting body should do so to test and discard unfair plans and not for the purpose of manufacturing artificial majorities in the legislative assembly. The rule should be sameness or fairness of treatment to all parties, that is, *neutrality* in this special sense. The vice to be avoided is differential advantage, one party over another, in the cause of manufacturing a congressional delegation majority out of a reasonably predictable statewide minority of the popular vote.

If a commission were to be barred from use of the political affiliation of registered voters, previous election results, or demographic information other than population head counts, then the bipartisan commission would have no rational function.[6] Indeed, it would be demeaning to serve on such a commission. The commission would be making some very basic decisions about the political future of the state—the make-up of its congressional delegation being the prize at issue—but would be doing so utterly in the dark. The bipartisan commission should be free to consider voting behavior data for the purpose of avoiding a set of districts that would favor one party over another in the contest for control of the legislature or state's congressional delegation. The congressional delegation, in states with several congressmen, offers opportunities for minority party representation that are not possible in the statewide election of one U.S. Senator at a time on a staggered-term basis. I submit that it should be unthinkable to pick as the final redistricing plan, from among the many "equally equal" plans available in population terms, the plan that predictably favors one party over another at the instant of enactment. Such a result should be equally abhorrent whether the built-in favoritism is purposely planned or the careless result of consciously uninformed decision making. Such an abhorrent result can be avoided only by considering political data to test the degree of predictable bias in the proffered plans.

The Constitutional Law of Reapportionment Districting

Historical Development

Until 1962 the courts followed a hands-off policy in respect to legislative districting. Justice Frankfurter in his 1946 controlling opinion in *Colegrove*

v. *Green*, which involved the congressional districts in Illinois, warned that it would be "hostile to a democratic system to involve the judiciary in the politics of the people."[7] The problem before the Court then, as in 1962 in *Baker* v. *Carr* when the Court decided to enter the political thicket, was gross population malapportionment. At the time of *Colegrove* v. *Green* the population disparity between the largest and smallest congressional districts in Illinois was the most extreme in the nation: 914,053 to 112,116. At the time of *Baker* in 1962, which was a challenge to the malapportioned state legislative districts in Tennessee, disparities between largest and smallest districts of ten to one or higher were common in most states for both congressional and state legislative districts. In Tennessee, for example, lower house districts ranged from 42,298 down to 2,340.

Baker v. *Carr* was responsive to the fact that political avenues for redress had become dead-end streets. With disparities of this dimension, any serious move toward equalization would destroy the districts of a substantial number of legislators. The ultimate rationale for *Baker* v. *Carr* was that some judicial intervention into the "politics of the people" had become necessary to make democratic politics effective. When the Supreme Court reached the merits two years later in 1964, it predictably announced a constitutional principle of population equality. It said in *Wesberry* v. *Sanders*[8] that congressional districts should be equal "as nearly as is practicable," and said in *Reynolds* v. *Sims*[9] that state legislative apportionments must be "based substantially on population." The difference in wording was inconsequential, and for a time the cases were cited interchangeably.

Within a short two or three years the problem that had given rise to these cases had been corrected. That problem, to repeat, was gross population malapportionment due to legislative nonaction, which normally resulted in substantial overrepresentation of rural and small town areas and substantial underrepresentation of the growing urban and suburban areas. In other words, the problem was one of *regional imbalance in political control*, in large measure.

However, the reapportionment-redistricting revolution quickly transcended its origin. Because the concept of substantial population equality is not a self-defining concept, there was a strong tendency in lower courts, with the Supreme Court following, to make the population equality requirement ever more stringent.

Two tactical factors contributed. First, the courts began to insist that all population deviations be justified in terms of a consistent, logical application of identifiable state policies. This was a practical impossibility, both because all lawmaking, including redistricting, is a compromise and adjustment process and not an exercise in logic, and more importantly, because nonpopulation policies—even a policy of following political subdivision lines insofar as practicable—cannot be made objective. Second, it was always easy for a plaintiff to offer a slightly more "equal" plan than the official state plan (albeit also more palatable to the plaintiff's political interests that motivated his suit). Hence, there was pressure on the state to move in the direction of ever-tighter equality to maximize the chances of prevailing in court. But plaintiffs still frequently prevailed with last-minute even tighter plans.

A direct corollary of insistence on ever-smaller population deviations—from 15 percent, which was an early rule of thumb, down to 10 percent, 5 percent, or lower—was to maximize the need to cut evermore political subdivision lines. This also maximized the freedom of choice in drawing new lines and consequently greatly increased opportunities for politically imbalanced districting, that is, gerrymandering.

A literal sea of litigation resulted and the issue likewise shifted. The issue shifted from the relatively simple question of safeguarding against *gross population disparities* to the complex question of safeguarding against *misrepresentation of interests*. The latter problem arose as district lines were fine-tuned nominally in pursuit of population equality but concurrently and predominantly in pursuit of one or another political result.

Some sense of this problem was signaled murkily in *Reynolds* v. *Sims*, but no solutions—no reliable guidelines—were given. Consider the following caveats in Chief Justice Warren's opinion:

> We realize that it is a practical impossibility to arrange legislative districts so that each one has an identical number of residents or citizens or voters.[10]

> [I]ndiscriminate districting without any regard for political sub-divisions or natural or historical lines, may be little more than an open invitation to partisan gerrymandering.[11]

> [F]air and effective representation for all citizens is concededly the basic aim of legislative apportionment.[12]

Especially significant is this last quote. It says that something more than equal numbers is needed. It suggests in effect that the payoff in terms of voice and influence inside a legislature is relevant, even predominant. Under this latter theme, what data are relevant? Are they necessarily essentially political data?

To a large extent we are still wallowing in the wake of the confusions implicit in *Reynolds* v. *Sims*. At the time, Paul Freund observed that the opinion reminded him of the little boy who had just learned how to spell the word *banana—ba-na-na-na-na*—but didn't know when to stop. Somewhat later Archibald Cox observed, in reference to several Warren Court initiatives under the equal protection of the laws principle, that "once loosed, the idea of Equality is not easily cabined" (Cox, 1966:91).

Current Population Equality Rules

As if in Pavlovian response to this observation the Supreme Court in two
congressional districting cases in 1969 from Missouri and New York went
all the way and mandated a virtual absolute equality rule for congressional
districting. In his opinion for the Court Justice Brennan said the Constitution "requires a State to make a good-faith effort to achieve precise mathematical equality (*Kirkpatrick* v. *Preisler*).[13] He then proceeded to eviscerate
every conceivable countervailing "fair representation" concept, including
all the caveats of Chief Justice Warren's opinion in *Reynolds* v. *Sims*. Four
justices—Harlan, Stewart, White, and Fortas—in strong terms rejected the
majority rationale and stressed the gerrymandering freedom under a rule
allowing district lines to run anywhere. Indeed, the plaintiff in the companion case from New York, *Wells* v. *Rockefeller*,[14] asked: "Can we appeal
from a decision that we won?" (Dixon, 1969: 219, 226). The maximum deviations from ideal population in the invalidated plans were 3.1 percent (Missouri) and 6.6 percent (New York).

Now it may be, to give Justice Brennan his due, that congressional districts are so large and amorphous that cutting in two any given hamlet—or
apartment house, as Justice Fortas hypothesized in bringing the new rule to
its *reductio ad absurdum*—in pursuit of absolute population equality is im-
material. At least, so I might have thought until three or four years ago
when I moved to Washington University and a home in Clayton, Missouri.
Clayton directly abuts the city of St. Louis and is the county seat of St.
Louis County, which now dwarfs the city of St. Louis. Yet I find that this
community has been split and a small part of it is in a congressional district
dominated by an adjacent part of the city of St. Louis with quite different
political representation concerns. Under any concept of fair and effective
representation, this does not make sense.

This "precise mathematical equality" rule of the 1969 congressional district rulings was reendorsed for congressional districts in 1973 in *White* v.
Weiser.[15] The anomaly of *Weiser* is that it endorsed a rule that three members
of the Court (the Chief Justice and Justices Powell and Rehnquist) said they
would not have supported had they been on the bench at the time of *Kirk-
patrick-Wells*, and that two other Justices (White, who wrote the opinion in
Weiser, and Stewart) had opposed at its inception in 1969. A further anomaly
is that although it is true, as Justice White observed, that a 1 percent deviation from ideal in congressional districts averaging 450,000 is 4,500 census
bodies, the plan the Court favored in *Weiser* transcended census accuracy.
There is an acknowledged margin of error in the census of 2 percent, which
yields 9,000 census bodies in the context of congressional districting. The districting plan the Court favored was claimed to have a maximum deviation
from ideal, in census terms, of 400 in excess of the ideal and 10 under the
ideal.

Concurrently in 1973, however, in state legislative reapportionment cases from Virginia and Connecticut—*Mahan* v. *Howell*[16] and *Gaffney* v. *Cummings*—the Supreme Court clarified the population equality ground rules for state legislative districts. In *Mahan* a plan in which the most deviant district was 9.6 percent from ideal passed muster because it allowed preservation of almost all political subdivision lines. It may be an atypical case because few states have such an even spread of population as that among the Virginia counties. In *Gaffney*, in more generally applicable terms for state legislative districts, the Court endorsed something analogous to a rule that districts are prima facie constitutional in population terms if the population deviations are de minimis in relation to the available census data. In this instance the deviations in terms of actual census head counts were under 800 and the average population of the census units available to work with was 1,100.

Gerrymandering

Meanwhile, on the issue of fair districting in terms of legislative payoff (gerrymandering issue) the Supreme Court has shown great disinclination to get involved. The present state of the law seems to be that gerrymandering claims may be justiciable; that is, courts can consider them, but plaintiffs have the burden of proving invidious discrimination. The earlier cases considered involve multimember districts, which of course tend to submerge both political and racial minorities under the winner-take-all rule (*Fortson* v. *Dorsey*,[17] *Burns* v. *Richardson*,[18] *Whitcomb* v. *Chavis*). However, because the underlying principle is a concern for fairness in political representation, logic dictates that gerrymandering claims against single-member districts likewise should be justiciable. In *Gaffney* v. *Cummings*, although the state's plan was upheld, Justice White did say that the Court "must . . . respond" to the claim that the plan was "invidiously discriminatory because a political fairness principle was followed."[19]

The question of whether invidious discrimination must be shown by proof of intent to construct a politically slanted districting scheme, or may be shown by evidence of a slanted electoral outcome in actual result, seems to have been resolved in favor of the former requirement. When the earlier cases mentioned the term effect, they always conjoined it with discriminatory *purpose*. More recently in a nonreapportionment case, *Washington* v. *Davis*,[20] the Court expressly rejected the idea that allegations of invidious discrimination in violation of the equal protection of the laws principle of the Fourteenth and Fifth Amendments could be sustained by bypassing proof of discriminatory purpose and showing only a disproportionate effect of the challenged practice. In that case plaintiffs could not show invidious racial intent in constructing the federal civil service examination but did show that blacks failed the test in higher proportion than did whites.

For the very reason that intent proof is difficult and courts may tend now to be satisfied with any "quite equal" redistricting plan, no matter how badly gerrymandered in actual result, it becomes all the more important that equality of political opportunity (which also can be called fairness or neutrality) be considered in the process of constructing the plan. It may be the first and last chance. Of course Justice White did offer a provocative line in *Gaffney* on the intent issue when he said:

> [A] politically mindless approach may produce, whether intended or not, the most grossly gerrymandered results; and, in any event, it is most unlikely that the political impact of such a plan would remain undiscovered by the time it was proposed or adopted, *in which event the results would be both known and, if not changed, intended*[21] (emphasis added).

We may well hear more of this warning in the litigation that will follow the 1980 census-induced redistrictings. But it would be unwise to place sole reliance on it as a safeguard for representative fairness.

Districting Standards

Contiguity

The contiguity requirement—that no part of one district be completely separated from any other part of the same district—has been universally accepted and poses no enforcement problem or serious challenge to districting flexibility in pursuit of other fair representation values.

Compactness

The requirement of compactness specifies that the boundaries of each district shall be as short as practicable. Although there is no federal constitutional requirement of compactness,[22] such a requirement may present a certain restraint on gerrymandering and may seem innocuous on its face. Rigid adherence to a compactness, however phrased, should be avoided. A district pattern of symmetrical squares, although conceivable, well can operate to submerge a significant element of the electorate. As a practical matter, absolute compactness (districts forming perfect circles that are even shorter lines than squares) is an impossibility. Furthermore, a benign gerrymander, in the sense of some asymmetrical districts, may well be required to assure representation of submerged elements within a larger area. Shape requirements focus on form rather than the substance of effective political representation.

Following Political Boundaries

The requirement of honoring political subdivision boundaries insofar as possible under the population equality requirements responds to a traditional and even instinctive sense of community as a significant basis for representation. It was mentioned by Chief Justice Warren in *Reynolds* v. *Sims*. The extent to which political subdivision boundaries may be honored is, of course, an inverse corollary of the degree of population stringency required. The Supreme Court's population equality stringency in *Kirkpatrick* v. *Preisler* and *White* v. *Weiser* had the effect of badly trampling any political subdivision policy for congressional districting.

Population Deviation

A 2 percent maximum deviation rule leaves some room for following political subdivision lines, without any demonstrable cost to any principle of fair and effective representation of which I am aware. In *Weiser* in 1973 the court voided an official state plan with a maximum deviation of 2.43 percent, under the force of the *Kirkpatrick* rule. The alternative plaintiffs' plan adopted by the Court cut eighteen more county lines than did the rejected state plan. I have already noted above that three members of the *Weiser* Court said they were disenchanted with this extremely stringent rule and two additional members had at least opposed the rule at its inception in 1969.

Incumbent Protection

Various groups (most notably Common Cause, 1977b), have advocated a flat prohibition on the consideration of addresses of incumbents in the drawing of district lines. In practice this prohibition may be no more enforceable than Prohibition itself, but I will lay that aside. From the standpoint of constitutional law, the Supreme Court said in *Weiser*, as it had earlier, that: "The fact that district boundaries may have been drawn in a way that minimized the number of contests between present incumbents does not in and of itself establish invidiousness."[23] On the question whether the prohibition is sound policy, persons will differ. There are virtues in having some continuity in office for the sake of experience, stability, and relations with constituents. There also are virtues in turnover, which is probably far better achieved—if we are at all serious about it—by limiting legislators to a specified number of terms.

Dilution of Minority Voting Strength

Rulings like the one made by the Supreme Court in *United Jewish Organizations* v. *Carey* suggest the likelihood that in many states, North as well as South, much of the state legislative reapportionment and congressional districting after the 1980 census will be controlled by the Attorney General of the United States under the Voting Rights Act. Under the *United Jewish Organizations* precedent the control would take the form of creation of safe districts for a specified number of black and language minority candidates, with consequent problems of adverse impacts on other groups. In that case the Hasidic Jewish community in Brooklyn was split in an attempt to create safe black districts.

Conclusion

In closing I must state that to me districting *method* is more important than districting *standards*. In general I favor a bipartisan commission with tie breaker.[24] Such a provision has much merit for a great majority of states. There may be some difficulty, and I suppose opposition, in heavily one-party states. Even there, however, there is virtue in getting the districting process out in the open through the bipartisan commission device so that it can be observed and alternative plans adequately tested. *Gaffney* v. *Cummings* indicates that there is no federal constitutional barrier to use of bipartisan commissions or use by such commissions of data on political behavior where done for the purpose of avoiding politically unfair districts.

It is important that the operation of a bipartisan commission not be unduly impeded by too detailed a specification of standards or attempted limitation on the kind of data that can be considered. A straitjacketed commission may be worse than no commission at all. A policy of blindly choosing one of the great many equally equal plans a cartographer or computer operator may produce, coupled with the unlikelihood of effective judicial policing of unfair results, could enshrine gerrymandering—perhaps unplanned but none the better for that—in an impregnable position.

Let me illustrate the point by reference one more time to the unfolding of the Connecticut case, *Gaffney* v. *Cummings*, back in 1972. While I was just beginning to take over the case and get a Supreme Court stay (which was granted) of the federal district court ruling adverse to the state's plan, the district court concurrently was proceeding to reapportion the state itself with the aid of a master. The appointed master was Professor Robert H. Bork of Yale University Law School. He worked with graduate students and a computer under severe time pressure and, under the instructions of the district court, essentially utilized census data alone. His resultant plan, though it certainly was not his intent, was so favorable to the Democratic party that, I am told, he was specially congratulated by the state Democratic chairman, John Bailey. Absent the continued litigation in the Supreme Court, this plan might well have gone into effect.[25] There is no substitute for using all the knowledge available and testing all proposed plans with all the knowledge available.

Notes

1. Baker v. Carr (1962) 369 U.S. 186.
2. Baker v. Carr (1962) 369 U.S. 186 at 269 (Frankfurter dissenting).
3. United Jewish Organizations v. Carey (1977) 430 U.S. 144.
4. Whitcomb v. Chavis (1971) 403 U.S. 124.
5. Gaffney v. Cummings (1973) 412 U.S. 735.
6. Limitations of this sort on the use of political data seem to be envisioned in Common Cause (1977).
7. Colegrove v. Green (1946) 328 U.S. 549 at 553-54.
8. Wesberry v. Sanders (1964) 376 U.S. 1.
9. Reynolds v. Sims (1964) 377 U.S. 533.
10. Reynolds v. Sims (1964) 377 U.S. 533 at 577.
11. Reynolds v. Sims (1964) 377 U.S. 533 at 578-79.
12. Reynolds v. Sims (1964) 377 U.S. 533 at 565-66.
13. Kirkpatrick v. Preisler (1969) 394 U.S. 526 at 530-31.
14. Wells v. Rockefeller (1969) 394 U.S. 542.
15. White v. Weiser (1973) 412 U.S. 783.
16. Mahan v. Howell (1973) 410 U.S. 315.
17. Fortson v. Dorsey (1965) 379 U.S. 433.
18. Burns v. Richardson (1966) 384 U.S. 73.
19. Gaffney v. Cummings (1973) 412 U.S. 735 at 751-52.
20. Washington v. Davis (1976) 426 U.S. 229.
21. Gaffney v. Cummings (1973) 412 U.S. 735 at 753.
22. Gaffney v. Cummings (1973) 412 U.S. 735 at 752, N. 18.
23. White v. Weiser (1973) 412 U.S. 783 at 797.
24. Editors' note: As additional material in his testimony, not included in this chapter, makes clear, Dixon was not advocating a 2 percent maximum deviation standard but rather arguing that such a guideline was superior to a rigid and impractical insistence on "perfect" equality of district population.
25. For details on bipartisanship and political fairness in the 1972 Connecticut reapportionment plan, see *Gaffney* v. *Cummings* (1973) 412 U.S. 735 Brief for Appellant, *45 et seq.* and Reply Brief for Appellant (with tables testing state plan, plaintiff's three plans, master's plan).

2 Threading the Political Thicket by Tracing the Steps of the Late Robert G. Dixon, Jr.: An Appraisal and Appreciation

Gordon E. Baker

There are occasions when our understanding of an institution or a historical development can be heightened by an examination of the contributions of a single individual. Such an enterprise can produce a sense of focus and direction in a kaleidoscopic and confusing scene. Such is the case with the works of Robert G. Dixon, Jr., whose life was cut short at the age of 60 on May 5, 1980. Dixon's name was so intimately associated with the subject of legislative reapportionment that his writings and activities since the early 1960s provide an invaluable reflection of the evolution of perhaps the most remarkable institutional transformation in twentieth century America.

This reapportionment revolution entailed, as few could have anticipated, an intricate nexus of politics and law. To understand and interpret such a development, Robert Dixon was uniquely qualified. His academic training included a doctorate in political science and a degree in law. After teaching the former subject for several years, Dixon joined the faculty at George Washington University's School of Law in the nation's capital. From this vantage point he witnessed all the major arguments in the series of reapportionment cases since *Baker* v. *Carr*[1] in 1962, discussed the legal issues with numerous counsel in these cases, served as a consultant to several public agencies, and ultimately presented to the U.S. Supreme Court a successful brief that helped trigger a shift in judicial direction. In 1975, Dixon was named Daniel Noyes Kirby Professor of Law at Washington University in St. Louis. While his scholarship spanned a wide range of subjects (for example, privacy, procedural safeguards, reverse discrimination), his interest and involvement in legislative reapportionment continued until the end of his days. Any future serious work on this subject will inevitably take account of his insights and wisdom, articulated with pungency and wit.

This chapter can deal with only a portion of Robert Dixon's work on reapportionment. Yet these highlights enable us to discern the route we have all traveled and to glimpse the potential that lies ahead.

Democratic Representation

Robert Dixon's magnum opus on the subject was published in 1968, a sufficient time after the landmark reapportionment decisions to permit a comprehensive account from the perspective of an institutional metamorphosis virtually completed. *Democratic Representation: Reapportionment in Law and Politics* won the Woodrow Wilson Foundation Award, presented at the 1969 annual meeting of the American Political Science Association, for being "the best book published in the United States in 1968 in government, politics, or international affairs." In this pioneering work, Dixon at the outset emphasized the unique and crucial nature of the Supreme Court's reapportionment decisions, since they represented judicial transfer of political power. "They question the legitimacy of arrangements by which legislative office is defined and filled. This constitutes a major innovation, not only for judicial review, but for democratic theory and practice." Distributing political power is more than either a legislative or judicial act, rather it is a *constitutive* act.

In the vortex of dispute over such momentous decisions, Dixon assumed a position of careful and dispassionate balance. On the one hand, he found that democratic theory led inevitably to the concept of one-person, one-vote as the basis of representation. At the same time, he faulted many of the doctrine's advocates for ignoring the complexities involved and for taking oversimplistic approaches to the theory and practice of representative equality. At the judicial level, he dissected the various opinions with incisive professorial analysis, sparing neither majority nor minority arguments.

But Dixon's balance was more than a sterile neutrality. He did not hesitate to express his considered opinions and conclusions on controversial or value-laden questions. A major theme running throughout the book was the author's distinction between majoritarian democracy and consensus democracy. An obsession with numerical equality, he insisted, can blind us to the need for the representation of all significant interests in society, including the rights of isolated minorities to be heard. For Dixon, political *equity* was fully as important as political equality, though he fell short of asserting the mutual incompatibility of the two concepts. In *Democratic Representation,* as in his subsequent writings, Bob Dixon urged courts, lawyers, and political theorists to explore the full import of Chief Justice Earl Warren's dictum in *Reynolds* v. *Sims,*[2] that "fair and effective representation of all citizens is concededly the basic aim of legislative apportionment." Hence Dixon pinpointed the priority of districting fairness, an ideal he found violated by such practices as gerrymandering or at-large elections in multimember districts that permit majorities to sweep all or most seats in a given area. He insisted that: "A mathematically equal vote which is politically worthless because of gerrymandering or winner-take-all districting is as deceiving as the emperor's clothes."

The evolving stress on population equality per se stemmed in large part from the Supreme Court's reliance upon the Fourteenth Amendment's equal protection clause. Dixon lamented that judicial entry into the political thicket had not instead been based on either of two constitutional provisions that he deemed more appropriate to the nature of apportionment. At that time he preferred that portion of Article IV guaranteeing to each state a "republican form of government." Next most appropriate would have been the due process clause of the Fourteenth Amendment. Either clause would have permitted judicial invalidation of representative distortions that allowed entrenched minorities to thwart political majorities. Within a few years, however, Dixon abandoned the neglected guaranty clause in favor of a due process clause that was showing substantive recognition to various forms of fairness. "A due process approach," he argued, "would not create, as the Court's rulings based on the equal protection clause have, a never-ending affirmative duty to try to equalize representation on the basis of census figures alone" (Dixon 1971).

This more flexible approach to the problem has considerable appeal, especially in view of an increasing judicial preoccupation with population equality and little else. Yet the alternative route entailed potential hazards that Dixon did not adequately address. His position appeared close to that argued by Justices Potter Stewart and Tom Clark in the reapportionment cases of 1964. While clinging to the equal protection clause, they limited its application to instances that lacked rationality in the light of a state's own characteristics and needs and that served "systematically to prevent ultimate effective majority rule."[13] Applying these criteria, Stewart and Clark dissented from some cases and concurred with the results (but not the Court's reasoning) in others. With this approach the judicial role would appear to be more cautious and limited, but the power to determine which districting patterns met the standards would necessarily involve the Court in difficult choices. And judges would surely differ in applying the criteria, as Stewart and Clark themselves did concerning Ohio in the second set of state cases decided in June of 1964. Even their joint dissent a week earlier from the invalidation of New York's apportionment pattern raised questions about ultimate effective majority rule in view of that state's partisan geography—a lack of political realism of which the dissenters accused the majority with its one-person, one-vote doctrine. Bob Dixon's due process approach would appear to entail similar hazards as the Stewart-Clark version of limited equal protection. As Dixon would be the first to admit, no formula can guarantee a consistent and reasonable implementation by well-meaning but fallible judges.

Whether the later stress on mathematical precision was inherent in the Supreme Court's majority opinions in the reapportionment cases of 1964 or was a subsequent development is an open question. In *Reynolds* v. *Sims*,

Chief Justice Warren held that "the Equal Protection Clause requires that a state make an honest and good faith effort to construct districts, in both houses of its legislature, as nearly of equal population as is practicable."[4] The thrust of this constitutional requisite, plus the Court's emphasis on the individual citizen's right to cast an equally effective vote, led Dixon at that time to trace the problem to the source: "The essence of *Reynolds* may be its simplistic, narrow, humorless quality. Although it has been said to be Chief Justice Warren's most prideful opinion, it has no trace of pragmatism, which also has been said to be his preeminent quality" (Dixon 1968, p. 273). Yet others of us at that time focused on some of the flexible and seemingly pragmatic features in the reapportionment cases— features that Bob Dixon played down as "puzzling caveats" (Dixon 1968; p. 271).

Central to understanding this ambivalence is the key role played by Solicitor General Archibald Cox's amicus curiae brief in the 1964 cases. Dixon gave full credit to Cox's importance, terming him the "chief theoretician and chief coordinator" (Dixon 1968, p. 201) for the plaintiffs, extraordinarily skillful at shaping the litigation tactics to judicial predilections. Yet Cox himself shied away from a rigid one-man, one-vote formulation. At one stage he had viewed the doctrine itself as good political science but dubious constitutional law (Navasky, 1977). While he eventually became more positive, some reservations remained. The result was a brief, tightly written, but full of subtleties that might appeal to justices on the fence. It argued the decisions ultimately taken by the Court but also acknowledged that the equal protection clause left room for accommodating "other permissible objectives" than simply per capita equality. Cox went on to argue that population equality is the "starting point" and fundamental standard, deviations from which must serve a "valid governmental purpose." The burden rested with the state to justify substantial district inequalities. Among permissible objectives could be the desire to represent communities or political subdivisions, so long as the result did not "submerge" the vital principle of voter equality and majority rule.[5]

The relevance of the solicitor general's brief is the close reliance placed on it by Chief Justice Warren, including use of the very phrases just quoted. The approach taken in *Reynolds* v. *Sims* left a considerable amount of flexibility in implementing the concept of representative equality. "We realize," explained Warren, "that it is a practical impossibility to arrange legislative districts so that each one has an identical number of residents, or citizens, or voters. Mathematical exactness or precision is hardly a workable constitutional requirement."[6] The opinion pointedly disavowed any uniform standard, applicable throughout the nation. "What is marginally permissible in one state," the option continued, "may be unsatisfactory in another, depending on the particular circumstances of the case."[7] This note of relativity implies that varying circumstances other than mere population may validly be given some attention by states. A specific example is then provided by the Court:

> A State may legitimately desire to maintain the integrity of various political subdivisions, insofar as possible, and provide for compact districts of contiguous territory in designing a legislative apportionment scheme. Valid considerations may underlie such aims. Indiscriminate districting, without any regard for political subdivisions or natural or historical boundary lines, may be little more than an open invitation to partisan gerrymandering. . . . Whatver the means of accomplishment, the overriding objective must be substantial equality of population among the various districts, so that the vote of any citizen is approximately equal in weight to that of any other citizen in the State. . . . So long as the divergences from a strict population standard are based on legitimate considerations incident to the effectuation of a rational state policy, some deviations from the equal-population principle are constitutionally permissible with respect to the apportionment of seats in either or both of the two houses of a bicameral state legislature.[8]

The highest tribunal went on to express confidence that lower courts could work out specific and appropriate standards in the context of actual litigation on a case-by-case basis. Needless to say, these 1964 Supreme Court decisions yielded less than clear-cut guidelines for others to follow. For example, in the Colorado case, the Court, while finding the total bicameral representation pattern nonseverable, suggested that the lower house, standing by itself, was "at least arguably apportioned substantially on a population basis."[9] The House districts in Colorado deviated from average population by plus 30 percent to minus 24.4 percent.

1969: Crusade for the "Holy Grail"

The 1964 opinions themselves, then, appeared to invite some flexibility so long as the principle of approximate voter equality was not eroded. Yet judicial trends, as Dixon had predicted, took the opposite direction. Why? For one thing, lower court judges, unlike academics, are not accustomed to exploring the nuances and implications of Supreme Court precedents. They look at the rulings and their justifications—and these are "the law." Moreover, most judges are anxious to avoid being overruled by higher courts, and such a result seems easier to avoid by upholding stricter numerical standards when presented with a choice. The course of events dismayed, but did not surprise, Bob Dixon. Perhaps he also had in mind the earlier observation of Oliver Wendell Holmes, Jr., that "judges are apt to be naif, simple-minded men," who "need an education in the obvious" (Mason, 1965, p. 704). In any case, as Dixon repeatedly insisted, even rational deviations were harder to justify whenever a plaintiff could present a more equipopulous district map—a situation that reinforced his aversion to the equal protection basis for reapportionment.

This inherent problem was squarely posed in a pair of key apportionment decisions handed down by the U.S. Supreme Court in April of 1969.
In *Kirkpatrick* v. *Preisler*, [10] the high tribunal affirmed a lower court rejection of a Missouri congressional districting plan with deviations ranging
from plus 3.13 percent to minus 2.84 percent, with an average deviation of
1.6 percent. In the companion case of *Wells* v. *Rockefeller*, [11] the Court
reversed a federal district court that had upheld a New York congressional
districting plan that had created constituencies with a maximum population
range from plus 6.49 percent to minus 6.61 percent.

While the Court majority reiterated some of the former state-by-state
approaches and did not spell out fixed numerical standards of equality, there
were ominous overtones signaling a radical departure from the spirit of the
1964 rulings. Now Justice William Brennan interpreted "as nearly as practicable" to mean that a state "must make a good-faith effort to achieve
precise mathematical equality," that any disparities "no matter how small"
had to be justified. [12] As Justice Abe Fortas objected, the Court "then pro-
ceeds to reject, seriatim, every type of justification that has been—possibly
every one that coud be—advanced. [13] In this concurring opinion, Fortas rejected Brennan's reasoning by pointing out:

> Whatever might be the merits of insistence on absolute equality if it could
> be attained, the majority's pursuit of precision is a search for a will-o'-the-
> wisp. The fact is that any solution to the apportionment and districting
> problem is at best an approximation because it is based upon figures which
> are always to some degree obsolete. No purpose is served by an insistence
> on precision which is unattainable because of the inherent imprecisions in
> the population data on which districting must be based. [14]

Moreover, a single-minded quest for mathematical equality of districts
at the expense of some adherence to local governmental subunits carries
with it the potential for extensive gerrymandering. In his dissenting opinion
to the 1969 Missouri and New York congressional districting cases, Justice
Byron White cogently summed up the implications and portent of the
Court's emphasis on virtually precise population:

> Today's decision on the one hand requires precise adherence to admittedly
> inexact census figures, and on the other downgrades a restraint on a far
> greater potential threat to equality of representation, the gerrymander.
> Legislatures intent on minimizing the representation of selected political or
> racial groups are invited to ignore political boundaries and compact
> districts so long as they adhere to population equality among districts using
> standards which we know and they know are sometimes quite incorrect. I
> see little merit in such a confusion of priorities. [15]

These decisions by a closely divided Supreme Court brought forth from Bob Dixon perhaps his finest single critique on reapportionment—"The Warren Court's Crusade for the Holy Grail of One-Man, One-Vote" appearing in *The Supreme Court Review* for 1969. Dixon took full advantage of his strategic opportunity to persuade all who would listen that the time was clearly at hand for an agonizing reappraisal of the nature and purpose of our representative institutions and their relationship to a democratic politics. "Just as the political system seemed to need some Court help in 1962, it now is becoming obvious that the Court needs help from the political system in managing the equality concept in apportionment-districting" (Dixon 1969, p. 220). After soliciting reactions from several staunch supporters of the 1964 decisions, Dixon reported widespread professional concern over these most recent interpretations of one-person, one-vote: "A surprising number of respected supporters both of this principle and the Supreme Court find dangerous, if not wholly unacceptable, the newly formulated absolute equality rule."[16]

What could be done? Hoping that the Court would shift back seemed unrealistic. Congress probably had the power under Article I and the Fourteenth Amendment (Section 5) to enact statutory guidelines of district equality. But Dixon preferred a constitutional amendment that would establish a presumption of constitutionality for congressional and legislative districts within a specified deviation (15, or 10, or 5 percent). This presumption could be overcome by a suit by any voter demonstrating "that the districts, although within the allowable percentage deviations stated, operate unreasonably to minimize the voting strength of racial or political elements of the voting population" (Dixon 1969, p. 236). Dixon's model of such an amendment was well drafted and had considerable merit in the context of that time. While it did not have the political disabilities of the ill-fated Dirksen amendment, by the same token it would doubtless attract less of a constituency. Whether Dixon felt that his proposal had real prospects or whether he felt that it would help dramatize the issue is uncertain. What was abundantly clear was that Dixon was using the art of advocacy in a most effective and eloquent manner. "The Warren Court Crusade for the Holy Grail" explores every important facet of the problem and does so within a compelling conceptual framework. Above all, Bob Dixon wanted to move the level of debate and analysis from that of sterile and mechanistic rituals to the fundamentals of representation theory and practice. His thesis is well stated in these words: "One-man, one-vote should be perceived as a symbol of an aspiration for fairness, for avoidance of complexity, for intelligibility in our representational process—indeed, for a sense of meaningful membership in the *polis*. These are legitimate aspirations, but there is no single, simple formula for their accomplishment" (Dixon 1969, p. 268).

1973: Political Fairness

Robert Dixon and other critics of the 1969 decisions in *Wells* and *Kirkpatrick* could take some comfort in the narrowing split on the Court—as well as the eloquent statements filed in opposition to Justice Brennan's reasoning. While Justice Fortas concurred in the result (apparently questioning the good-faith efforts of the states involved), he explicitly rejected the majority's quest for population precision. Even more significant was Justice White's dissent. White had steadfastly joined all previous decisions implementing the doctrine of one-person, one-vote and had written the opinion for the court in *Swann* v. *Adams* in 1967.[17] His previous commitment to Warren Court orthodoxy regarding representative equality made his dissenting voice in 1969 especially compelling.

Then, too, the Supreme Court itself was soon to undergo partial but rapid reconstitution. It seemed unlikely that President Richard Nixon's four new appointees would share the rigid approach to reapportionment set forth by Brennan in 1969. The wholesale redistricting activity among the states following the 1970 Census was bound to involve individuals or groups willing to seek further clarification and redefinitions from the high tribunal in the hope of finding a more moderate response.

The 1972 term of the Supreme Court marked a significant return to more flexible guidelines in state legislative apportionment. Yet no precedent was overturned, since Congressional districting standards remained stringent following the 1969 cases involving such constituencies. Perhaps as important as the cases decided was the judicial mood. While the Court made it clear that legislative districting would remain subject to judicial scrutiny, it made even more evident its hope that such recourse could be minimized, now that the guidelines of tolerable constitutional limits were reasonably clear. In Justice White's words, the high tribunal should recognize the "eminently reasonable approach of *Reynolds* v. *Sims*" and should not "become bogged down in a vast, intractable apportionment slough . . ."[18]

In the first of these four cases, the Supreme Court overruled a federal district court's holding that a recent redistricting of the Virginia House of Delegates strayed too far from the equal population principle, with a maximum overall population variance of 16.4 percent (plus 9.6 to minus 6.8). The Court found the apportionment to be "within tolerable constitutional limits," since the population deviations resulted from a legitimate state policy of consistently maintaining the integrity of political subdivision (city and county) lines. "While this percentage may well approach tolerable limits, we do not believe it exceeds them,"[19] declared Justice William Rehnquist, speaking for the Court.

Near the end of the term, on June 16, the Supreme Court handed down three more reapportionment decisions. One involved congressional redistricting in Texas, the other two, state legislative constituencies in Texas and Connecticut. In the latter two cases, the overall percentage variances from precise population equality were smaller than in Virginia—7.8 percent (plus 3.93 to minus 3.90) in Connecticut and 9.9 percent (plus 5.8 to minus 4.1) in Texas—but in neither instance was there the rationale of systematically preserving local boundaries as in the Virginia case. "Very likely," the Court suggested, "larger differences would not be tolerable without justification . . . ,"[20] but such variance ranges alone do not represent prima facie instances of invidious discrimination. In the Texas congressional districting case, as in the other three, the Court drew a distinction between the greater population flexibility permitted for state legislative constituencies and the more precise standard (as mathematically equal as reasonably possible[21]) expected for congressional districts.

The 1973 cases found Bob Dixon playing a crucial role, this time as a participant rather than observer-analyst, being named attorney for the Connecticut appellants before the Supreme Court in *Gaffney* v. *Cummings*. He was deservedly in fast company. Two of the companion cases were argued by Charles L. Black of Yale University School of Law and Leon Jaworski (later appointed Special Watergate Prosecutor), a special assistant attorney general of Texas. This was Bob Dixon's opportunity to put theory into practice, to persuade the most important audience of his career, and he made the most of it. Justice White's opinion for the Court in the Connecticut case followed much of Dixon's analysis and reasoning.

In the Connecticut case Dixon faced the delicate challenge of defending a state plan that had consciously taken political factors into account. But he made a virtue of necessity. The Connecticut redistricting of 1971 had been drawn by a bipartisan board of three judges (one Democrat and one Republican state superior court judge appointed by party leaders in the House; the two judges, in turn, chose as a third board member a justice from the state supreme court). The state legislature and, later, an eight-member bipartisan commission, had been unable to agree on maps before specific deadlines. In *Gaffney*, Justice White noted that the board cut the boundary lines of forty-seven of the state's one hundred sixty-nine towns[22] to reach what it thought to be substantial population equality. In the words of the Court:

> The Board also consciously and overtly adopted and followed a policy of "political fairness," which aimed at a rough scheme of proportional representation of the two major political parties. Senate and House districts were structured so that the composition of both Houses would reflect "as closely as possible . . .the actual (statewide) plurality of vote on the House or Senate lines in a given election." Rather than focusing on party membership in the respective districts, the Board took into account the party voting results in the preceding three statewide elections, and, on that

basis, created what was thought to be a proportionate number of Republican and Democratic legislative seats.[23]

According to a staff member of the Board, the plan for the House resulted in approximately seventy safe Democratic seats and fifty-five to sixty safe Republican seats, with the balance characterized as probable or strong Democratic or Republican, or just plain swing.[24]

As evidence that this goal had apparently been achieved, Robert Dixon presented statistics as shown in table 2-1.

These figures were then contrasted with five alternate districting plans that had been submitted or urged by plaintiffs. The others uniformly projected stronger Democratic success ratios. The critical difference centered around the election of 1970, where the board plan was the only one to project an electoral majority into a legislative majority (all plans did this in the remaining three elections). However, this factual point was in dispute. The actual statewide vote showed a slim Democratic margin. In the projections appellants estimated a normal Republican vote in three uncontested Democratic districts. Moreover, appellants' staff experts conceded that the figures necessarily involved a certain amount of judgment or estimating, but they believed the margin of error to be no more than four seats in each computation.[25]

In a single-member district system, a party winning a statewide majority of votes generally wins an even larger majority of seats. Accordingly, the board districting plan yielded a significantly better payoff for the Republicans in 1972 than it projected for Democratic majorities in 1966 and 1968. This situation brought charges from appellees in *Gaffney* that the board plan was a Republican gerrymander. It could nonetheless be argued that the 1970 election, however computed, was virtually a tossup, that the board plan, projecting a slim Republican legislative majority, more closely approximated electoral preferences than the actual lower house election of 1970, in which the Democrats won 56 percent of the seats. When the several

Table 2-1
Connecticut Lower House Elections: 1966-1972

Year	Statewide Vote Percentage		State Board Plan Percentage of Seats	
	Republican	Democrat	Republican	Democrat
1966 (projected)	45.5	54.4	39.1	60.9
1968 (projected)	47.9	52.1	39.1	53.6
1970 (projected)	50.25	49.75	51.0	49.0
1972 (actual)	52.88	46.86	61.6	38.4

Source: Adapted from Robert G. Dixon, Jr.'s Appellants' Reply Brief, Gaffney v. Cummings (No. 71-147b):3a.

alternative plans presented are also considered, one can easily conclude that the choice in Connecticut was between one Republican gerrymander and several Democratic gerrymanders.

In this context, the Supreme Court concluded that any of the alternate plans might also be constitutional but that a state's normal political processes should not be overturned when a reapportionment plan is within tolerable population limits and no invidious discrimination is demonstrated. The Court was obviously impressed with Bob Dixon's arguments that the board plan was animated by a spirit of political fairness, that such an approach is not only permissible but desirable. Mr. Justice White and the majority were convinced that the state plan undertook "not to minimize or eliminate the political strength of any group or party, but to recognize it and, through districting, provide a rough sort of proportional representation in the legislative halls of the state."[26]

1979: Standards, Methods, Goals

The possibility of achieving a rough sort of proportional representation is intriguing. Where equipopulated single-member districts predominate, a party's statewide voting majority tends to elect a disproportionately larger legislative majority, since a number of winner-take-all constituencies accumulate. The same result is even more likely in areas with multimember districts elected at large. Under these conditions, the degree of proportional representation may be very rough indeed. The central desideratum—the one most vital to the democratic ideal—is to so construct districts that significant shifts in public opinion are reflected in the legislature and that a political party winning a clear-cut majority at the polls will also capture a majority of legislative seats. As Bob Dixon pointed out, however, "The core problem can be stated somewhat simply: Our *ideals* about political representation and our implementing *election system* do not fit together neatly."[27]

This problem continued to plague Dixon. In several of his writings he seemed tempted by proportional representation as the logical institutional expression of the one-person, one-vote concept. But he conceded that it runs counter to the American inheritance of a district system and some important corollary values (such as community representation). With the possible exception of large multimember districts, he concluded that it had little future here.

For better or worse, then, the single-member district system remains the major product of the apportionment process. While at one point Dixon sardonically declared that "all districting is gerrymandering (Dixon 1968, p. 462), he ordinarily used the latter term to refer to discriminatory cartography resulting in political or racial malrepresentation. As the 1980 round of reapportionment approached, he felt that the major challenge continued to be fair and effective representation, which meant devising checks on at least the more blatant forms of gerrymandering.

This then leads to the question: Who shall draw the district lines? When he wrote *Democratic Representation* in 1968, Dixon preferred that the function remain with the legislatures (or, in some cases, the courts). Bipartisan commissions might be acceptable, he felt, but not nonpartisan ones or neutral computer systems. Since redrawing district lines has profound political consequences, the relevant political factors should be made known so that meaningful compromises can take place. But can fair representation be obtained from self-interested legislators? Dixon ultimately reconsidered in favor of a bipartisan, nonlegislative agency. But he continued to insist that the quest for nonpartisan agencies or for a *deus ex machina* was a dangerous illusion:

> The key concept to grasp is that there are no "neutral" lines for legislative districts. Whether the lines are drawn by a ninth-grade civics class, a board of Ph.D.'s, or a computer, every line drawn aligns partisans and interest blocks in a particular way different from the alignment resulting from putting the line in some other place.[28]

In the summer of 1979 Dixon had a chance to summarize his views on redistricting criteria and methods to a committee of the U.S. Senate considering a bill spelling out procedures to be used in establishing congressional districts. Here he concluded that *method* is more important than districting *standards*. He then expressed his support for the idea of a bipartisan commission with tie breaker as the most promising mechanism for improving our procedures for redistricting. But he warned against the attempt to insert blinders that would shield the commission from political life. He argued: "It is important that the operation of bipartisan commission not be unduly impeded by too detailed a specification of 'standards,' or attempted limitation on the kind of data that can be considered."[29] Dixon pointed to recent research by political scientists Niemi and Deegan to the effect that the partisan division of the vote must be incorporated into criteria for fair districting if we are aiming for legislatures responsive to electoral change (Niemi and Deegan 1978). We might add that attaining this ideal of fair and effective representation is no easy matter. Even assuming dispassionate motives by a commission, it is difficult to find the magic formula ensuring the right proportions of safe and swing constituencies. Too many of the former negate voter choice and responsiveness to change, while too many of the latter produce lopsided legislative majorities.

Conclusion

In reviewing the contributions of Robert G. Dixon, Jr., to the theory and practice of reapportionment, one cannot help but be impressed at the totality of their impact—in this instance, the whole is greater than the sum of the parts, however compelling separately. Consistently, Bob Dixon prided himself on being a tough-minded realist at a time when utopian reform was popular. If he frequently seemed more critical of these reformers than of conservatives, the reason seems clear. He was convinced that political egalitarianism was in the ascendancy, that the vital issue was not the goal but the means of attaining it. That goal, he felt, could not be achieved unless its advocates faced up to the nature of representation in a complex, pluralistic society. There were no easy answers. Each step into the political thicket brought consequences hitherto unforeseen. As he looked back in 1979 at the course reapportionment had taken, he found four key facts: (1) there are no neutral district lines; (2) any numerical range of population equality can encompass countless alternate boundary plans; (3) equal population stringency cannot guarantee (and can even undermine) meaningful equality and majority rule. Then he concluded: "The fourth key fact, and the saddest of all because seventeen years have passed since *Baker* v. *Carr*, is that the first three key facts are not understood by judges who rule on these matters, many journalists who report these matters, and many members of the general public."[30] Here Dixon may have underestimated his own influence, at least in the long run.

For all his professed realism, however, Bob Dixon was at heart an idealist deeply committed to equity, fairness, and democratic values. Speaking to Justice Felix Frankfurter's assertion that apportionment plaintiffs in *Baker* v. *Carr* were asking the Court to choose between competing theories of political philosophy, Dixon asked: "Difficult though it may be, what is wrong with a court commitment to a democratic political philosophy?" (Dixon 1968, p. 136). It is revealing that the one portion of Chief Justice Warren's opinion in *Reynolds* v. *Sims* that Dixon liked wholeheartedly was the statement that fair and effective representation for all citizens is the basic aim of legislative apportionment. If the redistricting activity of the 1980s should result in progress toward achieving that elusive goal (as well as a more sophisticated understanding of what progress is), no one would have been more pleased than Robert Dixon. And no one could claim more credit.

Notes

1. Baker v. Carr (1962) 369 U.S. 186.
2. Reynolds v. Sims (1964) 377 U.S. 533.

3. Lucas v. 44th General Assembly of the State of Colorado (1964) 377 U.S. 713, 754.

4. Reynolds v. Sims (1964) 377 U.S. 533, 577.

5. For summary and citations see Baker (1966).

6. Reynolds v. Sims (1964) 377 U.S. 533, 578.

7. Reynolds v. Sims (1964) 377 U.S. 533, 578.

8. Reynolds v. Sims (1964) 377 U.S. 533, 578-579.

9. Lucas v. 44th General Assembly of the State of Colorado (1964) 377 U.S. 713, 730, 735.

10. Kirkpatrick v. Preisler (1969) 394 U.S. 526.

11. Wells v. Rockefeller (1969) 394 U.S. 542.

12. Kirkpatrick v. Preisler (1969) 394 U.S. 526, 530-531.

13. Kirkpatrick v. Preisler (1969) U.S. 526, 537 (Fortas, J., concurring).

14. Kirkpatrick v. Preisler (1969) 394 U.S. 526, 538-539.

15. Wells v. Rockefeller (1969) 394 U.S. 542, 555.

16. Dixon (1969:231). Dixon discussed and quoted responses from David Wells, William J.D. Boyd, William M. Beaney, Malcolm E. Jewell, Robert B. McKay, and Gordon E. Baker.

17. Swann v. Adams (1967) 385 U.S. 440.

18. Gaffney v. Cummings (1973) 412 U.S. 735, 745, 749-750.

19. Mahan v. Howell (1973) 410 U.S. 315, 329.

20. White v. Regester (1973) 412 U.S. 755, 764.

21. White v. Weiser (1973) 412 U.S. 783, 790.

22. In Connecticut, towns rather than counties are the basic units of local government.

23. Gaffney v. Cummings (1973) 412 U.S. 735, 738.

24. Gaffney v. Cummings (1973) 412 U.S. 735. Appellant Gaffney, chairman of the State Republican Party, was permitted to intervene in support of the board plan.

25. Adapted from Robert G. Dixon Jr.'s Appellant's Reply Brief, Gaffney v. Cummings (No. 71-147b): 18, 19.

26. Gaffney v. Cummings (1973) 412 U.S. 735, 754.

27. Statement of Robert G. Dixon, Jr., (1979) at hearings on S.596 before the Committee on Government Affairs, U.S. Senate (June 20):4.

28. Statement of Robert G. Dixon, Jr., (1979) at hearings on S.596 before the Committee on Governmental Affairs, U.S. Senate (June 20):2.

29. Statement of Robert G. Dixon, Jr., (1979) at hearings on S.596 before the Committee on Governmental Affairs, U.S. Senate (June 20):25.

30. Statement of Robert G. Dixon, Jr., (1979) at hearings on S.596 before the Committee on Governmental Affairs, U.S. Senate (June 20):3.

3 The Effects of Districting on Trade-offs among Party Competition, Electoral Responsiveness, and Seats-Votes Relationships

Richard G. Niemi

Discussions of fairness in legislative districting assume that a chief criterion is that neither political party be greatly advantaged in seats relative to its proportion of votes. While it is easy to agree that such a criterion is important, it is not the only one to consider—even if we restrict our attention to the relationship between seats and votes. I have begun some work in which I attempt to specify several criteria by which districting plans can be evaluated. I do not maintain that this work is finished or that these are the only criteria to use. Moreover, since the criteria conflict with one another, as I will show, the result is not a single, simple statement. Decisions would still have to be made (as with population equality) about how far one can deviate from particular standards. Nonetheless, I suggest that this represents a beginning at establishing in more precise terms than was previously done just what it means to develop a districting plan that is fair to both parties.

The fairness criteria focus on the characteristics of a set of districts, such as those for an entire state. (Criteria such as equality of size, contiguity, compactness, adherence to local boundaries, and social homogeneity have been discussed elsewhere at length, and I will not deal with them here.) I begin with two general requirements that seem hard to argue with initially, although they are both heavily laden with political and partisan implications. First, following Tufte (1973), I suggest that a districting plan should be neutral (that is, treat all parties alike) and that it should be responsible to changes in votes. Obviously it would be difficult to call a districting plan fair if it favors one party. Just as obviously, it hardly seems fair or consistent with democratic principles to have a districting plan such that changes in seats are heavily insulated from changes in votes.

Since these requirements, as stated, are relatively vague, they need to be specified more clearly. I suggest that four parameters or characteristics should be used to specify these requirements:

1. *Neutrality*: A districting plan that treats all parties alike in allocating seats per given vote totals is said to be neutral.
2. *Range of responsiveness*: The range of responsiveness of a districting plan is defined as the percentage range of the total popular vote (for the entire state) over which seats change from one party to the other. In other words, the low end of the range is the minimum percentage of the total vote required to win at least one seat, while the upper end is the minimum percentage of the total vote required to win all seats.
3. *Constant swing ratio*: The swing ratio of a districting plan is defined as the rate at which a party gains seats per unit increment in votes. When this rate is identical for all vote percentage points over a specified range, the swing ratio is said to be constant over that range.
4. *Competitiveness*: The competitiveness of a districting plan is defined as the percentage of districts in which some normal or expected vote is within a fixed distance of 50 percent.

Implicit throughout this chapter are the parameter values I tentatively favor—neutrality, a wide range of responsiveness, a constant or nearly constant swing ratio over relatively wide ranges, and a fairly high degree of competitiveness. I would add, however, that these parameters are important features by which to judge the quality of a districting plan even if one favors widely different values.

What I want to do now is to examine each of these criteria alone. Then I need to put them together—because the way in which they all relate to one another is extremely important. Finally, having shown that one cannot design a set of districts that is completely satisfactory on each of these criteria, I will propose some possible standards for fair districting. I will not define precisely here the underlying model upon which my reasoning is based. I think the general points will be eminently clear without all of the complications brought about by such precision. (A more formal presentation is found in Niemi and Deegan, 1978.)

Without being absolutely rigorous, then, let me first examine *neutrality*. A districting plan is neutral when the distribution of expected votes in each district is symmetric around the total expected vote. This neutrality has at least two implications. One is that if a party were to win exactly 50 percent of the total votes, it would win exactly 50 percent of the seats. This is, of course, the only way in which a districting plan can treat two parties equally at the 50 percent vote point. Second, it implies that if one party wins, say X percent of the seats when it wins Y percent of the votes, then the same must be true for the other party. That is, if the other party wins Y percent of the votes, it should win X percent of the seats. Neutrality in this sense is achievable regardless of how one-sided the state vote (within very broad limits), how wide the range of responsiveness, and no matter what the distribution of expected votes in the districts (as long as the distribution is symmetric about the overall expected vote).

The *range of responsiveness* is easily manipulated since it is a function of the greatest deviation of the expected district votes above and below the total state vote. Rather informally, one can think of it this way. If there is an extremely Democratic district, say, one in which the Democrats can expect to get 95 percent of the votes, then that seat will be won even if the Democrats win many fewer votes than anticipated. With some simple assumptions about how the votes are distributed among districts, the Democrats would win that seat even if they won almost 45 percent fewer votes than expected. Conversely, if there is a district in which the expected Democratic vote is extremely low, the Democrats have to win many more votes than anticipated before they would win all of the seats in the state. The range of responsiveness that can be achieved is restricted somewhat in one-sided states. Nevertheless, within the constraints imposed by one-party states, any desired range of responsiveness can be achieved simply by creating districts with expected votes as far as one wishes above and below the overall state vote.

The *swing ratio* over the range $(50 - X)$ percent to $(50 + X)$ percent is constant if the expected votes in the districts are distributed uniformly X percent above and below the state vote. One can think of the situation in this way. As the vote changes from 0 percent Democratic upward, the most Democratic district will be won at some particular point. Then, because of the uniform distribution of expected district votes, every 1 percent increase in the vote will yield a constant increase in the number of seats (that is, the average gain per 1 percent increase in the vote will be constant) until all seats are won. In figure 3-1 I illustrate how a large set of districts can be distributed so that there is a constant swing ratio. Two different examples are shown, one with a swing ratio of 2.0 and one with a swing ratio of 5.0. Note that the range of responsiveness in these examples varies and that both districting plans are neutral. In general a constant swing ratio over the entire range of responsiveness guarantees neutrality.

Competitiveness, by itself, can be maximized quite simply. (One could also minimize competitiveness in similar fashion if one so chose.) If the expected statewide vote falls within the competitive range, an obvious solution is to make all of the districts have the same expected vote as the statewide average. If the statewide expected vote is outside the competitive range, one would simply pile up as many as possible districts just inside the competitive range. I should note, of course, that such a solution might not be terribly satisfactory, and there is not always a unique solution. Moreover, if the expected statewide vote is quite far from 50 percent, no amount of juggling (with equal size districts) can make a large proportion of the districts competitive. Nevertheless, by itself, maximizing the number of competitive districts is not a difficult task.

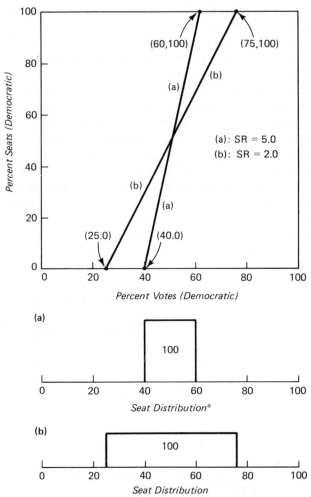

Source: Reprinted by permission of *American Political Science Review* from "The Effects of Districting on Tradeoffs among Party Competition, Electoral Responsiveness and Seats-Votes Relationships."

[a]District expected votes are distributed uniformly across the range shown.

Figure 3-1. Two Examples of Constant Swing Ratios

Putting Together the Four Criteria

An unfortunate fact of life is that there are interdependencies among these four criteria. As simple as it is to achieve desired values of these parameters individually, it may be impossible to attain certain desired combinations of the parameter values in a given districting plan. Consider figure 3-2, which is again a very simple situation in which the statewide expected vote is exactly 50 percent. Figure 3-2 illustrates a districting plan that is neutral, has the maximum possible range of responsiveness, and has a constant swing ratio throughout that range. However, very few seats are competitive by commonly used standards (40-60 percent or 45-55 percent). Obviously more seats could be made competitive simply by creating a large number of districts with expected votes close to 50 percent. If this were done "symmetrically," neutrality would be maintained. Moreover, if one district were left completely Democratic and one completely Republican, the range of responsiveness would not be narrowed. Obviously, however, as more seats are made competitive, the swing ratio will no longer be constant. At the extreme, the modified districting plan would still be neutral, have the maximum range of responsiveness, and all but two of the districts would be extremely

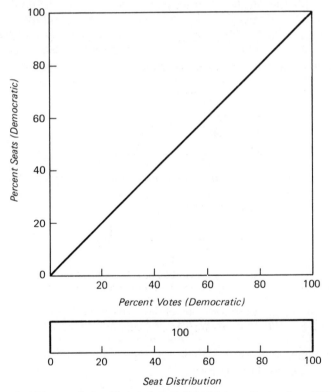

Seat Distribution

Source: Reprinted by permission of *American Political Science Review* from "The Effects of Districting on Tradeoffs among Party Competition, Electoral Responsiveness and Seats-Votes Relationships."

Figure 3-2. Neutral, Maximum Range of Responsiveness, Constant Swing Ratio, Little Competition

competitive. However, it would also have a swing ratio of 0—that is, be totally unresponsive to vote changes—throughout most of the range of votes.

In general, since district-expected votes must be spread out uniformly around the statewide vote to obtain a constant swing ratio but bunched together in the competitive range to maximize competition, it can be seen that these two parameter values are basically incompatible. (This is clearest when the statewide vote equals 50 percent, as in figure 3-2, although it just as surely holds when the statewide vote does not equal 50 percent.)

It is not merely the incompatibility between obtaining a constant swing ratio and maximizing competitiveness that forms the root of the problem. If the statewide vote is not 50 percent, maintaining neutrality and maximizing competitiveness can also be mutually incompatible. If the statewide vote is outside of the competitive range, neutrality requires that at least half of the districts be safe since their district votes must be at least as extreme as the statewide vote. In contrast, a nonneutral set of districts might include a larger number of districts that are competitive. As an example, consider a political unit in which the statewide vote equals 60 percent and assume for simplicity that there are only three districts, 1, 2, and 3. Neutrality would require district-expected votes such as these:

Districts	(a)	(b)		(c)		(d)		(e)	
1	. . . 60	59	. . .	55	. . .	50	. . .	45	. . .
2	. . . 60	60	. . .	60	. . .	60	. . .	60	. . .
3	. . . 60	61	. . .	65	. . .	70	. . .	75	. . .

At most, only one district is highly competitive (45-55 percent). In contrast, a nonneutral set of districts would contain two highly competitive seats, along with one very safe seat, such as:

Districts	(a)	(b)	(c)
1	50	50	52
2	50	55	53
3	80	75	75

Thus, in some circumstances, attempting to maximize the number of competitive districts might require violating neutrality, and conversely, retaining neutrality might require less than the maximum number of competitive districts.

Standards for Fair Districting

Prescribing standards for fair districting is a risky business, especially in light of the incompatibilities examined. Moreover, recall that I will set up some exact standards, but no districting plan could be expected to match them exactly. I will focus only on the simplest situation—that of a large number of districts in which the statewide vote is 50 percent. While other situations are more complicated, the basic considerations are similar.

When the statewide expected vote equals 50 percent, I think that the best districting plan is one that is neutral with a fairly wide range of responsiveness, in which the swing ratio is constant over significant portions of that range and in which there is a reasonably large number of competitive districts by virtue of a higher swing ratio near the statewide expected vote than farther away from it. In support of such a prescription, I note first of all that there is no a priori reason to violate neutrality. Second, a fairly wide range of responsiveness will virtually assure a major party of some representation without creating extremely one-sided districts. Third, a constant swing ratio insures that vote changes will lead to seat changes in a relatively well-specified manner. Having a large number of competitive districts means that the rate at which seats respond to votes is relatively high. And fourth, having a swing ratio near the lower ends of the range of responsiveness rather than in the middle makes it possible to have relatively constant swing ratios both in the middle and near the ends of that range (but a lower swing ratio at the ends rather than in the middle) without creating a large number of safe seats for each party.

In figure 3-3 I illustrate two districting plans with these prescribed features. Both are neutral. The range of responsiveness (20-80 percent or 30-70 percent) seems quite acceptable assuming the expected statewide vote really is a meaningful predictor of future votes. With the wider range of responsiveness, the actual vote could deviate almost 30 percent from normal before one party would be completely denied representation. The swing ratio is constant across ranges of at least 10 percent and there are no flat spots where the swing ratio is zero. And the number of competitive districts, especially in figure 3-3(a), is quite high.

Let me simply say, without proof here, that slight variations are needed to take care of situations when the statewide vote is not 50 percent. Some variation, more problematic, is also necessary when the number of districts is small. Nonetheless, the principles are the same.

In concluding, I simply repeat that I have no illusions that my prescriptions will solve all or most problems in districting. Nor will everyone agree on the standards that I propose. Nonetheless, I hope that I have made clear, if nothing else, some of the elements that must be considered if a commission or legislature is to go beyond population equality to incorporate other politically relevant data in determining what constitutes a fair set of legislative districts.

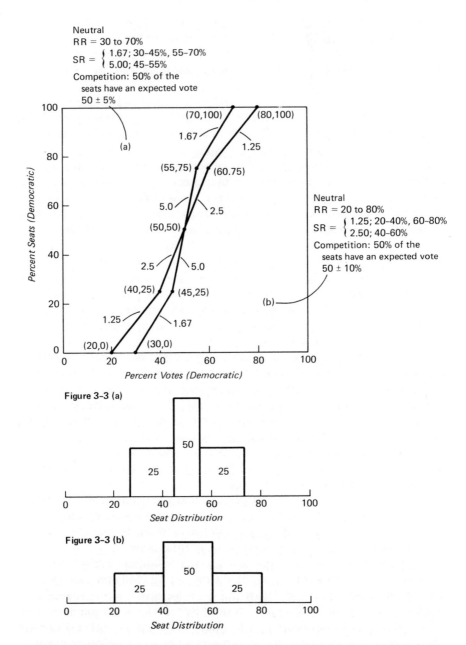

Figure 3-3 (a)

Figure 3-3 (b)

Source: Reprinted by permission of *American Political Science Review* from ''The Effects of Districting on Tradeoffs among Party Competition, Electoral Responsiveness and Seats-Votes Relationships.''

Figure 3-3. Fair Seats-Votes Curves

4 Problems of Implementing Redistricting

Charles H. Backstrom

Implementation of public policy has become a major topic of study in political science. We have at last begun to realize that it is neither judges stating constitutional principles nor legislative statute writers that really determine how things happen. Instead it is street-level bureaucrats who are the real policymakers, based on their daily activities. They decide who really is eligible for welfare, whether students pray together in school, what constitutes a crime.

No less is this true in legislative redistricting. The U.S. Supreme Court pronounced that one-person, one-vote shall be the law of the land, but in the actual realignment of legislative districts, ordinary people have to draw the specific lines. To do that, they have to decide what data to use and what to reject, what principles and other parameters should constrain the district draw process, and whether and how to try to estimate in advance the possible political and personal effects any plan that is adopted might have. A court, assuming it is not itself doing the districting, may take a second look at the choices made on these points, and of course the U.S. Supreme Court may be persuaded to rule on the acceptability of a local decision. But usually the problems of implementation of redistricting must be handled by those with the responsibility for doing the job. What is news is that they have no option whether to redistrict—that would surely trigger a challenge—but scholars should scrutinize the actual implementation of redistricting at every stage.

There are two broad areas of concern when it comes to implementing redistricting: (1) applied theoretical concerns, in the sense of philosophical questions of what the goal of representation can be and how these principles can be achieved in practice and (2) more strictly practical concerns, in the sense of problems relating to the location and handling of data.

First let us look at principles. The object of an elected legislature is to provide representation. (We shall not here go into the more profound aspects of this topic. But see H. Pitkin 1967.) The Supreme Court has referred to representation of people, enunciating the rule of one-person, one-vote,[1] and that one man's vote is worth as much as another's.[2]

As a basic constitutional standard, the Equal Protection Clause required that the seats in both houses of a bicameral state legislature must be apportioned on a population basis. Simply stated, an individual's right to vote for state legislators is unconstitutionally impaired when its weight is in a substantial fashion diluted when compared with votes of citizens living on other parts of the state.[3]

And "simply stated" it was, leaving a number of difficult questions unresolved.

For example, unless the Chief Justice could be accused of sloppy writing, the language in *Reynolds* appears to exclude aliens. The Fourteenth Amendment distinguishes between the "privileges and immunities of citizens"—a term that can be restricted to natural born or formally admitted participants in the polity—and the rights of "persons"—a designation based on humanness and therefore not to be denied someone just because he may have sneaked across the border. If the Court really meant to exclude aliens, they should be cut from the district count. Yet the 1980 Census specifically did not ask about the illegal status of people, in its desire to encourage a full count. And, repeated attempts by Congressmen—from states that were about to lose in reapportionment—to disallow the use of Census figures that included aliens, by riders on appropriations bills late in 1980, failed.

Elsewhere in *Reynolds* the Court speaks of requiring "equal number of residents, or citizens, or voters."[4] This phrase introduces a related problem in the definition of *population*. If the full population count is used as a base for redistricting, substantial inequalities among voting power can result. Legislative districts vary considerably in the portion of the population who are children—from some with 50 percent under eighteen to some with only 5 percent under that age. The effect, of course, is to let the people in one district have about twice the strength of people in another. Using only age-eligible voters as a base might make more sense. Of course, it can be argued that children have stakes in the policy process too, so they should be counted—and in effect the parents would cast their children's votes along with their own. This may be desirable social policy, but it would be healthful to acknowledge the political effects of what is being done. We might be more hesitant to allocate legislative seats on numbers of *voters,* which, while correcting for the differing proportions of youth, would discriminate against those people choosing not to vote in the particular election just before reapportionment when they might desire to participate another year. Again, it would be well to acknowledge the result of choice that is made in counting all adults—which is to give those who do vote in low-voting districts greater power than those who vote in high-participation areas.

Leaving the question of whom to count and turning instead to the question of what aspect of people is to be represented, the Court appears to have said that citizens (or persons) are undistinguishable from each other and that equality can be achieved for representation by simply counting their heads and dividing by the number of seats available. But satisfactory representation in reality requires more than simple math (as soon became evident when black people wanted to be represented as blacks and not merely as people). The Supreme Court had already agreed to that before *Baker* v. *Carr*,[5] in the Tuskeegee case (*Gomillion* v. *Lightfoot*)[6] in 1960, with Frankfurter, who didn't like political thickets, writing the opinion. The Court has continued to be solicitous of blacks' representation as blacks, outlawing multimember districts in Texas that appeared to be discriminatory against them[7] even though multimember districts per se, when drawn by legislatures, have not been invalidated.[8,9]

Futhermore, Republicans wanted to be represented as partisans and Hasidic Jews as religious people, and the question of just whose interests were to be represented was revealed in all its complexity.

It is not at all clear whether the best strategy for effective representation comes from having people of the same type (say, blacks) spread throughout many districts (for example, constituting 25 percent in each district) so that all of the representatives of whatever race must pay attention to what blacks want, or whether it would be better to have blacks concentrated in one or two districts, where they could constitute a majority and be more or less sure of getting one or two of their number elected to the legislature. For the present at least, minority groups will accept nothing less than the latter strategy, whatever the policy effect differential may be.

On the matter of partisanship as a criterion for representation, the Supreme Court has recognized its relevance to fair representation but has so far refused to invalidate a reapportionment plan on grounds of partisan gerrymandering.[10,11] This lack of success is probably largely due to the lack of a precise definition of partisan gerrymandering and the lack of recognized measures of it. V.O. Key (1932, p. 105-151) very early recognized that court action on population malapportionment had to await more scientific underpinning of its exact nature and degree. It was another thirty years after his observation before these critera were developed enough that the courts had no hesitation in ruling on what constituted population inequality.

Elsewhere we have proposed a definition and measurement for partisan gerrymandering (Backstrom et al., 1978). We have insisted that gerrymandering is not merely an optical judgment as to whether districts snake too scandalously over a map. Instead it consists of one group of partisans gaining undue advantage over another, even in regular-shaped districts. The problems of satisfactory measurement of party advantage are severe. Designation of a typical state-base race or an index of several races is required so as not to condemn the victorious party for having benefited from a gerrymander when they have selected good candidates and run good campaigns. A partisan test must be made with the results of a previous election, so that a redistricting plan can be judged before it goes into effect.

We have insisted that the test of fairness for contending parties be that the majority party, when it has received a mere 50 percent plus of the base race statewide, be in a majority in a bare majority of the districts. This standard allows the "balloon effect" to operate, giving the majority party dominance in a greater percentage of districts than its state-wide average as that percentage rises above 50 percent. We have stressed that the natural concentration of partisans in certain parts of most states might make it impossible to draw a plan that is entirely fair, but that this situation cannot be called a gerrymander—only a remedial disadvantage that has not in fact been remedied can be so classified.

What this chapter illustrates is the vast complexity in practice of trying to implement a fair districting plan, accommodating all possible representation goals. In any event, the desire of some reformers to try to sterilize the redistricting process from all partisan input and measures is a hopeless, if not misguided, effort. Just because the drafter of a redistricting plan is unconscious of partisan criteria does not mean that the resulting plan will be fair. There is simply no way of drawing a redistricting plan without effects, both representational and partisan political. Give a chimp in a zoo a crayon and a map, and the resulting plan will have differential effects on people. Therefore, the principles underlying a plan should be explicitly stated, clearly defined, realistically operationalized, and the probable partisan and other representational effects estimated in advance.

Let us turn now to practical data problems in implementing redistricting. Phrases here too are tossed around glibly: *One person/one vote, contiguity,* and *compactness* are common criteria required or sought in districting. These words are all clichés that must be given concrete meaning by the people who sit down to institute a districting plan. Let us take them up in turn.

Equal population is not easy to ascertain. No one needs to be reminded of the inaccuracy of the every-household count. With so much federal aid based on census counts at stake, ever since the census was tabulated cities have been demanding recounts or taking the Census Bureau to court to demand a general inflation of the results. In 1970 the full Census count was off, by Bureau admission, by 5.3 million, or a 2.5 percent undercount. But since there is an area bias to this loss, census officials admit 7.7 percent of the blacks were not included. This bias has representational consequences because of diminished voting power for important minorities. But the entire undercount also has implications for what constitutes equality. It is *false precision* for a reapportioning authority to try to come within 2 percent of an average for each district (as the court required in Minnesota) or within 0.5 percent (as in Michigan). The result of such ridiculous tolerances has been contorted district lines, as pieces of municipalities had to be thrown into the next district. Sometimes single blocks were split or apartment complexes divided. (We joke about a district line drawn through a double bed separating husband and wife in the name of greater equality.) Whatever other goals could be sought by easing up on these population standards, we should require no closer equality than the data warrant. A tolerance of 5 percent or more could be justified on this basis. After explicitly rejecting *de minimis* ("the court will not concern itself with trifles") in a 1969 case,[12] the Supreme Court began to retreat from "unrealistic emphasis on raw population figures" and spoke specifically of *de minimis,* allowing deviations of 7.8 percent in Connecticut (*Gaffney*), 9.9 percent in Texas (*White*), and 16.4 percent in Virginia (*Mahan* v. *Howell*).[13]

The Court is willing to tolerate more deviation in state legislative districts than in congressional districts, and more deviation in legislature-drawn plans than in court-drawn plans.

The application of a single standard of allowed population deviation works differently depending upon the relative size of the legislative body to population of the state. A 2 percent deviation in California with Senate districts of half a million allows 10,000 more people in one district than in another. In Minnesota (near the median state in number of constituents per legislative district) the difference could be only 560 people, far fewer than reside on some city apartment blocks. No wonder California districters had such an easy time getting data—they moved only whole tracts, compared to the block-level data employed in Minnesota. One wonders if it is the relative (percentage) deprivation of citizens in different districts or the number of people who are "excess" that should constitute an impermissible disparity.

In *Mahan* the Court acknowledged the legitimate goal of recognizing local government boundaries. Enforcing hair-splitting equality had had the effect of producing artificial districts. In Minnesota, representation of community of interest was sacrificed. Although the social or psychological boundaries of communities are not precise, they are real. People think of themselves as belonging together in counties in rural areas, in cities or sectors of metropolitan areas, and in neighborhoods of central cities. This feeling is a clue to community, which is in turn the only rationale for geographically defined districts. People's other interests can be better represented by interest-group membership, or proportional representation through ideological-based parties. Since, however, it is unlikely that these hoary alternatives will gain any headway in our representation systems, we may as well continue to concentrate on redistricting present seats by area.

Community of interest itself is not easy to operationalize. To achieve it may require following a river valley, rather than have the river divide two districts. It may mean putting all of a certain ore deposit together in a district since all the people there are connected in some way to the mine, which could mean domination of a district by a single powerful interest that might be less oppressive if split up. As one legislator commented, his district illustrated the perfect community of interest. He had a little bit of everything in it and, therefore, the district was an exact microcosm of the state. The issue arises when deciding if central city areas should constitute some districts exclusively, or if districts should contain both suburban and central city areas to avoid personifying their conflict of interest with separate legislators.

Merely obtaining usable population data for redistricting is not easy. The Census Bureau has promised easy access to 1980 census data and even has a computer software program (CENSPAC) that is reputed to allow ordinary users to reaggregate census data to any geographic area. Perhaps this will work. The 1970 tapes could not be used in the form received for redistricting but had to be reformatted. For another thing, the tapes of 1970 were based on initial returns. Subsequent corrections were made to state and congressional district totals and were printed as errata in the front of census publications. But the tapes were never changed. Thus one could cumulate all enumeration districts (EDs) for a state from the tape and not come out with the official state population total. It was necessary to update the tape locally to include these corrections to get accurate totals. In 1980 the Bureau invited early comment by municipalities on preliminary figures. Perhaps this will catch many errors before the tapes are released, but caution is always advised.

Figures, when printed in census books or computer tabulations, have an aura of authenticity. Figures contained in a legislative committee report have the ring of being official. Yet the assertions of accuracy are not necessarily borne out after a mathematical check. The Minnesota legislature in 1965, in their response to *Reynolds,* asserted that their new districts met the test of a maximum 20-percent deviation from the average size district. The present author's calculation for the governor of Minnesota (done in the twenty-four hours between the unveiling of the bill and its enactment) showed a 100-percent deviation: the largest district was exactly twice the size of the smallest (the home district of the Speaker of the House.) What had happened, most probably, was that errors compounded as pieces were subtracted from some districts and added to others to accommodate various requests, without checking the new totals for omissions and duplications of parts of municipalities. Part of the problem arose from the typographical style of the census report, which did not distinguish between the total population of a village reported separately and the same people counted together with the rest of the people in the rural township surrounding it. The mistakes were caused partly by fatigue, partly by cocksure clerical help, and partly by a deliberate decision that any figures were good enough to release since no one would ever likely check. The program used for the governor made all these checks automatically, so that he could be confident of the accuracy, but it is an interesting case study of the practice of public relations that the figures justifying the Governor's veto never caught up in the press or on the hustings with the claims of legislative leaders that their reasonable bill had been unfairly shot down.

This example illustrates a fundamental problem of the implementation of redistricting. Because redistricting is episodic—happening only once in ten years—it is not efficient to keep a trained bureaucracy employed to handle it—as is done for tax collection, which happens once or twice a year, or drivers license renewals, which go on every day. Thus the personnel handling the details of redistricting are most likely novices—or at least very rusty as they tool up again to tackle the job. The time lapse between redistricting efforts has a positive aspect. Each decade finds a large number of people eager to do legislative districting. One discovers that these are always people who have never done it before. Those who have gone through it are trying to hide behind another job in hopes they are not called upon this time! The Hobbesian lust for power is rapidly sated by a single orgy of redistricting.

Despite the foregoing discussion, equal population is the easiest aspect of districting to understand. Other concepts are harder to operationalize.

Contiguity seems self-evident, but it can be deceptive. Are counties that touch only on a corner contiguous? Moreover, do districts that appear to touch on a corner actually do so? One plan passed by the Minnesota state senate contained a district that, when a very large-scale highway map was procured, had counties that actually missed touching by a few hundred feet because of a survey correction line.

Even if two areas touch, are they really contiguous if it is not possible to get from one to another without going through another district, as when no roads connect the two parts? Do rivers without bridges in the district join or separate the adjacent land? Where cities have extraterritoriality, as when they own a water reservoir or a park completely outside their boundaries, can the district include the whole city in one district and the interposing city in another? If the remains of a township after various incorporations consist of eleven discontiguous parts, can these parts be put into a single district without carrying along the municipalities that lie between? (Incidentally, figuring the population of these parts, even with the aid of the census ED maps, is a puzzle of some magnitude.)

Compactness is another simplistic trap. The most common lay definition of gerrymandering is visual—a district that winds irregularly over the map. The supposed remedy for this has been to require compactness, often without further specification. But what constitutes a compact district, and how compact should a district be required to be?

Some practitioners have suggested counting the number of sides—the fewer (down to three) there are, the more compact is the district. Of course, following the boundaries of a river or of a governmental unit, the least suspect of gerrymandering, may stairstep a district line into a visual monstrosity. Another test is to draw lines between opposite extemities of a district and count the number of times the line crosses the border. Still another test for compactness is to figure the ratio of actual area of a district to the area of a circle that circumscribes the district. If the district is round, therefore, it will have a perfect compactness of 1.00. Obviously not all districts in a state could achieve this sort of compactness without, like round cookie cutters, leaving a lot of scraps. Nature's solution, the hexagon, is a more reasonable gauge. The Minneapolis city charter, trying to insure compactness, stipulates that no ward shall be more than twice as long as it is wide. (In practice this didn't ensure compactness at all, because the designers of a toothpick-shaped ward merely turned it into a skinny L, which violated community interest while satisfying the charter provision.

The CROND (Delaware) computer program judges compactness by a transportation model that weights population centers by distance into moments of inertia—a large city far from the center makes a district that rates low in compactness. A similar algorithm can be used with area spread regardless of the population it contains.

Those who are redistricting a state, or judging the product of that redistricting, need to have explicit instructions and standards for judging compactness.

Besides the separate complications of implementing the various criteria for districting mentioned here, the several criteria *interact* to produce effects on each other. Achieving close population equality, as mentioned, will tend to reduce compactness. It will also require the breeching of county and municipal lines, generally an undesirable feature both for citizen understanding of their contacts with government and for election administrators trying to be accurate and efficient.

Population equality certainly constrains partisan gerrymandering somewhat. Yet, as we demonstrated in our Minnesota example, hewing to very tight population critera and specified standards of compactness can still result in plans with a range of from 33 percent to 58 percent of the districts being dominated by one of the parties (Backstrom et al 1978, p. 1155).

Everyone agrees that compactness inhibits party gerrymandering, but most are unaware that it doesn't cure it. Another oft-expressed value in districting—having as many possible districts marginal so as to increase overall competitiveness, and thereby make the state responsive to party swings—could be more widely achieved if compactness were relaxed so that partisan areas could be combined counter to the way the dominant party probably wishes. (The incumbents at least want safe districts.) There is a limit, however, to how many marginal districts can be created, depending on the concentration of party members in certain areas, unless contiguity is given up.

The bottom line is that reformers should be cautious of glibly stating that all standard criteria of good redistricting should be simultaneously applied. It can't be done. Moreover, many people probably wouldn't want to do it. If the criteria are to be anything more than hortatory desiderata, however, methods of calculation—and the extent to which each is to be considered or traded off—should be specified in the charge to the districting authority.

Let us look now at the use of the *computer* in redistricting. Hopefully, there is no one who thinks the computer is a black box with magical problem-solving capacity of its own. Everyone now realizes that the steps through which the computer is to proceed and the criteria by which a plan is to be evaluated and rejected in favor of continued manipulation must be programmed by a human being.

Should the computer divide the state in two, and then each part in two again, and so forth, until the right number of oblong districts are drawn? If so, at which dimension of the state should it start? How should it treat large lakes and ocean inlets—cross them to include both sides in one, or stick to the shore? Should the computer instead be instructed to start in a corner of the state and proceed like a crawling cookie cutter, stamping out nearly equal size districts (by population) as it goes? Or should the computer merely start with existing districts, with untouchable centers (the incumbents' homes), trading units only at the borders (like the Nagel program used in California, Nagel, 1965, 863)? And can other criteria constitutionally be used—party strength and percentage of black or Spanish-surnamed—at the outset of the district drawing? Inevitably, practical politicians will use these criteria when critiquing a districting plan, but should they be introduced specifically at the beginning in an effort to do affirmative districting in favor of constitutionally recognized minorities? If not, the resulting plan will be subject to court challenge as discriminatory if it doesn't do the best possible for such groups.

The desire to apply many criteria variably has up till now usually led district drafters to avoid the computer except as a testing tool for a districting plan created intuitively. Computer freaks always promise fancy software that will allow district designers to move areas around on a cathode ray tube by light pen, with instant reports of new population totals and political effects by district. But these are horrendously expensive in time and money, and for the same reason that the programs have only a once-per-decade use, usually don't get finished before the deadlines for ordering a plan into effect. (See W. Craig 1973, for uses and limitations of the computer in reapportionment.) Perhaps the 1980s will see a big breakthrough in computer-assisted redistricting, but otherwise most drafters will opt for the manual, patient, experimental approach (Morrill, 1973, pp. 463, 472).[14]

The traditional authorities for districting are, of course, most often legislators—usually a few leaders who get themselves put on the elections committee. The resultant committee is usually a mix of people with strong majority party interests plus a few innocuous appointees from the other party (unless the minority is allowed to name their own members). In the old days in Minnesota, the leaders always installed as chairman of redistricting the senator from the smallest district, assuming he wouldn't get carried away with a desire for complete equality. But he always managed to commit suicide with the districting plan, while murdering the fewest of his colleagues, usually those who were near electoral death or about to retire anyway.

Reapportionment bills have always been among the most difficult to pass in a legislature, however, even without the party squabbling associated with split house control or the governor being of the opposite party from the legislature. Redistricting is one of the few bills that every single member wishes to be concerned with the details of. That is, each member wants to dictate one particular part of the bill—his or her own area—and each has seemingly simple requests: Just give me another slice of my old district (where the big contributors live), or just move my district away from the university a little more so that I don't have to contend with too many obstreperous students. Each member in turn looks over the shoulders of the mapmakers and says helpfully that all they have to do is compensate at the other end of the district by moving that line a little. What they don't understand is that every move affects every other district around theirs, not only the first tier. The effect ripples through at least one fourth of the state before the needed equality can be regained.

The stigma of conflict-of-interest charges and the desire of some leaders to free their agenda for substantive bills have combined to put forth an argument for *nonlegislative reapportionment commissions.* These commissions would be one step removed from direct self-interest, but the hope that they would be free from partisan politics or pleas to save individual careers is naive. Illinois will be remembered for its deadlock in a bipartisan commission that resulted in the disaster of having the whole legislature elected at large. Minnesota in 1980 proposed a constitutional amendment for a commission of four legislators who would then unanimously elect five more nonlegislative members. While this proposal would not eliminate legislative influence from redistricting, the fact that it was proposed at all shows that court-enforced constitutional criteria and public scrutiny have taken away some of the uncurbed discretion that the legislature formerly exercised in district-making and has made them ready to yield some power over the process. The amendment was narrowly defeated, so how it might have worked must remain speculative. The appointment process would likely have resulted in a procedure called "striking the brains out of the commission"—each side vetoing anyone proposed by the other who knows anything about reapportionment.

However constituted, a redistricting authority must decide whether to formulate its own plan in camera and then hold hearings on it or to solicit plans from outsiders, and decide which one to adopt. The commission's final product is unlikely to satisfy all activists, just as judicially imposed plans have been subject to a charge of favoritism. The point was made earlier that every plan has political effects. There is no technical or mechanistic way to redistrict. Those who want to remove legislators from the process are denying a say to the people who have the most practice in what representation means on a day-to-day basis.

Representative government has so little public confidence today that anything that could provide more sensitivity for all aspects of representation, more rationality of election district lines, and more stability of representative service, would be welcome. We should not let technical goals in reapportionment obscure these deeper needs. Yet public confidence in the fairness of the representative system can be further increased by continuing to develop and implement understandable and appealing criteria for reapportionment.

The issues raised in this chapter should serve as a challenge to improve the implementation of redistricting.

Notes

1. Gray v. Sanders (1963) 372 U.S. 368.
2. Wesberry v. Sanders (1964) 376 U.S. 1.
3. Reynolds v. Sims (1964) 377 U.S. 533, 564.
4. Reynolds v. Sims (1964) 377 U.S. 533, 577.
5. Baker v. Carr (1962) 369 U.S. 186.
6. Gomillion v. Lightfoot (1960) 364 U.S. 339.
7. White v. Regester (1973) 412 U.S. 755.
8. Fortson v. Dorsey (1965) 379 U.S. 433.
9. Whitcomb v. Chavis (1971) 403 U.S. 124.
10. Gaffney v. Cummings (1973) 412 U.S. 736.
11. Wells v. Rockefeller (1969) 394 U.S. 542.
12. Kirkpatrick v. Preisler (1969) 394 U.S. 526.
13. Mahan v. Howell (1973) 410 U.S. 315.
14. Editor's note: At least two states, New York and California did make use of highly sophisticated computer-graphics terminals in drawing up 1980's legislative and congressional districts.

5 For Single-Member Districts Random Is Not Equal

Bernard Grofman

Senator Danforth:	I don't know how many black members there are in the Congress. Maybe you do.
Mr. Wells:	I don't know the actual figure, no.
Senator Danforth:	But it is roughly fifteen, something like that, whereas it is about 10 or 11 percent of the population of this country is black. So, they are about one third of what their representation would be (15/435 = 3.4 percent).
Senator Levin:	Suppose it could be shown that to use what amounts to the chance method is going to result in even a lower black representation. I don't see how that is possible.
Mr. Wells:	I agree with you, Senator. I don't see how it is possible. Even if it is possible in one particular district, it may not be in the next one. That is the beauty of operating on a chance pattern.
	In the long run, if I understand mathematical logic, a chance pattern will, over the long haul, operate in such a way as to make the percentage of the population and the percentage of representation more or less equal. It may not do that in any given redistricting arrangement. But, in looking at it over a series of years, it should accomplish that (Wells 1979, p. 529).

Dave Wells's assertion that, for single-member districts, "a chance pattern will, over the long haul, operate in such a way as to make the percentage of the population and the percentage of representation more or less equal" is a view I suspect is widely held. For example, David Cohen of Common Cause in his testimony on S.596 also calls attention to the discrepancy between black and Hispanic population figures and the percentages of black/ Hispanic congressional representatives as evidence of nonrandom (and discriminatory) districting. Unfortunately, except under very special circumstances, unlikely to be ever achieved in practice, random districting will not yield proportionality between a group's vote percentage and the percentage of seats it wins. We show in table 5-1 potential expected average long-

This research was supported by NSF Grant #SOC 77-24474, Political Science Program. I am indebted to Nick Noviello for programming the selection simulation reported in figure 5-1.

run relationships between aggregate vote percentages and seat percentages in a single-member election system with a large number of randomly drawn equal population districts under the assumption that there are two distinct groups competing in each district so that whichever seats are lost by the one group will be won by the other. The parameter k is an index of proportionality (Theil, 1969, 1970; Taagepera, 1973; Tufte, 1973; Grofman, 1975; Niemi and Deegan, 1978). Only for $k = 1$ will the percentage of seats won equal the percentage of votes received.

At one time it was thought that $k = 3$ was the most likely k value. This conjecture is known as the *cube law of politics* (Kendall and Stuart, 1950). Recent work (see esp. Tufte, 1973) has found a wide variation in k, with only parliamentary elections in Great Britain approximating the magic value of 3. Estimated values range from .71 (U.S. congressional elections in the period 1966-1970; Tufte, 1973) to 4.4 (the U.S. Electoral College, 1828-1968; Taagepera, 1973). Most of the fitted values are, however, in the range 2.2 ± .8. For example, Tufte finds k for U.S. congressional elections (1900-1970) to be 2.2. The value $k = 3$, does, however, provide a *quite good* approximation to the situation where partisan/group strength is randomly distributed across districts. We show in figure 5-1 the results of a simulation of a 99-district election. The cube law fits the data remarkably well.

As is apparent from table 5-1, the higher the k value the less successful will be the minority party/group in terms of translating its votes into seats. Moreover, for $k > 1$, the smaller the minority, the less well it does in achieving a proportionality between its vote share and its seat share. For example, for $k = 2$, 10 percent of the vote achieves only an expected 1.2 percent of the seats ($1.2/10 = 12$ percent) on average but 20 percent of the vote achieves an expected 5.8 percent of the seats ($5.8/20 = 29$ percent) on average, while 40 percent of the vote achieves an expected 30.8 percent of the seats ($30.8/40 = 77$ percent) on average.

Table 5-1
Average Expected Seat Percentage (S) as a Function of Vote Percentage (V) and k:$\left(\dfrac{1-S}{S}\right)=\left(\dfrac{1-V^k}{V^k}\right)$

V(%)/S(%)	K=.75	K=1	K=1.25	K=1.5	K=2	K=2.5	K=3	K=3.5
10	16.1	10	6.0	3.5	1.2	.4	.1	.04
15	21.3	15	10.3	6.9	3.0	1.2	.5	.2
20	26.1	20	15.0	11.1	5.8	3.0	1.5	.8
25	30.4	25	20.2	16.1	10.0	6.0	3.6	2.1
30	34.6	30	25.8	21.9	15.6	10.8	7.3	4.9
35	38.6	35	31.5	28.3	22.4	17.4	13.4	10.2
40	42.4	40	37.6	35.2	30.8	26.6	22.9	19.5
45	46.3	45	43.8	42.5	40.2	37.8	35.5	33.3
50	50.0	50	50.0	50.0	50.0	50.0	50.0	50.0

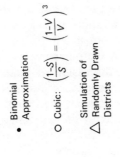

• Binomial
  Approximation

○ Cubic: $\left(\dfrac{1-S}{S}\right) = \left(\dfrac{1-V}{V}\right)^3$

△ Simulation of
  Randomly Drawn
  Districts

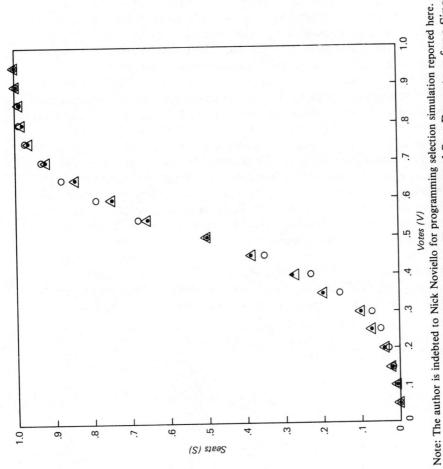

Note: The author is indebted to Nick Noviello for programming selection simulation reported here.

Figure 5-1. Relationship between Vote Percentage and Seat Percentage for a Single-Member District Legislature Whose Equipopulation Districts Have Been Randomly Drawn

In any actual election system, the value of k will depend upon the spatial distribution of partisan/group support across districts. Roughly speaking, the more the distribution of partisan/group strength is similar in all districts (that is, the lower the variance), the higher will be k. (See Johnston 1976; Niemi and Deegan 1978, for a discussion of related issues.) Wildgen and Engstrom (1980) note that, in general, minorities will do better if their strength is geographically concentrated; while majority seat share is maximized the more evenly distributed is its vote strength.

Backstrom, Robins, and Eller (1978) and Engstrom and Wildgen (1977) have proposed to measure fairness of apportionment (that is, proportionality between vote share and seat share), as relative to that which would be statistically expected under a random drawing of (equal population) district lines *given the actual pattern of minority concentration.* It is possible to establish confidence limits around predicted values at any desired level, for example, 95 percent. Observations that fall outside these limits can be assumed to be due to deliberate gerrymandering.

As we see from table 5-1, for any given level of minority voting strength, what would be a reasonable minority seat representation depends very much on k, which in turn depends upon the spatial distribution of minority strength. For example, under a random drawing of district boundaries, a minority with a 30 percent vote strength could expect on average 21.9 percent of the seats if $k = 1.5$ but only 7.3 percent of the seats if $k = 3$. In the U.S. Congress, were $k = 2$, then, an 11 percent black population minority could only *expect* to get 1.5 percent of the seats on average, while a 9 percent Hispanic minority could only *expect* to get .9 percent of the seats on average, even were districting completely unbiased. That blacks win more congressional seats than Hispanics (3.4 percent versus about 1 percent) relative to what might be expected is, in our view, at least in part due to the fact that blacks are somewhat more geographically concentrated than are Hispanics. Only where minority strength is at least 45 percent is seat share relatively insensitive to variation in k.

In sum, blind districting is extremely unlikely to give rise to proportional results, except when minority and majority are near equal in size.

6 Compromise Districting

Lee Papayanopoulos

The quest for districting criteria and measures of gerrymandering, nearly two decades after *Baker* v. *Carr*,[1] is beginning to seem quixotic. When apportionment creates conflict, controversy, and confrontation—as it frequently does—there are no adequate, let alone universal, criteria by which to judge its effects. Only a sincere compromise plan reflecting the political sentiments of the various political groups can be fair.

We contend that the conflict between parties facing redistricting is analogous to that between a union and management negotiating a contract. Consequently, the conflict may be resolved by some method of rational compromising akin to binding arbitration.

Nondistricting methods of apportionment are not prone to gerrymandering and therefore are not competitive in the above sense. They include weighted voting,[2] at-large representation,[3] and the allocation of congressional seats to states[4] that are important but outside our present scope.

In this chapter we take a fresh look at equipopulous cartographic districting with singular representation. We propose that fairness can be achieved through a methodology of compromise—aided by a set of principles—rather than by the invention and imposition of more districting criteria. This is consistent with Dixon's view, which "concluded that *method* is more important than districting *standards*"—as Baker points out.[5]

Terminology

A few definitions will facilitate the following development. A *districting plan* (or *plan*) is a specified geographic correspondence between constituencies and their representatives. The ordinary *districting process* is an arbitrary sequence of actions taken by an appointed individual, committee, or agency to obtain a plan.

A *definitive districting process* is a specified sequence of steps that leads to a unique plan or a set of equivalent plans.[6]

Districting criteria are *reasonable* if they are intended to discourage gerrymandering. Districting criteria are *absolute* if they conform to some universal democratic notion such as equality or symmetry.[7]

A plan is *fair* if it meets a set of reasonable criteria. It is *absolutely fair* if it meets a set of absolute criteria. A plan is fair to a constituency if it gives it at least as much representation as an absolutely fair plan.

Subjectivity in Districting

From attempting to reconcile the behavioral, political, and game-theoretic aspects of districting, a number of observations and logical conclusions emerge. We summarize these into a set of propositions that later lead to an operational model of districting.

The potential benefits rendered by a particular district plan are not always accurately quantifiable. Measurable or not, the benefits enjoyed by the constituencies are finite and their distribution depends on the way the districting plan is drawn.

> *Proposition 1:* A districting plan is an allocation of limited (social/political/economic) resources among competing population groups.

Anyone appointed to segment the political pie, no matter how well intentioned, is predisposed by his own perceptions of democracy and political idealism. Some unresolvable questions that underlie the conventional districting process are: Is a legislator a delegate or a free agent? Should incumbency be protected? By extension, should a legislature be stable or responsive?[8]

> *Proposition 2:* Any pronouncement regarding the fairness of a plan must necessarily be subjective.

Proponents of fair districting purport that a large set of concurrent criteria limit gerrymandering because they restrict aberrant choice. However, arbitrary criteria make districting more subjective and controversial than it has to be. We hope that in this development it will become apparent that definitive districting coupled with a few absolute criteria will produce plans that are more equitable and less prone to criticism.

Districting under Conditions of Conflict

In the utopia of perfect homogeneity, all citizens and representatives share common viewpoints on all matters. There exists no conflict and both elections and legislative decisions are by assumption, unanimous.

> *Proposition 3:* Under conditions of total concordance every apportionment is absolutely fair. Every plan is equivalent to every other.

As the polity becomes more heterogeneous, it deviates from this ideal forming two or more distinct political groups, which by definition are in conflict. Apportionment plans are no longer equivalent but subject to group preference. The groups in question, also referred to as *parties*, may include political parties, ethnic or racial blocks of population, and so forth. Our discussion will revolve around a two-party model for the sake of exposition, but it is by no means limited in that respect.

> *Proposition 4:* Under conditions of conflict, a districting plan is fair to all parties only insofar as it is absolutely fair.

This of course is a consequence of the definitions of fairness and of propositions 1 and 2. The key question then is how to sidestep the arbitrary and subjective construction of a plan and come up with one using only absolute means.

> *Proposition 5:* Under conflict, an absolutely fair plan can be derived only through a definitive procedure that seeks a true compromise.

This deliberately strong statement becomes plausible if apportionment is identified as merely a member of a class of familiar conflict situations. Society has successfully institutionalized the way to resolve the others, and if our taxonomic analogy is valid, then, surely, we can be guided by it.

The judicial system resolves conflict by means of well-defined procedures. Competitive conflict in athletics is arbitrated similarly. In these and other arenas, a judge or umpire whose career rides on his reputation for impartiality is the ultimate peacemaker between adversaries whose optimal strategy is maximally selfish. Arbiters are individuals, not committees, with roles that limit subjectivity.

Actually, we prefer to draw the parallel between districting and still another member of the class of conflict situations, namely labor-management contract negotiations under binding arbitration. The analogy is closer because each side's expectations are made known, they are negotiable, politics are involved, the conflict occurs at fixed intervals of time and, miraculously, when everything is said and done, all parties emerge victorious. The arbitrator hears all sides, obtains their demands and all supporting data, and proclaims his Solomonian verdict, which is essentially an average or midpoint compromise. The procedure is definitive, the criteria symmetrical, the conflict resolved.

In this context, proposition 5 becomes substantive and constructive for it leads us to a rational procedure to resolve apportionment conflict. One may notice that such a procedure need not strive to control gerrymandering through artificial criteria but can be made to fight fire with fire. That is, it accepts gerrymanders as inputs and then allows them to cancel one another.

Proposition 6: A true compromise of extreme and opposite gerrymanders
proposed by each and every party is absolutely fair.

To illustrate, consider a hypothetical state with 70 percent Democrats
and 30 percent Republicans. Under certain special, but not entirely unusual,
conditions for which the theorem of gerrymandering[10] may be invoked, the
Republicans can come up with a gerrymander that gives them 60 percent of
the seats while the Democrats can produce a map with no districts going to
the Republicans. A true compromise of these extremes gives the
Republicans 30 percent, which conforms exactly with our intuitive sense of
fairness *and* with the democratic edict of symmetry.

Population distribution being irregular as it is, the "band of
discretion"[11] may be narrower[12]—but a plan of compromise at the midpoint
will still be absolutely fair by symmetry.

A General Blueprint for Compromise Districting

Propositions 4, 5, and 6 become operational in the framework of the
following model of a districting procedure. During a post-census period of
reasonable duration, each party prepares a plan with a prescribed number
of equal population districts. Since no judgment of the plan is intended, no
further conditions are placed on it.

The party plans are then submitted to a jointly agreeable arbitrator who
is mandated to obtain the final and binding compromise map. Clearly, it is
difficult to reach a purely cartographic compromise because averages involve
numbers. Thus, the arbitrator requests (and it is in the parties' best interest to
provide) everyone's best estimates regarding such matters as voting patterns.
"Cheating," which is probably not possible in the first place, has no rewards.
In fact, both over- and understating party strength can be detrimental.

Among the important differences between blind, unilateral districting
and the compromise approach is that the latter uses the party plans as
reference points. These plans have already absorbed all the subjectivity inherent in districting. They reflect political realities to their fullest, and it is
the arbitrator's responsibility to preserve and protect them as equitably as
possible. He is in a better position to do it because, unlike the apportionment committee, he is a referee and not a player.

Conclusions

The theory of systematic apportionment must deal with methodological
questions because effective antigerrymandering criteria are difficult to obtain

and next to impossible to enforce. A committee (of any composition) may comply with all the rules of compactness, contiguity, and such, and still create a masterful gerrymander.

Under arbitration there is no hypocritical self-regulation. All "parties"[13] provide their inputs into the districting process. Not so paradoxically, what would otherwise be blatant gerrymandering is now legitimized. In game-theoretic terms it is actually the *optimal* strategy of the parties.

We strongly favor the notion of a single individual in the role of arbitrator for sharper definition of responsibility and reputation. His optimal policy is to be fair. Whether or not it is necessary to define more precisely how this is to be accomplished remains to be discussed elsewhere. It must be pointed out, however, that mediation methods of labor disputes are certainly not standardized.[14]

Compromise districting is a definitive, structured approach that ought to be more equitable and straightforward than that which relies on a multitude of criteria. Judging from the success of the well-established process of binding arbitration, it should be less controversial as well.

Notes

1. Baker v. Carr (1962) 369 U.S. 186.
2. See Imrie (1973, p. 182).
3. See Bernard Grofman "Alternatives to Single-Member Plurality Districts: Legal and Empirical Issues," chapter 12, this volume.
4. See Balinski and Young 1974.
5. See Gordon E. Baker, chapter 2, this volume.
6. Traditionally, districting has been carried out in a nondefinitive way. On the other hand, modified weighted voting reapportionment is definitive and so is congressional apportionment.
7. Examples: Compactness is reasonable. Equality of population is absolute.
8. Mutually exclusive terms: A stable legislature maximizes reelection of incumbents; a responsive one changes with political tides.
9. Best defined as an average.
10. See L. Papayanopoulos (1973), footnote on p. 185.
11. Term used by Backstrom, Robins, and Eller (1978, p. 1137).
12. Say 5 percent to 55 percent for the previous example.
13. Identification of political groups is straightforward and can be legislated.
14. But great care is exercised in selecting a highly competent arbitrator.

7 Nondiscrimination in Districting

Armand Derfner

The year 1980 was the twentieth anniversary of the decision in *Gomillion* v. *Lightfoot*,[1] the case in which the Supreme Court first held that the Constitution prohibits a state or local government from manipulating political boundary lines to the disadvantage of black voters. In that case, the Court struck down a statute that fenced most of the black voters (but none of the white voters) out of the city of Tuskegee, Alabama, by changing the shape of the city from a square to "an uncouth twenty-eight-sided figure."

In the next four years, the Court built on the *Gomillion* case in *Baker* v. *Carr*[2] and *Reynolds* v. *Sims*[3] to declare that malapportionment in general could be challenged in court and that all voters were entitled to have their votes counted equally, without dilution. Since that time there have been countless reapportionments at every level of state and local government, and mathematical devaluation seems to be a thing of the past. At the same time it has become increasingly evident that gerrymandering—stacking the deck—has continued to flourish, and for blacks and other minorities has often made reapportionment virtually meaningless or even regressive.[4] The process has now come full circle with the decision of the Supreme Court upholding racially discriminatory at-large elections in *City of Mobile* v. *Bolden*.[5] Apart from the nationwide implications of that case, the ironical immediate result is that the white voters of Mobile, who as plaintiffs in *Reynolds* v. *Sims* wrested power away from the rural areas, have now been freed of any obligation to share that power with their black neighbors.

Professor John H. Ely seems to have hit the nail on the head when he recently wrote that the one-person, one-vote standard "is certainly administrable. In fact, administrability is its long suit, and the more troublesome question is what else it has to recommend it" (Ely, 1980).

Many attempts have been made to devise a reapportionment process that would be immune, or at least resistant, to gerrymandering. These attempts have focused chiefly on such devices as putting the process in the hands of neutral technicians, depriving the plan drafters of poisonous information (such as racial or political population figures, or incumbents' addresses), and imposing strict standards that would eliminate discretion (such as a rigid compactness requirement). Unfortunately, all these proposals come up against the reality that reapportionment is an inherently political process, and even though there have been some encouraging experiences with reapportionment commissions, it is still undoubtedly wishful to think that the process can be squeezed dry of politics and prejudice.

The governing principle is that a reapportionment plan must not discriminate on account of race,[6] or as it is often put in terms that sound more precise but only deepen the mystery, "avoid diluting or minimizing representation." The courts, which have felt free to enter into consideration of the mathematical validity of reapportionment plans, have made it extraordinarily hard for a challenger to prove that a plan is racially gerrymandered. For a time it appeared that the proof was easier in attacks on multimember districts and at-large elections. But, the Supreme Court has now made it clear that a successful challenge must be based on proof of discriminatory *purpose* in creating or maintaining the at-large elections, not simply proof of discriminatory effect or disparate impact. The Court has gone further and, even while acknowledging that proof of discriminatory purpose need not be subjective proof, it has rejected circumstantial proof of the strongest possible kind.[7] Proof of racial gerrymandering where there are districts rather than at-large elections has always been well-nigh impossible, and there are no more than a few cases in which the drawing of district lines has been found by a court to be racially gerrymandered.[8]

It is not the purpose of this chapter to go into detail about the proof requirements in court cases alleging gerrymandering. Rather the focus here is on what plans can be drawn, either voluntarily or under prodding by the Justice Department (under Section 5 of the Voting Rights Act)[9] or at the direction of a court. The theme of this chapter is that protecting the interests of minority voters does not necessarily devalue or dilute the rights of white voters. In other words, the degree to which affirmative action in this area goes beyond what is required to eliminate discrimination is minimal and acceptable.

Affirmative action is one (or two) of those code words that we use to stand for our overall views on a complex and controversial topic. Because we tend to incorporate those views into our definition of the term, the definition can be elusive. But, it seems to have two elements, a process and a goal (or result): It involves (1) taking race or another discriminating characteristic into account, (2) for the purpose of being fair to blacks or people who share the particular discriminating characteristic.

Of course, each element of the definition leaves a basic question unanswered: First, "taking race into account" in *doing what?* and second, *how much* is "being fair"? The answer that we each give to these questions reflects our views on where to locate the border between what is right, legal, and constitutional and what is not.

There is a corollary implicit in the element of "taking race into account" that some may think should be explicitly included in the definition. That corollary is the idea that discrimination against the people in the particular group is so historic or so likely that it must be *overcome* by something more than merely neutral or colorblind action. This feature is generally thought to distinguish affirmative action from simple non-discrimination and generally comes in only after less stringent measures have been unsuccessful.

Put in simpler terms, these elements boil down to the notion of setting the rules to come closer to a goal of proportionality.

The concept of affirmative action comes up in different areas. For example, in school desegregation it may mean assigning children to schools that are not the nearest to overcome segregated housing patterns. In employment or admission to professional school, it may mean selecting a black who has less seniority or a lower test score than a white applicant. In redistricting, it may mean drawing district lines (and perhaps dividing precincts or counties) to create a district in which black voters are a significant portion or a majority of the population of the district.

These illustrations all show that the crucial issue is not simply that race is an important factor but that it is deemed more important than some other factors, such as geography, test scores, or seniority. Courts have been scrutinizing the so-called neutral factors for many years, at least since the Supreme Court struck down the grandfather clauses used in Oklahoma and Maryland (which allowed someone to qualify for voting, even if he met none of the other qualifications, if his grandfather had been eligible to vote at the time of the Civil War—an obvious limitation to whites).[10] Where the competing factor is itself infected with discrimination (as with a grandfather clause or as with school attendance districts that have been gerrymandered by school officials), or where the competing factor is not sufficiently related to the selection being made (as with a test that does not in fact measure the skill for which the test is used), Congress and the courts have increasingly been skeptical of its use.[11] By and large, the process of rejecting such factors has not been called affirmative action because it involves the elimination rather than the use of race-conscious or race-selective grounds for decision. Affirmative action, under this view, comes into play when the factor overridden or ignored is one that is both untainted by discrimination and is strongly related to the decision to be made.

As discriminatory factors are eliminated, the tendency is to move toward proportionality, that is, a racial composition of the affected category that mirrors the racial composition of the population source. This is so because where there is no discrimination (valid or invidious) and where each person is treated as an individual, society's benefits and burdens would be distributed randomly by race, sex, hair color, length of fingernails, and so forth. Random distribution, in turn, should produce proportional distribution within different races, so that if 10 percent of the population has red hair or is black, the number of doctors and truck drivers who have red hair or are black should approximate 10 percent. Thus, the starting point for determining whether there is discrimination is a statistical comparison of the racial composition of the group in which discrimination may be suspected and the racial composition of the population source.

Of course, not all of society's benefits and burdens are distributed randomly by race and such. Many of these benefits and burdens are or should be allocated on the basis of characteristics that are not distributed randomly. Thus, the degree to which simple nondiscrimination can produce randomness or proportionality will vary significantly between, say, jury selection and admission to graduate school.

Jury selection is a process designed to be random and one in which legitimate nonracial factors are at a minimum. The essential thesis of the jury system is that one juror is like another. Thus, the initial pool is designed to be universal or cross-sectional, and the process of selecting the jury panel from a large list is also supposed to be neutral, involving such techniques as blindfolded selections and bingo game equipment. The end result should be a set of jurors that reflects the racial composition of the community. If not, that is sufficient proof that nonrandom feature has crept into the process, either because the initial list was skewed or because someone interfered with the randomness of the process of selecting the jury panels.[12] Of course, while randomness should assure proportionality over a number of juries, it cannot make each jury a separate microcosm—and need not, since the overall process has already achieved proportionality and there is therefore no need to take any stronger action.

As we move away from the truly random process of jury selection to something like employment decisions, qualifying factors obviously come into play, and the goal of proportionality will generally be distorted by the intervention of a qualifying requirement—such as an engineering degree or fluency in French—that is not distributed randomly by race. Even here, the starting point for analyzing discrimination is the statistical comparison. Deviations from proportionality must be explained, and the explanation is more difficult for positions that seem within the reach of the average person.[13] Here the nondiscrimination principle eliminates many of the selection factors that cannot be justified or validated, and when there remain selection factors that are justifiable yet that produce unacceptably low levels of participation by minorities, the use of more stringent measures is what has created controversy under the name of affirmative action.

Affirmative action is currently associated principally with discrimination in employment and analogous selection processes. The two recent affirmative action cases decided by the Supreme Court involved the apprenticeship program at the Kaiser Aluminum plant in Louisiana (*United Steelworkers of America* v. *Webber*)[14] and admission to the medical school of the University of California at Davis (*Regents of the University of*

California v. *Bakke*).[15] The elements of the affirmative action plan in each case included these common features: the general use of certain selection criteria, which there was no claim that *this* employer or school had used unfairly;[16] a race-conscious decision to displace those criteria for blacks for a specified number of places, that is, a quota system; a showing that the results were changed by use of the quota system; and a justification based on the theory that because of the legacy of historic discrimination, use of the standard selection criteria would disfavor blacks and consequently unfairly lower their number.

Thus, in the *Weber* case, where half the places in the apprenticeship program were reserved for blacks (until the employment figures by race should approximate the racial composition of the local labor force), selection for the program was based on seniority. In the *Bakke* case, where sixteen of one hundred places in the medical school class were reserved for blacks, selection was based on an aggregate of factors including undergraduate grades, a test score, letters of recommendation, extracurricular activities, other biographical data, and an interview. In both cases, the effect was to set up separate tracks, which changed the results so that some blacks who were admitted to the apprenticeship program or to the medical school ranked lower in seniority or in the aggregation of medical school admission factors than some whites who were rejected. Thus, each of these affirmative action programs not only foreordained the race of some of those to be selected but foreordained it differently from the outcome if the other factors had been followed.

The benchmark of selection was chosen with reference to the proportion of blacks in the available population *rather than* the percentage of blacks who would have qualified for selection under the nonracial criteria that were being relied on. And, the reason for the selection of a benchmark different from that related to the selection process was the historic patterns of discrimination that were thought to leave a legacy by which blacks in general would rank lower in seniority at Kaiser Aluminum and lower in the aggregation of medical school factors than they would have without the discrimination. There was no proof in these cases, though, that this employer and this medical school had themselves discriminated against any blacks,[17] much less that they or anyone else had discriminated specifically against the blacks who were seeking admission to the school or the apprenticeship program.[18]

What about reapportionment? Like jury selection, it is arguably a random process in which few if any legitimate nonracial factors have any role. A number of factors are generally thought to be useful—such as contiguity, compactness, and some degree of maintenance of existing political and geographic boundaries—but these are of limited utility, especially because they do not go very far toward minimizing the number of reapportionment plans that can be drawn. Moreover, what may look good on a map may not be appropriate in reality.[19]

Yet there are at least two major factors that distinguish reapportionment from jury selection. First, whereas juries are selected frequently from a relatively unchanged population, reapportionment is done rarely (generally decenially) and there are almost certain to be major shifts in the population distribution between times. As a result, the analysis of juries in the aggregate is simply not appropriate for reapportionments. Second, unlike a juror who can be identified by race, sex, age, or other characteristic, a district cannot be so easily identified or typed. Thus, a district may be regarded as majority white whether its population is 55 percent white, 75 percent white, or 95 percent white. The difference is significant not only for that district but for its effect on the composition of adjacent districts and, for that matter, all of the districts.[20]

Analysis of reapportionment plans for racial effect, or any other effect, generally focuses on the number of districts (compared to the total) in which a given group or faction has a controlling majority. The most common anlaysis along these lines is political, and reapportionments are generally considered *fair*, for these purposes, if the relationship between the number of districts controlled by each party is equivalent to the relationship of their numerical strength.[21] Courts have uniformly, and rightly, rejected any notion that achieving this proportionality is a mandatory result, either on political lines or on racial lines. Any such attempt is likely to be impossible because residence patterns are not uniform, which means that even a totally random drawing of district lines will produce a smaller-than-proportional number of preponderantly minority districts; too energetic an effort to achieve proportionality is likely to result in a grotesque (or "uncouth") plan that too greatly minimizes other values.[22]

At the same time, proportionality is an essential benchmark, and because there is virtually no limit to the ways in which a plan can be drawn, or the number of plans that can be drawn, any greater a deviation than necessary from proportionality is likely to be suspect. One way to determine how close a plan should come to proportionality is to draw alternate plans, preferably from different starting points and with different guiding principles, to determine the probable range of the number of, say, majority black districts.[23] Another method is to look particularly at concentrations of black population and observe whether they are maintained, dismembered, combined with larger white population areas, or dealt with in some other way.

In Hinds County, Mississippi, the black population was concentrated in a portion of Jackson, the major population center, located in a corner of the county. The drafters of the reapportionment plan dismembered this population concentration by sending slivers of each of the five districts into this area. The result was districts in which anticompactness was the goal—a goal the governing body sought to justify by pointing out that each of the five county supervisors was responsible for maintaining roads in his district, and the plan was designed to equalize the road mileage among districts. The court of appeals struck the plan down, finding that "the supervisors' plan fragments a geographically concentrated minority voting community in a context of bloc voting."[24]

In Brooklyn, on the other hand, the legislature (under prodding from the Attorney General pursuant to the Voting Rights Act) drew a number of majority black districts that still left 70 percent of the districts' majorities white, in a 65 percent white county. This race-conscious districting was upheld by the Supreme Court, which saw it essentially as a way of minimizing the effect of winner-take-all politics:

> Rather, that plan can be viewed as seeking to alleviate the consequences of racial voting at the polls and to achieve a fair allocation of political power between white and nonwhite voters in Kings County.
>
> In this respect New York's revision of certain district lines is little different in kind from the decision by a State in which a racial minority is unable to elect representatives from multimember districts to change to single-member districting for the purpose of increasing minority representation. This change might substantially increase minority representation at the expense of white voters, who previously elected all of the legislators but who with single-member districts could elect no more than their proportional share. If this intentional reduction of white voting power would be constitutionally permissible, as we think it would be, we think it also permissible for a State, employing sound districting principles such as compactness and population equality, to attempt to prevent racial minorities from being repeatedly out-voted by creating districts that will afford fair representation to the members of those racial groups who are sufficiently numerous and whose residential patterns afford the opportunity of creating districts in which they will be in the majority.[25]

Race-conscious apportionments may be unfortunate, but the reality of discrimination may make them necessary. Chief Justice Burger argued for drawing reapportionment plans "along neutral lines," without defining what those were or offering any advice on how to get that done. Moreover, and most fundamentally, the persistence of racial discrimination in this society makes a black minority qualitatively different from ethnic, political, economic, or other minorities.

Many minorities exercise considerable influence. Voters tend to form politically oriented interest blocs, and because voters' interests are multiple, these blocs tend to shift, fragment, coalesce, and overlap. Thus, voters in a minority on one issue may combine with others to form a majority on other issues or at other times. For this reason, members of a mobile minority in a fluid political system cannot be ignored. Each of these ordinary minorities (such as union members, students, veterans, or blacks in some places) has the potential to form the balance of power; therefore, even its minority influence over a number of officials may amount to substantial power. Therefore, putting such people in a minority position is not necessarily a permanent arrangement.

None of this analysis applies where a minority is isolated. In such a case, as with blacks in much of the South, minority influence is essentially no influence. An isolated minority has difficulty in forming coalitions, finds its members discriminated against or disfavored by others, and finds it difficult for its candidates or positions to gain support from other groups. *Neutral lines* in this context is simply a synonym for overrepresenting the majority (generally white voters).

As a district court said in striking down a multimember district in Bexar County, Texas (San Antonio): "All these factors confirm the fact that race is still an important issue in Bexar County and that because of it, Mexican-Americans are frozen into permanent political minorities destined for constant defeat at the hands of the controlling political majorities."[26]

In cases involving racial minorities, proof of isolation may include the following types of evidence: a pattern of racial divisiveness and bloc voting in the electorate; a fairly recent history of racial discrimination, public or private; instances of racial appeals by candidates; a showing that minority votes have little effect on the election results; the absence or weakness of a white opposition party or faction (which might compete for minority votes); a sharp rise in white turnout when minority candidates run; a relative paucity of minority candidates; and a showing that in elections involving clear racial choices the wishes of minority voters are generally opposed and overborne by the wishes of the overall (white) electorate. In short, the isolation of a racial minority will be shown when racial issues are influential in politics to a significant degree, in determining the lines of political division or in diverting the attention of the electorate from nonracial issues.[27]

Of course these conditions, while they are deeply rooted and extraordinarily persistent, do evolve over time and place, and in some situations have been eroded almost to the vanishing point. It is therefore dangerous to base any actions on an assumption that they will remain true for all times and places, and it is frustrating to speculate that some actions (such as affirmative redistricting) may well root these unfortunate realities more deeply.[28] It would, however, be even more dangerous to imagine that they are simply transitory.

The final question here concerns the size of a deliberately created black majority. One of the complaints in *United Jewish Organizations* v. *Carey* was that the black districts were created with 65 percent black populations. This does not seem to be an independent ground of complaint, for the empirical evidence suggested that that percentage was the equivalent of a simple majority. Voting projections and political power are affected by several statistical realities, including the facts that a higher proportion of blacks than of whites are children who are not of voting age and that (both because of historical voting discrimination and current economic conditions) blacks register and vote at lower rates than whites, which in turn add up to the fact that there must be a substantial black population majority to produce a majority black turnout.

For these reasons, control of an election is generally thought to be possible in most places where blacks comprise 65 percent of the district's population. This situation does not guarantee that a black candidate will represent that district. A black population of 65 percent gives black voters in that district a realistic opportunity to win or control the election, but it does not guarantee it. In light of the factors noted above, a 65 percent black district is probably a toss-up or only a slight black advantage, and thus does foster competition—competition in which all segments of voters have a real opportunity to win. Also there is no guarantee in any district that black voters with the power to control the election will necessarily choose a black candidate. Many black districts have returned white candidates who were politically responsive, effective campaigners—or just familiar incumbents. The failure to elect a black in a black district does not necessarily signify failure of the exercise.[29]

Professor Kelley and his associates have shown how illusory the appearance of neutrality can be. Writing about registration, they concluded that "our study indicates, not only that electorates are much more the product of political forces than many have appreciated, but also that, to a considerable extent, they are *political artifacts*. Within limits, they can be constructed to a size and composition deemed desirable by those in power" (Kelley, Ayres, and Bowen 1967, p. 121).

Until we find a way of drafting reapportionment plans that we can be sure are truly nondiscriminatory, and perhaps until there are no isolated minorities in our society, the only protection we have against reapportionment plans that discriminate on account of race is to do them with our eyes open and seek to achieve fairness. That approach may be called affirmative action, but it is no more than is necessary to eliminate discrimination.

Notes

1. *Gomillion* v. *Lightfoot* (1960) 364 U.S. 339.
2. *Baker* v. *Carr* (1962) 369 U.S. 186.
3. *Reynolds* v. *Sims* (1964) 377 U.S. 533. The one-man, one-vote rule (as it was then known, before we became conscious of sex discrimination) was suggested in two intervening cases, *Gray* v. *Sanders* (1963), 372 U.S. 368 and *Wesberry* v. *Sanders* (1964) 376 U.S. 1 before being made explicit in *Reynolds* v. *Sims*.

4. By the mid-1960s, the longtime failure to reapportion had created many rotten boroughs in southern states (and elsewhere) that had large black population majorities but were, of course, controlled by the few white voters and were represented by white officials because blacks were still largely disfranchised. Just about the time that rapid growth in black voting (since 1965) would have elected blacks from many of these rotten boroughs, they were abolished or submerged in the course of reapportionment. In many cases, the result was precisely what Justice Frankfurter hoped to avoid in *Gomillion* v. *Lightfoot*: "the achievement by a State of any impairment of voting rights whatever so long as it was cloaked in the garb of the realignment of political subdivisions."

5. *City of Mobile* v. *Bolden* (1980) 48 L.W. 4436.

6. Throughout this chapter, reference to racial gerrymandering can refer to blacks, Hispanics, and perhaps Indians and Orientals. Other categories of discrimination that are common in education, employment, and housing (such as discrimination based on sex, age, and physical handicap) rarely come up in reapportionment, probably because these groups are not concentrated in large geographic clusters. There are other forms of gerrymandering (for example, those based on political party, incumbency, and economic status), which are the subject of constant debate over whether they are legitimate or legal, and which are not meant to be covered here.

7. *City of Mobile* v. *Bolden* (1980) 48 L.W. 4436. The proof rejected was along the lines spelled out in *Zimmer* v. *McKeithen* (1973) 485 F.2d 1297 (5th Cir), affirmed on other grounds, *East Carroll Parish School Board* v. *Marshall* (1976) 424 U.S. 636.

8. See *Klahr* v. *Williams* (1972) 339 F. Supp. 922 (D. Ariz.); *Kirksey* v. *Board of Supervisors* (1977); 554 F.2d 139 (5th Cir.); *Robinson* v. *Commissioners Court* (1974) 505 F.2d 674 (5th Cir.).

9. 42 U.S.C. § 1973c. This statute was involved in *United Jewish Organization of Williamsburgh* v. *Carey* (1977) 430 U.S. 144.

10. *Guinn* v. *United States* (1915) 238 U.S. 347; *Myers* v. *Anderson* (1915) 238 U.S. 368. The grandfather clause was simply one exemption from the literacy test, that is, it was a means of adopting a literacy test that could exclude blacks without necessarily having to exclude illiterate whites. The Supreme Court held that the remedy should include invalidation of the literacy test itself; that is, a requirement from which white people were exempted was essentially fictitious and the proper remedy was elimination of the fictitious requirement.

11. For example, *Griggs* v. *Duke Power Co.* (1971) 401 U.S. 424, 431:

Congress has now provided that tests or criteria for employment or promotion may not provide equality of opportunity merely in the sense of the fabled offer of milk to the stork and the fox. On the contrary, Congress has now required that the posture and condition of a job-seeker be taken into account. It has—to resort again to the fable—provided that the vessel in which the milk is proffered be one all seekers can use. The Act proscribes not only overt discrimination but also practices that are fair in form, but discriminatory in operation. The touchstone is business necessity. If an employment practice which operates to exclude Negroes cannot be shown to be related to job performance, the practice is prohibited.

12. *Castaneda* v. *Partida* (1977) 430 U.S. 482.

13. *Hazelwood School District* v. *United States* (1977) 433 U.S. 299.

14. *United Steelworkers of America* v. *Weber* (1979) 61 L.Ed.2d 480.

15. *Regents of the University of California* v. *Bakke* (1978) 438 U.S. 365.

16. The absence of any claim or proof in either case that Kaiser or the medical school had ever discriminated was due in part to the way in which the case arose. In each case, a rejected white applicant sued the institution; no beneficiaries of the affirmative action program, nor any other blacks, were made parties. None of the existing parties had any incentive to prove any background or history of discrimination. Certainly the rejected white applicant had no such incentive; neither did the institution since doing so could have opened it up to additional suits from blacks, as well as decreasing its flexibility in regard to the affirmative action program. It has been claimed that proof was available, if a proper party had intervened, that would have shown discriminatory acts on the part of Kaiser and of the medical school that would have clearly justified affirmative action as a remedy for specific discrimination.

17. Had there been proof of discrimination the question would not have involved affirmative action but only the simpler question of the appropriate remedy for a proven violation. Here the law is quite clear in allowing and requiring broad remedies. *Dayton Board of Education* v. *Brinkman* (1979) 61 L.Ed.2d 720.

18. As it happens, the Kaiser Aluminum plan was upheld in *Weber*, while the Davis medical school plan was struck down in *Bakke*. The principal reason is that the medical school is public and therefore has a greater obligation to provide equal treatment, under the equal protection clause of the Fourteenth Amendment to the Constitution than Kaiser, a private employer whose duties are defined by the somewhat looser provisions of Title VII of the Civil Rights Act of 1964. Too much should not be made of this difference, though, because it really represents only the shift of a single Justice's vote: Justice Stewart, who voted for Allan Bakke and against Brian Weber.

19. On a map a street may look like a convenient dividing line, but in reality it may be more appropriate to split the block in the middle or up the alley, so that residents of both sides of a street will be in the same district.

20. See the discussion of "stacking," "cracking," and "packing" districts in F. Parker (1973). This is not to judge the comparative value to a particular group of voters of having greater control over a small number of

districts versus a lesser amount of influence over a greater number of districts. It is worth noting, though, that those who have the opportunity to choose (majority parties) invariably opt for majority control over a district rather than some amorphous wider spread of districts in which they will have only a minority influence—that is, no control.

21. See *Gaffney* v. *Cummings* (1973) 412 U.S. 735.

22. In any event, residence patterns change, often bringing about surprising results. Thus, in *City of Richmond* v. *United States* (1975) 422 U.S. 358, 371, the city and a set of black litigants had both drawn plans that called for four majority-white and four majority-black wards; they were divided over the composition of the ninth, swing ward. The Supreme Court accepted the city's plan on the ground that the plaintiffs' plan would have artificially perpetuated a black majority in a city that according to the 1970 census was majority white. By the time elections were held, however, the ninth ward even under the city's plan was majority-black, and a black was elected from that district, giving blacks a 5-4 majority on the city council (and a black mayor too, since the mayor is elected from among the nine councilmen).

23. In the course of litigation (unsuccessful) to require single-member districts in the South Carolina Senate, single-member plans were drawn by the black plaintiffs, by the Republican Party, and by the senate's statistician. Each of the plans, which were otherwise quite different, created either four or five majority black districts out of forty-six.

24. *Kirksey* v. *Board of Supervisors of Hinds County* (1977) 554 F.2d 139.

25. *United Jewish Organizations* v. *Carey* (1977) 430 U.S. 144, 167-68.

26. *Graves* v. *Barnes* (1972) 343 F. Supp. 704, 732 (W.D. Tex. 1972), affirmed sub nom. *White* v. *Regester* (1973) 412 U.S. 755.

27. These factors and similar ones were set forth in *Zimmer* v. *McKeithen* (1973) 485 F.2d 1297 (5th Cir. 1973), affirmed on other grounds sub nom. *East Carroll Parish School Board* v. *Marshall* (1976) 424 U.S. 636. In *City of Mobile* v. *Bolden* the Supreme Court held that the Zimmer criteria are insufficient to prove a constitutional violation because they do not prove a racially discriminatory purpose.

28. Indeed, because white officials draw most of the districting plans, a basic problem of affirmative districting is that any justification of subjective (for example, race-conscious or politics-conscious) districting may perversely open the door to more discrimination in other cases.

29. Some judges and lawyers characterize claims of proportionality as representing a theory that only blacks can represent blacks and that that result should be guaranteed. This characterization is at best a red herring and is more generally a knowing bit of hypocrisy.

8 Against Affirmative Gerrymandering

David Wells

During the decade following *Baker* v. *Carr*,[1] the United States Supreme Court was called upon to decide many cases dealing with apportionment and districting. The bulk of these dealt with population differences among legislative districts: How much of a departure from precise equality was permissible. Some involved partisan gerrymandering and presented the question of whether that practice was consitutionally allowable. A few other aspects of legislative representation also engaged the attention of the Court. But in the early 1970s a new question, not previously considered, was presented: Whether or not a deliberate attempt to predetermine the composition of a legislative body through use of the districting process was sanctioned by the federal Constitution.

Although the most widely noticed—and most controversial—form in which this question came before the Supreme Court posed the issue in a racial context, the Court's initial encounter with the question did not involve race at all. Rather, it dealt with *political party* structuring—with numbers of Democrats and Republicans rather than numbers of blacks and whites. The case, *Gaffney* v. *Cummings*,[2] decided in June, 1973, sprang from a redistricting of the Connecticut State Legislature.

One of the grounds on which the Connecticut redistricting had been attacked was that it reflected a deliberate effort to create specific numbers of Democratic and Republican districts in rough proportion to the "normal" political party division within the state. The required gerrymandering necessitated by this effort was referred to by the attorneys who defended the Connecticut redistricting as "benevolent consideration of past election results"—that is, as a kind of *benevolent gerrymander*.[3]

The plaintiffs in Connecticut charged that this deliberate political structuring violated the rights of minorities: Democratic minorities in districts which the state had preordained would be Republican and vice versa. But the Supreme Court saw it differently. It opined that such "benevolent, bipartisan gerrymandering" was not merely permissible but that it was indeed commendable. "The very essence of districting is to produce . . . a more politically fair result than would be reached with elections at large," wrote Justice Byron White, who authored the decision. "(N)either we nor the district courts have a constitutional warrant to invalidate a state plan . . . because it undertakes, not to minimize or eliminate the political strength of any group or party, but to *recognize it and, through districting,*

provide a rough sort of proportional representation in the legislative halls.''
(emphasis added).[4]

The apparent thrust of the *Gaffney* decision was to sanction gerrymandering as long as that practice was used to produce a result the Court deemed politically fair. (The Court has never ruled on the question of whether gerrymandering that produces an "unfair" result is constitutionally permissible. Indeed it appears to have deliberately skirted that issue on several occasions.)

Four years later the Court confronted what was in many respects the same basic question, predetermination of representational patterns through the districting process, but this time the emotionally supercharged issue of race was involved.

At the beginning of the decade, the New York Legislature had redrawn that state's legislative and congressional district boundaries. It was that redistricting that became the subject of litigation and led eventually to the Supreme Court's landmark 1977 decision in *United Jewish Organizations of Williamsburg* v. *Carey.*[5]

The case revolved around state legislative lines in two New York City boroughs, Brooklyn and Manhattan, and congressional district lines in Brooklyn alone. Early in 1974, the U.S. Department of Justice, acting on the basis of complex provisions of the Voting Rights Acts of 1965 and 1970, had ruled that New York State had failed to prove, as required under the Voting Rights Act, that its redistricting had not had the effect of abridging the right to vote because of race or color. Specifically, it was charged that blacks and Hispanics had been unduly concentrated in several Brooklyn and Manhattan districts and that minority strength in adjacent districts had thereby been diluted—the result being that those groups were under-represented in the legislature and congressional delegations.[6] (It is ironic that this case arose from a situation involving application of Section 5 of the Voting Rights Act to counties in a northern state, for that legislation had clearly been designed by its framers to combat the classic forms of antiblack discrimination in the South: direct and indirect denial of access to participation in the political process. The law was applicable to part of New York State only because of a technicality: because the state had in the past had a literacy qualification for voting and because the voting participation level in the counties involved had fallen below the 50 percent mark in 1968.)[7]

The effect of the Justice Department's 1974 ruling was to invalidate New York's redistricting laws and require substitution of new districting arrangements designed to yield a legislative and congressional delegation that reflected the racial composition of the counties involved. Informally, the Justice Department apparently indicated that it would approve a districting pattern only if a number of additional districts were created in which the non-white majority was in the neighborhood of 65 percent—a figure apparently believed to be high enough *to overcome the effects of lower minority-group voting-participation.*[8] In effect, the legislature was told that it must not merely avoid efforts to minimize minority representation but that it was required to take positive action to maximize the number of minority representatives.[9] Thus the concept of affirmative action—positive steps to atone for alleged past injustices—was applied to the districting process.[10]

Ironically, critics of New York State's redistricting practices had, over the years, alleged many past injustices—but these had been political, not racial, in character. They had usually been characterized by Republican efforts to minimize Democratic representation or, more recently, by bipartisan "arrangements" to protect the seats of incumbents of both parties.[11] After 1970 there had been a clear effort by the Republicans, then in control of the legislature, to perpetuate their majorities. So, the lines had been laid down in the first instance by the GOP to hold down the number of Democratic districts and, in areas of the state where that was not possible, selected Democrats had been given a say in the placement of the lines to assure some Democratic votes for the plan in the legislature and thus to counter some threatened GOP defections.[12] If any Democratic legislators were "protected," it was not whites who were protected from potential black or Puerto Rican challengers but rather regulars who were protected from potential threats posed by Reform Democrats—all of whom were white. (It is noteworthy that with regard to the four Manhattan assembly districts cited by the Justice Department, one was represented by a white Reform Democrat who voted *against* the 1971 redistricting whereas the other three were represented by blacks, all of whom *supported* the measure! Indeed, nine of the fifteen members of the legislature's black and Puerto Rican caucus had voted for the redistricting bill in the face of the strong opposition of their own party leadership (*New York Times* April 7, 1974)!

In 1974, in line with the Justice Department's action, the legislature redrew the congressional lines in Brooklyn and the legislative lines in both boroughs. The new plan did not change the number of districts with nonwhite majorities but did alter the size of those majorities to create a number of additional districts in which the nonwhite majorities were close to 65 percent.

This new element in redistricting evoked a variety of reactions. Even the minority groups themselves were not united in support of the new arrangement or even of the Justice Department's reasoning. Manhattan Borough President Percy Sutton complained that the new lines, rather than adding to the number of minority legislators, would probably jeopardize the seats of several already in office (*New York Times* May 29, 1974). (This complaint echoed a controversy within the black community a decade earlier when the late Congressman Adam Clayton Powell opposed a move by black plaintiffs who had charged discrimination because Powell's district had been given an

86 percent black majority. This situation indicated an effort, they had alleged, to concentrate blacks in one district to keep the adjacent districts as white as possible. But Powell argued that any change would make his district vulnerable to a nonblack challenger and was thus inimical to black interests.)[13]

Puerto Rican leaders in Brooklyn also complained that even if the new 1974 redistricting did succeed in increasing the number of black legislators, nothing in the revised districting law would do the same for them (*New York Times* June 23, 1974). By contrast, black leaders in Manhattan protested that a new district in East Harlem, ostensibly drawn to assure the election of a Puerto Rican, would place two previously secure black districts in jeopardy. And a noted black academician challenged the whole concept underlying the redistricting, pointing out the fact that ultimately black and Puerto Rican politicians must assume responsibility for their own political mobilization. It was not the courts' responsibility to require district lines predicated on turnout. If minority voters did not exercise their right to vote, the problem was not a legal one but a political one. "The situation calls for the skills of precinct captains, not plaintiffs," he concluded (Hamilton, 1974).

One group especially aggrieved by the 1974 redistricting was the Hasidic Jewish community in the Williamsburg section of Brooklyn. Prior to the realignment, virtually the entire community had been located within a single assembly and state senate district. In the attempt to create additional districts with the requisite-sized black and Puerto Rican majorities, however, the legislature had drawn the new district lines in a way that split the Hasidim among two assembly and two senate districts. This redistricting, their leaders felt, eroded their political influence. The new lines, they contended, had been drawn to give special favor to two specific minority groups but in the process they—another minority group—had suffered serious political injury. They consequently brought suit to have the new lines overturned. The central complaint was that there was no justification for the state to have given special consideration to *any* specific ethnic group.

While this case was making its way through the courts, the Justice Department gave its approval to the new lines and they were used in the election of 1974 (and subsequently). Ironically, only one of the five new safe (65 percent plus) nonwhite state legislative districts in Brooklyn actually elected a nonwhite representative. And the Fourteenth Congressional District, also redrawn to assure the election of a nonwhite, instead sent its white incumbent back to Congress again!

On March 1, 1977, the Supreme Court, by a seven-to-one majority, held that the complaint brought by the Hasidim was without merit and that the state did indeed have the legal right (and in this case the obligation imposed on it by the Voting Rights Act) to draw district lines with the specific purpose of maximizing black and Puerto Rican legislative representation.

The majority opinion was authored, like the one in *Gaffney,* by Justice White—who recognized and even drew on the parallels between the two cases. "(N)either the Fourteenth nor the Fifteenth Amendment," he wrote, "mandates any per se rule against using racial factors in districting and apportionment. . . . Moreover, in the process of drawing black majority districts in order to comply with Section 5, the State must decide how substantial those majorities must be in order to satisfy the Voting Rights Act. . . . Because . . . the inquiry under Section 5 focuses ultimately on the position of racial minorities with respect to their effective exercise of the electoral franchise . . . , the percentage of eligible voters by district is of great importance to that inquiry. We think it was reasonable for the Attorney General to conclude in this case that a substantial nonwhite population majority—in the vicinity of 65 percent—would be required to achieve a nonwhite majority of eligible voters."[14]

Justice William Brennan, in concurring, spoke of "benign discrimination," which "may be permissible because it is cast in a remedial context with respect to a disadvantaged class rather than in a setting that aims to demean or insult any racial group."[15]

To many observers, the gist of this decision appeared to move in precisely the opposite direction from an earlier Court decision that had also been widely viewed as a judicial landmark. In *Gomillion* v. *Lightfoot* (1960), the Court held that "when a legislature . . . singles out a readily isolated segment of a racial minority for special discriminatory treatment, it violates the Fifteenth Amendment."[16] (That case arose when Alabama deliberately altered the boundaries of Tuskegee to lessen black voting power.) Now, by contrast, the Court appeared to be saying instead that under certain circumstances it was not merely permissible but desirable for a state to single out a specific minority for special advantages in the delineation of political boundary lines.

The only dissent in the 1977 decision was registered by Chief Justice Warren Burger, who noted the contrast with the 1960 ruling. "I begin with this Court's holding in *Gomillion* v. *Lightfoot,* . . . the first case to strike down a state attempt at racial gerrymandering", wrote Burger.

"If *Gomillion* teaches anything, I had thought it was that drawing of political boundary lines with the sole, explicit objective of reaching a predetermined racial result cannot ordinarily be squared with the Constitution. . . . The words *racial quota* are emotionally loaded and must be used with caution. Yet this undisputed testimony shows that the 65 percent figure was viewed by the legislative reapportionment committee as so firm a criterion that even a fractional deviation was deemed impermissible. I cannot see how this can be characterized otherwise than a strict quota approach, and I must therefore view today's holding as casting doubt on the clear-cut principles established in *Gomillion.* . . . While petitioners certainly have no constitutional right to remain unified within a single political district, they do have, in my view, the constitutional right not to be carved up so as to create a voting bloc composed of some other ethnic or racial group. . . . If districts have been drawn in a racially biased manner in the past (which the record does not show to have been the case here), the proper remedy is to reapportion along neutral lines. Manipulating the racial composition of electoral districts to assure one minority or another its "deserved" representation will not promote the goal of a racially neutral legislature. On the contrary, such racial gerrymandering puts the imprimatur of the State on the concept that race is a proper consideration in the electoral process. The device employed by the State of New York and endorsed by the Court today, moves us one step further away from a truly homogeneous society."[17]

This decision in effect endorses a radical departure from the traditional American concept of legislative representation. Formerly, legislators have been considered the representatives of individual citizens who happened to reside together within a single geographic area, but here the Court appears to view lawmakers as representing not individuals but specific groups *as groups*—in this instance, as ethnic groups. Indeed, Justice White was quite explicit on this point: "(T)he white voter who is in a district more likely to return a nonwhite representative will be represented, to the extent that voting continues to follow racial lines, by legislators elected from majority white districts. The effect of the reapportionment on whites in districts where nonwhite majorities have been increased is thus mitigated by the preservation of white majority districts in the rest of the county."[18] In the same vein, Justice Brennan wrote that: "(T)o the extent that white and nonwhite interests and sentiments are polarized, . . . petitioners still are indirectly protected by the remaining white assembly and senate districts. . . ."[19,20]

Both Justices White and Brennan were careful to qualify their view by basing it on the assumption that racial polarization exists, but Justice Burger challenged the validity of that premise:

The assumption that "whites" and "nonwhites" . . . form homogeneous entities for voting purposes is entirely without foundation. The "whites" category consists of a veritable galaxy of national origins, ethnic backgrounds, and religious denominations. It simply cannot be assumed that the legislative interests of all "whites" are even substantially identical. In similar fashion, those described as "nonwhites" include, in addition to Negroes, a substantial portion of Puerto Ricans. . . . The Puerto Rican population, for whose protection the Voting Rights Act was "triggered" in Kings County[21] . . . has expressly disavowed any identity of interest with the Negroes, and, in fact, objected to the 1974 redistricting scheme because it did not establish a Puerto Rican controlled district. . . . The notion that Americans vote in firm blocs has been repudiated in the election of minority members as mayors and legislators in numerous American cities and districts overwhelmingly white.[22]

Burger's dissent was reminiscent of one written thirteen years earlier by Justice William O. Douglas—who belonged to a very different ideological segment of the court. In *Wright* v. *Rockefeller,* the case referred to above that involved the district of Congressman Powell, Douglas wrote: "The principle of equality is at war with the notion that District *A* must be represented by a Negro (and) that District *B* must be represented by a Caucasian. . . . That . . . is a divisive force in a community, emphasizing difference between candidates and voters that are irrelevant in the constitutional sense. . . . Government has no business designing electoral districts along racial or religious lines."[23]

An inevitable consequence of acceptance of the concept of *representation by group*, which is inherent in the majority opinions in both *Gaffney* and *United Jewish Organizations*, is that, at least in general elections, the individual voter is reduced to the status of a pawn or chip in a game played by the political parties or ethnic groups. (This is less true in primary contests. At that level, the individual voter's choice still plays a role; but in the general election, the deck has been stacked. The outcome has been prearranged. The individual voter may as well stay home. His vote is meaningless!) And whether or not, in individual situations, specific groups or parties are benefited, the system as a whole is bound to victimize whole categories or voters: Republicans who live in districts allocated to the Democrats, Democrats in districts preordained to be represented by a Republican, nonwhites in districts carved out for whites, and so on. Without deliberate structuring a candidate belonging to a minority party or ethnic group within a district might have a fighting chance of winning; but under the procedures condoned in these two cases, victory has been placed effectively beyond such a candidate's reach—not because of the irregular distribution of party strength or the random pattern of ethnic concentration but because of a deliberate state policy.

The judicial blessing given to the practice of purposefully carving out districts for specific groups is troublesome in yet another respect. The minority groups involved in the New York situation at which the Court was looking in 1977 happened to live in relatively compact geographic areas. It was therefore possible to apply the quotas sanctioned by the Court. But how could this approach be used in situations in which a minority group is *not* conveniently gathered together in easily discernible chunks of territory? It would be virtually impossible, using even the most egregious kind of gerrymandering, to establish districts for groups that might even form a larger proportion of an area's population than those at issue in this case but that are geographically dispersed.[24]

The Chief Justice's dissent touched on this point:

> The result reached by the Court today in the name of the Voting Rights Act
> is ironic. The use of a mathematical formula tends to sustain the existence
> of ghettos by promoting the notion that political clout is to be gained or
> maintained by marshalling particular racial, ethnic, or religious groups in
> enclaves. It suggests to the voter that only a candidate of the same race,
> religion, or ethnic origins can properly represent that voter's interests, and
> that such candidate can be elected only from a district with a sufficient
> minority concentration.[25]

Actually, the question of how the practice of deliberately carving out
specific districts for specific groups would work in a situation in which the
groups in question were geographically scattered need not be limited to
hypothetical situations, for the events in Connecticut that gave rise to the
Gaffney case posed just such a circumstance—although there, unlike the New
York situation of the later case, the groups in question were political rather
than ethnic. Because of the pattern of party strength in Connecticut, it is
necessary, in order to create numbers of Democratic and Republican districts
in proportion to the normal statewide vote totals of the two major parties, to
ferret out scattered pockets of Republican strength outside Fairfield County
and string enough of them together to form legislative districts. Unless this is
done, there is no way of "compensating" for the top-heavy majorities the
GOP usually wins in Fairfield. But doing so requires the construction of
many districts with grossly contorted, geographically illogical shapes.

The plaintiffs who attacked the Connecticut redistricting pointed to the
outlines of many such districts and alleged that this classic, telltale sign of
gerrymandering—outlandishly shaped districts—clearly indicated that gerrymandering was the inevitable result of the state's efforts to predetermine
the political composition of the legislature.[26] But Justice White's response
clearly indicated that the Court viewed gerrymandering as an acceptable
tool for achieving results it deemed desirable: "Compactness or attrac-
tiveness have never been held to constitute an independent federal constitutional requirement", he wrote.[27] In effect, the 1973 and 1977 decisions do
not merely sanction gerrymandering; they mandate it, for without it, the
desirable results are virtually impossible to achieve. Indeed, the attorneys
who defended Connecticut's action in the earlier case contended quite openly
that: "(N)oncompactness could be the only way to provide even minimal
representation of a scattered minority, racial or political.[28]

The practice endorsed by the Court in both cases is in effect an attempt
to superimpose one system of representation upon the structure of another.
It would be more consistent with the approach the Supreme Court appears
to have espoused if the idea of representation by districts were scrapped
altogether (Neighbor 1979) or if the concept of a district as a single contiguous unit of territory were eliminated. Instead of having legislators

represent specific geographic areas, perhaps they should represent ethnic groups or political parties per se, with no specified geographic base. Or, as an alternative, they might represent groups in noncontiguous districts. In New York, for example, the Puerto Rican areas of the South Bronx, the lower East Side of Manhattan, and parts of East Harlem and northern Brooklyn might be designated a single congressional district! In this way, it would be quite easy to impose a quota and provide each ethnic minority or political party with its fair share of seats. Indeed, in an action apparently motivated by a desire to maintain Hispanic majorities in two out of four court districts in El Paso County, Texas (an action subsequently sustained by the Justice Department in the exercise of its reviewing power under the Voting Rights Act), a noncontiguous district, consisting of two segments separated from one another by ten miles and an uninhabitable mountain range, was recently pieced together.

But the Supreme Court has not directly proposed such overt abandonment of the traditional concept of a district as a single piece of land; instead it has acquiesced in the superimposition of political and ethnic quotas on a geographically based system of representation. The result of this attempt to divide apples by oranges is a hybrid system in which *neither* approach— representation by groups *or* representation by geographic areas—can work properly. The only possible way to affect a mixture of two such basically incompatible approaches is by the most blatant kind of gerrymandering—and even then, the mixture is only minimally effective.[29]

This approach to legislative representation—one that permits the state, acting in the pursuit of a desirable end, to decide how many whites and nonwhites or Democrats and Republicans shall sit in a legislature or in Congress—has been characterized by its defenders as benign or benevolent gerrymandering. The characterization is revealing, for like *benevolent despotism,* benevolent gerrymandering is a distinctly elitist concept. Just as benevolent despotism takes power away from the people who are presumably too ignorant or unskilled to manage their own affairs and turns it over to a just and wise dictator, so does benevolent gerrymandering take from the voters their power to determine the composition of the lawmaking body and turn it over instead to those presumed to be wise and fair enough to know what that composition *ought to be.*

Benign or benevolent gerrymandering, like all forms of gerrymandering, has yet another consequence of which its advocates take insufficient note. Gerrymandering tends to maximize the number of politically and racially *homogeneous* districts and to minimize the number of politically unstable swing (contestable) districts and racially mixed districts. Because homogeneous districts are usually *safe* districts (more or less certain to be won by one party or represented by one ethnic group), gerrymandering invariably inflates the number of safe districts. Barring a successful primary challenge, the individual incumbent is virtually assured of continued reelection for as long as he or she cares to hold the seat. This has the effect of insulating the legislative body against the consequences of changing sentiments and circumstances, for gerrymandering has provided the individual legislator, the legislative leadership, and the legislature as a whole with rather strong guarantees of continued office and power. The political and ethnic composition of the legislature has been effectively frozen for a decade, and changes are possible only within a limited, narrow range. The representation system, because it has been made less politically sensitive and therefore less responsive, has thus been rendered less able to perform its most fundamental task—the translation of public sentiment into public policy as accurately as possible.

In rendering its decisions in both *Gaffney* and *United Jewish Organizations,* the Court was essentially addressing the question of how to prevent a dominant party or racial group from carving out districts in such a way as to disadvantage other parties or groups. If one rejects the solutions approved by the Court, one is still left with the problem itself: How *can* that practice be effectively curbed?

Perhaps the best way to make sure that whoever draws the district lines cannot do so in a manner calculated to bestow special advantages on any ethnic group or political party or partisan faction or favored candidates or geographic area is to establish firm, explicit, enforceable, politically and ethnically neutral districting *guidelines* or *groundrules.* Such rules would eliminate the discretion held by those who draw the lines, and it is precisely that discretion—that power to decide where district boundaries shall be placed—that is the very essence of gerrymandering.

The way to eliminate one evil is not to substitute a counterevil. The way to preclude the imposition of special disadvantages on any group is not by providing that group with compensating advantages beforehand (often to the consequent disadvantage of others who may be innocent bystanders). Rather, it is to make certain that no special, unwarranted advantages or disadvantages can be imposed by or against any group.

Politically and ethnically neutral criteria (such as equality of population, geographic compactness to the greatest degree achievable, geographic contiguity, and avoidance of needless fracturing of existing political units) would make it impossible for *whoever* draws the lines to deliberately maximize or minimize the power of any group.

The districting provisions of the state constitution of Colorado, for example, read in part as follows:

> In no event shall there be more than 5 percent deviation between the most populous and the least populous district in each house. . . . Each district shall be as compact in area as possible, and the aggregate linear distance of

all district boundaries shall be as short as possible. . . . Each district shall consist of contiguous . . . precincts. . . . Except when necessary to meet the equal-population requirements . . . no part of one county shall be added to all or part of another county in forming districts. . . . The number of cities and towns whose territory is contained in more than one district shall be as small as possible (Constitution of the State of Colorado, Article V, Sections 46-47).

Such provisions, properly enforced, eliminate the possibility of any type of gerrymandering by precluding any deliberately built-in advantages or disadvantages for anyone. They do not, of course, guarantee that each political or ethnic group will end up with a proportionate share of the seats. But, they do guarantee that no group can be purposefully victimized by another. By so doing, they allow the political process to work as it ought to work—with neutral rules to make sure that "the great game of politics" is played fairly.

Notes

1. Baker v. Carr (1962) 369 U.S. 186.
2. Gaffney v. Cummings (1973) 412 U.S. 735.
3. Appellant's Motion for Expanded Consideration and Jurisdictional Statement and Brief, Gaffney v. Cummings, (1973) 412 U.S. 735, p. 42.
4. Gaffney v. Cummings (1973) 412 U.S. at 753-754.
5. United Jewish Organizations of Williamsburg v. Carey (1977) 430 U.S. 144.
6. See letter of J. Stanley Pottinger, Assistant Attorney General, Civil Rights Division, U.S. Department of Justice to George D. Zuckerman, Assistant Attorney General, State of New York, April 1, 1974; and *The New York Times,* April 2, 1974.
7. For a thoughtful analysis of the way the Voting Rights Act has come to be applied in states outside the South, see Thernstrom (1979, p. 49-76).
8. Such "informal suggestion" is apparently the standard way in which the Civil Rights Division of the Department of Justice transmits its recommendations for "improvements" in electoral arrangements to local officials (Thernstrom 1979, p. 74).
9. Referring to this, Thernstrom (1979, p. 60) observed that "the Attorney General made the bizarre assumption" that if historically an ethnic group demonstrated low voter turnout, "it is necessary to draw district lines in such a way as to increase the concentration of that group!"
10. Noting the analogy to the question of numerical quotas in the area of school admissions, Thernstrom (1979, p. 60) writes: "Whether we want a society in which citizens are assigned slots on . . . race or ethnicity

is . . . precisely the question *Bakke* . . . raised with reference to higher education.''

11. See Tyler and Wells (1962, pp. 221-248) and Wells (1978, pp. 9-13).

12. See Wells (1979, pp. 8-14). For the role of Democrats in passage of the Republican-sponsored 1971 state legislative redistricting bill, see pp. 9-10.

13. Wright v. Rockefeller (1964) 376 U.S. 52.

14. United Jewish Organizations of Williamsburg v. Carey (1977) 430 U.S. at 161-162, 164.

15. United Jewish Organizations of Williamsburg v. Carey (1977) 430 U.S. at 170.

16. Gomillion v. Lightfoot (1960)364 U.S. 339 at 346.

17. United Jewish Organizations of Williamsburg v. Carey (1977) 430 U.S. at 181-187.

18. United Jewish Organizations of Williamsburg v. Carey (1977) 430 U.S. at 166 fn.

19. United Jewish Organizations of Williamsburg v. Carey (1977) 430 U.S. at 178.

20. "Yet incorporating this depressing political assumption (of racial polarization) into the Voting Rights Act is costly, for it produces a society in which political interests are defined by racial and ethnic identity and representation is guaranteed in proportion to groups' numerical strength.'' Thernstrom (1979, p. 60).

21. The initial grounds on which Section 5 of the Voting Rights Act was ruled to be applicable to parts of New York State related to the fact that the state had conducted elections using ballots printed only in English. In the light of New York's heavy Puerto Rican population, this was interpreted by the Civil Rights Division of the Department of Justice as being, in effect, a literacy test—thus bringing Section 5 into play.

22. United Jewish Organizations of Williamsburg v. Carey (1977) 430 U.S. at 185, 187.

23. Wright v. Rockefeller (1964) 376 U.S. at 66.

24. This writer was recently made aware of an actual situation involving precisely this problem in the State of Alaska. There, the "native Alaskan" population makes up a significant proportion of the total population but is scattered in small villages in many areas of the state. The construction of districts designed to provide this minority with proportionate representation in the legislature is therefore virtually impossible. A similar situation may exist in parts of the southwest with regard to small, scattered urban and rural Hispanic enclaves.

25. United Jewish Organizations of Williamsburg v. Carey (1977) 430 U.S. at 186.

26. Brief for Appellees, Gaffney v. Cummings (1973) 412 U.S. 735, p. 41.

27. Gaffney v. Cummings (1973) 412 U.S. at 752 fn.

28. Brief for Appellant, Gaffney v. Cummings (1973) 412 U.S. 735, p. 72.

29. As Thernstrom (1979, p. 63) notes (and as the eventual electoral outcome in New York points up), "Even the most careful drawing of ward lines does not guarantee the representation of minorities in proportion to their size. Proportional racial and ethnic representation is a dubious end, and single-member districting an inadequate means."

Affirmative Gerrymandering

Robert B. McKay

The issues of reapportionment and redistricting have been of great interest for twenty years. Since I have not been actively involved in the day-to-day developments relating to reapportionment, I find it particularly fascinating to think again about the relevant concerns surrounding these issues that have emerged during these two decades.

It is interesting to think back to the beginnings in the 1960s when many people were optimistic that the disgraces of egregious malapportionment and discriminatory gerrymandering could indeed be ended. The 1970s suggested the need to qualify our enthusiams somewhat. Here in the 1980s I am optimistic once more that events will point anew the way to secure the benefits of truly fair reapportionment and redistricting. The task is not necessarily easy. Even now individuals who are essentially like-minded as to goals perceive differently how best to achieve those ends.

During the early 1960s many people reached agreement on two basic propositions that I believe are still basic. The first proposition is that reapportionment issues are justiciable in federal courts. I believe there is no substantial dissent from that proposition now despite Justice Frankfurter's caution against entering the political thicket. Although he was wrong to conclude that courts must avoid reapportionment issues, he was surely right in noting the many brambles in the thicket. It is not necessarily easy for judges, to some extent isolated in their chambers from the tumultuous world of politics, to keep up with the antics of legislators determined to achieve political advantage out of every drawing of voting districts. As an analogy to the problem of the political thicket, we might recall the experience of Br'er Fox and the Tar Baby. The more Br'er Fox sought disentanglement after his first encounter with Tar Baby, the more stuck he became. So, too, with reapportionment and redistricting. Each attempt at a solution reveals new problems. Nevertheless, I, for one, continue grateful that the Court is still actively engaged in seeking solutions to these seemingly intractable problems. While we may not all agree with every resolution, we can, I think, agree that the federal courts are better guardians of the electoral cabbage patch than the legislative goat.

The second proposition on which there was early agreement, and for which I believe there still is support, is that equality is the basic standard for testing the legislative districting process. As I look back to those innocent days of the 1960s, when all seemed clear, at least to me, I am tempted to compare *Reynolds*[1] with first feelings about *Brown* v. *Board of Education*[2] ten years earlier. It may be recalled that many people greeted with enthusiasm the decision in *Brown* that discrimination on grounds of race is unconstitutional, that dual school systems are forbidden, and that the Constitution is color blind. As we now know, it is not that easy, whether the issue is school desegregation or election districts. In both instances the beginning proposition—and still the central point—is that equality of treatment, as nearly as practicable, is the constant objective.

There is, I believe, another parallel between *Brown* and *Reynolds*. Armand Derfner (chapter 7, this volume) makes the point that the Constitution is not necessarily color blind; race must sometimes be taken into account, even in the pursuit of equality. So it is that we came to *Bakke*,[3] permitting affirmative action in higher education; *Weber*,[4] permitting affirmative action in private employment; and *Williamsburg* v. *Carey*,[5] permitting affirmative action in legislative districting.

It is not always easy to anticipate the hard problems, so perhaps it is enough to begin with the large generalizations about fairness and equality, working from these to the more particularized responses to the issues that later surface. It may be that early reliance on equality as a standard to resolve all questions was naive, but there should be no regret at the accomplishment of that important beginning. Perhaps we expected miracles that the political process does not encourage, does not even permit. For example, when I moved from academic consideration of apportionment into what I shall loosely call the real world of legislative districting as the chairman of a commission charged with drawing new lines, I learned much about the real world of politics. One house of the New York Legislature, seeing some political advantage in our proposal, was quite willing to enact it, while the other house, with an opposite perception of the political results, was quite unwilling. (In our earnest attempt at neutrality, we sought no information as to the residence of incumbents, with the result that an important legislative leader would under our plan have had to run in unfamiliar and potentially hostile territory. So much for neutrality!)

In the late 1960s I also made an effort at third-branch persuasion. The case in the Supreme Court was *Wells* v. *Rockefeller*,[6] and David Wells was my client, for the usual academic fee. We were, in an odd way, more successful than we had hoped because we won on the numerical equality issue despite narrow population differentials among the congressional districts in New York. I do not mean that we had not challenged the numerical differences, but we more earnestly sought to upset what we thought (correctly I still believe) was an outrageous political gerrymander. But the Court was not much interested in that complex, more nearly political-thicket issue, so it resolved the case on strict equality grounds. To this day the Court remains unwilling to consider political motivation in the drawing of election district lines. And my own metamorphosis is evident in that I now support the gerrymander for the limited purpose of assuring representation to minority racial and ethnic groups that might otherwise be left without reasonable representation in the political process. This, it seems to me, is quite distinguishable from the gerrymander done out of political motivation to benefit the party in power or to damage those out of power.

It would in my judgment be intolerable for Congress or a state legislature to transact business affecting all its constituents with no representation, or only token representation, of blacks, Chicanos, or other minority groups relevant to the particular jurisdiction. To leave representation of substantial minority interests to the not always benign mercy of a legislature, concerned first of all with continuance of its own incumbency, would suggest that the centuries-old pattern of discrimination has not yet ended. As in the case of higher education and employment, I believe race must still sometimes be taken into account. And so it is that on this issue I must record some disagreement with Dave Wells. Since he is no longer my client, the Code of Professional Responsibility does not require that I speak for him without regard to my own beliefs.

The Voting Rights Act of 1965, as amended, authorizes intervention by the Attorney General, when certain conditions are met, to vindicate the election rights of previously disadvantaged minorities. That is what happened in New York State leading to the litigation in *Williamsburg* v. *Carey.* The New York State Legislature, acting, to be sure, at the instance of the Department of Justice, drew election district lines in a manner designed to favor racial and ethnic minorities even though to the disadvantage of a religious minority. Although it is for me a hard case, the balance is ultimately tipped by the good-faith effort to comply with the congressional mandate to provide modest redress to those who had long suffered discrimination because of race or ethnic background.

The issue in *Williamsburg* was not whether the redistricting was well or sensitively done, but whether courts should defer to Congress and the executive branch where the action taken is not clearly invalid. Accordingly, *Williamsburg* is not in conflict with *Gomillion* v. *Lightfoot.*[7] The discrimination in that case was against the protected class; thus the districting was suspect and ultimately invalid.

Williamsburg is important for another reason as well. It was the precursor to the later affirmative action cases of *Bakke* and *Weber,* making the approval of the affirmtive action results in those cases predictable if not altogether inevitable.

Williamsburg demonstrates the difficulty of current redistricting dilemmas. When two favored groups are put against each other, it is not easy for a legislature or a court to make decisions that can immediately be pronounced right. Another more recent example of the hard cases is *Mobile* v. *Bolden,*[8] decided earlier in 1980. In this instance I believe the court made a misstep, putting an end to what I consider the salutary suspicion of multimember election districts. The consequences of approving the multimember districts there at issue are likely to be quite serious. Since, as Justice White observed in dissent, this was an instance in which the discriminatory intent was clearly demonstrated, other states are encouraged to adopt multimember districts when that action will serve to submerge a disfavored minority. Single-member districts will be preferred when they may be expected to serve similarly discriminatory purpose or other legislative selfish interests. The danger is that minorities will be effectively frozen out of the electoral process. This possibility presents one of the most serious threats to constructive race relations and effective representational democracy in this country. These are matters to worry about.

Notes

1. Reynolds v. Sims (1964) 377 U.S. 533.
2. Brown v. Board of Education (1954) 347 U.S. 483.
3. Regents of the University of California v. Bakke (1978) 438 U.S. 365.
4. United Steelworkers of America v. Weber (1979) 61 L. Ed. 2d 480.
5. United Jewish Organization of Williamsburg v. Carey (1977) 430 U.S. 144.
6. Wells v. Rockefeller (1969) 394 U.S. 542.
7. Gomillion v. Lightfoot (1960) 364 U.S. 339.
8. City of Mobile v. Bolden (1980) 48 LW 4436.

10 Comments on Criteria for Single-Member Districting

Carl A. Auerbach

Robert McKay (chapter 9, this volume) and I are among the few academics who supported the reapportionment cases. So it is with some distress that I find myself in disagreement with him now and in the role of a second to David Wells (chapter 8, this volume), who hardly ever needs a second. Unlike Wells, though, I think there is a difference between *Gaffney* v. *Cummings*[1] and *United Jewish Organizations of Williamsburg* v. *Carey*.[2]

Affirmative action gerrymandering must be evaluated in the context of a larger question: What is it that we expect geographic districting to accomplish? This question, in turn, can be answered only in the light of one's philosophy of democracy and views as to how districting should help to shape the electoral process so that it realizes the assumptions of our political democracy. It cannot be said that the electoral process now performs this function adequately.

As Austin Ranny (chapter 18, this volume) points out, the influence of our political parties is waning. The media contribute to this decline by giving candidates for political office unparalleled opportunity to appeal directly to the mass of voters over the heads of the political parties. National Convention delegate selection procedures minimize the influence of political leadership and deliberation and magnify the influence of single-issue groups that abhor the very notion of compromise and accommodation so essential to our democratic system. Single-issue groups multiply and make it difficult to achieve a consensus that reflects our common or shared interests and has the potential for expanding the area of agreement.

Is there any way geographic districting can help to overcome these difficulties, which make it impossible to put together a majority and effectuate its will? The theory of the reapportionment cases offers a guide and so I will remind you of it.

The dissenters in the reapportionment cases attack the Supreme Court's majority opinion on the ground that it emphasizes mathematical equality and regards people as "ciphers" or "faceless numbers." The charge is mistaken. True, the majority sees individual citizens, not groups or interests, as the principal actors in the electoral process and, therefore, the ones to be represented. Each individual, in a measure, is the product of what Georg Simmel describes as the "web" of the groups with which the individual is affiliated or with which the individual identifies for particular purposes. For a whole personality to emerge, the individual must reconcile the various, often conflicting, pressures exerted by these groups. Because, in the last analysis, only the individual votes; the same process of reconciliation should be encouraged when the individual is deciding for which political candidate or political party to vote. The overall judgment expressed in the vote will then reflect some concept of the public interest that the individual will seek to further by voting. This concept may be selfishly motivated, but it will reflect a reaching out to others to advance the sum total of common or shared interests. By this reaching out, the individual becomes a citizen.

Only if the individual succeeds in this inner reconciliation of the many group pressures affecting the individual's behavior will the single-mindedness of each group be tempered. Only then will political parties, elected representatives, and legislatures be able to accommodate and conciliate the various groups that seek to influence their behavior and act to advance the public interest.

For these reasons, I agree with David Wells's conclusion that *United Jewish Organizations of Williamsburg* v. *Carey* is inconsistent with the fundamental assumptions of the reapportionment cases. Racial, ethnic, and interest groups have many ways to influence the political process. They should not be permitted to do so by way of geographic districting, which should be oriented only to the individual citizen-voter. In the long run, I doubt that the creation of districts in which particular racial or ethnic groups predominate will benefit minority groups. They may benefit more by exerting political pressure in a large number of districts than having assured representation in a few. In any case, diversity should be the principle guiding districting.

I do not, however, agree with Wells's call for neutral principles of districting. The difficulty with this proposal is that neutral principles are blind to the inevitable political consequences they produce. Districting must be conscious of these political consequences and yet be fair—objectives not easy to attain. (See Backstrom, this volume.)

Notes

1. Gaffney v. Cummings (1973) 412 U.S. 735.
2. United Jewish Organizations of Williamsburg v. Carey (1977) 430 U.S. 144.

11 Should Representatives Be Typical of Their Constituents?

Bernard Grofman

In my observations on the issues raised by affirmative gerrymandering I wish to draw attention to the seminal work of Hannah Pitkin (1967) and her discussion of competing views on the nature of representation. Early in her book Pitkin distinguishes between two seemingly antithetical views of the nature of representation. The first of these she refers to as the *authorization view* (whose leading spokesman is Hobbes). In this view a representative "is an agent who has been delegated the power to act in the name of the one represented and to make commitments binding on him (it)." The second view (which lacks a single clear articulation) she labels the *accountability view*. In this view a representative is one who must answer to another for his actions. "(A)n elected official is a representative because (and insofar as) he will be subject to election or removal at the end of his term" (Pitkin, 1967:56).

> Where the one group defines a representative as someone who has been elected (authorized), the other defines him as someone who will be subject to election (held to account). Where the one sees representation as initiated in a certain way, the other sees it as terminated in a certain way (Pitkin, 1967:58).

Both views are sterile and formalistic according to Pitkin (1967:58-59) because "(n)either can tell us anything about what goes on *during* representation, how a representative ought to act or what he is expected to do, how to tell whether he has represented well or badly . . . (T)heir defining criterion for representation lies outside the activity of representing itself—before it begins or after it ends."

The accountability view of representation and the authorization view both lead one to downplay the importance of the characteristics of the representative since, in a two-party system at least, the representative has been chosen by a majority of his constituents and might be expected to follow the preferences of his constituents as a precondition to his own reelection. Thus, it might not seem to matter much how constituency boundaries get drawn. However, in a situation that is politically polarized, representatives may represent only that *element* of their constituency they

97

see as responsible for their own election and whose continued support they see as crucial to their own *reelection* chances. Thus, important elements of a constituency may go unrepresented.

Pitkin also considers an alternative approach to the authorization and accountability views of the meaning of representation, which emerges from writers concerned with "the proper composition" of a legislative assembly." John Adams, for example, argued that a representative legislature "should be an exact portrait, in miniature, of the people at large, as it should think, feel, reason, and act like them" (Adams, *Works*, Vol. IV, Boston 1852-1865, p. 284, cited in Pitkin, 1967:60). The clearest advocacy of what we shall call the *mirror view* is by some early twentieth-century proponents of proportional representation, whose aim is to secure a representative assembly reflecting with more or less mathematical exactness the various divisions in the electorate.

One difficulty with the mirror view is that it is not clear what characteristics of the electorate need to be mirrored to insure a fair sample. The mirror view, carried to its extreme, would argue for a random selection process for legislative assemblies (see also DeGrazia, 1951:185). To the extent that public officials constitute a fair sample of the people, "their opinion will be the same as that the public itself would form, if it could spend time enough to examine the matter thoroughly" (Lowell, 1921:239-240; cited in Pitkin, 1967:74). For example, as Pitkin (1967:76) points out, few would seriously argue that the "best legislator is one who is typical and average in every conceivable respect including intelligence, public spiritedness, and experience." Furthermore, few would wish to replace elections with a controlled random sample, Lowell's (1921:239-240) argument that choice by lot "would secure the same probability of impartial judgment that is expected of jurors" to the contrary, notwithstanding. More importantly, however, few would seriously argue that a legislator (legislature) must be typical of his (its) constituents to be an *effective* representative of them. Furthermore, voters may or may not desire representatives "like" them. A voter may choose a representative because of a likeness of characteristics, or because a representative possesses characteristics that the voter may lack but he *nonetheless* sees as desirable.

I, like Pitkin, am generally unsympathetic to the mirror view.[2] More specifically, affirmative gerrymandering is, in my view, misconceived if it is seen as a mechanism to guarantee that blacks will be represented by blacks, Hispanics by Hispanics, and whites by whites; rather, the proper use of affirmative gerrymandering is to guarantee that important groups in the population will not be substantially impaired in their ability to elect representatives *of their choice*. If district lines have been drawn so that the voting strength of some groups is consistently unrepresented (or underrepresented) throughout the districts in the unit, then we have the beginnings of a case for affirmative gerrymandering to redress this imbalance. Of course, under-representation must be measured relative to the appropriate statistical baseline, which in general will be a standard far less than proportional representation. (See chapter 5, this volume.)

Being typical may be roughly synonymous with being representative, but it is neither a sufficient nor a necessary condition for being an effective representative. Or, to put it somewhat paradoxically, that a representative is *not* representative of those whom he represents does not *prevent* him from representing them well, and that a representative *is* representative of those whom he represents does not *guarantee* that he will represent them well. There is no necessity for spaghettis to rejoice when linguines are elected.

Notes

1. A variant of the mirror view emphasizes the representative characteristics of individual legislators rather than focusing on the legislature as a whole. Stuart Rice's pioneer study (Rice, 1928) of the characteristics of legislators correlates the characteristics of state legislators with those of their constituents, taking the degree of correlation as the measure of "the extent to which they [legislators] represent their consti-tuents," and the specific characteristics on which there is high correlation are seen as providing "the respects in which legislators actually represent" (Rice, 1928:189, 206; cited in Pitkin, 1967:76). (See also Hoag and Hallett, 1926.)

2. Pitkin emphasizes that we must look beyond formal criteria—whether of typicalness, delegation, or accountability—to ascertain what the *task* of representing is all about and to develop criteria for whether it is be-ing done well or done badly.

Part II
Election Mechanisms Other than Single-Member Plurality Districts

Introduction to Part II

Arend Lijphart

Both American and foreign observers of American politics tend to think of the single-member plurality district system as the typical electoral method used in the United States. To a large extent, this picture is correct: the U.S. House of Representatives and most of the state legislatures are elected according to this method. But at the state level and even more at the level of county and city governments, various other electoral mechanisms occur, especially multimember districts, at-large elections, and weighted voting. And, of course, U.S. Senators are elected in two-member districts—a fact which is obscured by the staggering of the senatorial terms of office.

This part of the book deals with actual and potential alternatives to single-member plurality districts. Bernard Grofman (chapter 12, this volume) reviews the recent court decisions on multimember districts and at-large elections as well as the evidence concerning the effects of these methods on minority representation, and he analyzes the relatively infrequent instances of weighted voting and proportional systems in the United States. In his commentary, Malcolm Jewell (chapter 13, this volume) agrees with Grofman that single-member districting is the most favorable method from the point of view of achieving minority representation. This does not mean that it is impossible for minorities to be elected in multimember and at-large systems. In fact, minorities may well be overrepresented, for instance, if they manage to nominate a proportional share of the candidates of the majority party that then wins all or most of the seats in an at-large election. But the general tendency of districts with more than one member is to discourage minority representation. Hence it is not surprising that most minority politicians advocate single-member districting.

In addition to the number of representatives elected per district, there are several other factors that affect minority representation, such as the political cohesiveness of the minority and its geographical concentration. Especially if the minority is geographically dispersed to some extent, its chances of being represented are also enhanced by having relatively many districts—and a relatively large legislature. The general rule is that districts that are small—in terms of both the number of representatives elected from the district (preferably one) and the number of voters in the district—enhance minority representation.

There appear to be two ways in which the damage to political, ethnic, and other minorities in at-large and multimember elections can be minimized without resorting to single-member districting. One is to give each voter a

number of votes that is smaller than the number of seats in a district. For instance, in a four-member district and one vote per voter, a minority of
slightly more than 20 percent can elect its own candidate by concentrating
its vote on that candidate. If each voter has two or three votes in this four-
member district, the chances for the minority are less good—but still better
than under the normal plurality system of four votes per voter. Electoral
methods that prescribe fewer votes than there are seats in a district are
usually referred to as the *limited vote*. A special category of the limited vote
is the *single nontransferable vote,* in which each voter has only one vote; the
best-known example of its use is for the election of the Japanese House of
Representatives. It should be pointed out, however, that the limited and
single nontransferable votes are semiproportional methods. They entail
fundamental deviations from the plurality principle in the direction of proportionality.

The second method to minimize the damage to minorities in
multimember and at-large elections is for the minority to follow a strategy
that resembles the single nontransferable vote: Instead of using all four
votes available in a four-member district, minority voters can increase the
likelihood of electing their own representative by casting only a single vote
and withholding the other three votes. Such *single-shot* or *bullet* voting is
only effective, of course, when the majority divides its votes among
several—in our example of a four-member district, more than four—
candidates.

Whenever a majority scatters its votes among too many candidates, the
probability increases that a minority candidate will be elected. This is true
not only for at-large elections and multimember districts but also for single-
member districts. For the former category, this may be considered an advantage, but in single-member districts it presents a serious problem: The
minority candidate is elected not *in addition to* one or more majority candidates, but *instead of* a candidate whom the majority would prefer. This is
the problem to which Steven Brams (chapter 14, this volume) addresses
himself and for which he proposes the solution of approval voting. Approval voting is definitely an improvement over the usual single-member
district plurality rule when there are many serious candidates, as is often the
case in presidential primary elections in the beginning of the primary season.
One of the great advantages of the single-member plurality method is that it is
a very simple and understandable electoral system. Most of the methods that
try to be fairer, more effective, and more proportional are also more complicated. Approval voting is exceptional in this respect since it represents an
improvement that is also remarkably simple and straightforward.

The preceding pages have focused on questions of minority and majority
representation. It should be emphasized, however, that districting has many
other important consequences. As Jewell points out, campaign tactics and

the costs of campaigns in single-member districts tend to be very different from those in multimember districts and at-large elections. These differences almost inevitably result in different policy outcomes, too, although it is difficult to find unambiguous evidence for this proposition. And both Grofman and Jewell call attention to the strong impact of districting on the representatives' service role and their communications with the voters.

The alternative to single-member plurality districts that entails a more radical change and that is, in the United States, more unusual than multimember and at-large plurality elections, is *proportional representation*. About twenty-five cities and the state of Illinois have used some form of proportional election method, but, as Grofman shows, all but one have abandoned it. This is a paradoxical trend because it runs counter to the growing feeling that elections should yield proportional results and that minorities deserve to be fairly represented. The main conclusion of Arend Lijphart's (chapter 15, this volume) analysis is that the plurality rule and geographical districts—whether single-member, multimember, or at-large—are incompatible with the desire to attain proportional election outcomes. Hence a fundamental choice has to be made: If one's highest priority is to achieve proportionality, one has to opt for proportional representation; conversely, if one is unwilling to abandon plurality and geographical districting, one can try to minimize extreme disproportionalities—mainly by insisting on single-member districts—but one has to reconcile oneself to not getting proportional or nearly proportional results.

Proportional representation is the normal electoral method in most of the twenty-odd Western democracies. In fact, in this group only the United States, Great Britain, Canada, and New Zealand use single-member plurality districts at the national level. The great advantage of proportional representation is not only that it facilitates minority representation but also that it does not try to, and does not need to, predetermine which minorities should be represented. As John Wahlke (chapter 16, this volume) points out, the single transferable vote is the optimal form of proportional representation in this respect, because it allows candidates to run as individuals instead of on party lists and because it allows voters to express their preferences for these individual candidates instead of for groups of candidates organized as party lists. At the same time, Wahlke also warns that minority *representation* is merely the first step toward effective minority *power*.

Although the single transferable vote is theoretically superior to the list method of proportional representation, the latter is the one that is much more frequently used in Western democracies—a reflection of the power of political parties. The final point that should be made in this introduction is that there is an interesting parallelism between the three principal methods used to distribute parliamentary seats to party lists according to the votes received by these lists, mentioned in Lijphart's chapter, (chapter 15, this volume) and the methods of apportionment of the seats in the U.S. House of Representatives according to the constitutional requirement that Representatives "shall be apportioned among the several States . . . according to their respective members" (Balinski and Young, 1978; Balinski and Young, 1980; Brams, 1976b: 137-166).

The basic problem of allocating seats to parties in list proportional representation (PR) systems is the same as that of apportioning the 435 seats in the House of Representatives to the fifty states: When the parties' percentage shares of the total vote, and the states' percentage shares of the total population of the United States, are multiplied by the total number of available seats, we normally fail to get whole numbers. The simplest and most obvious solution appears to be to give each party list, or each state, the whole number of seats to which it is entitled, and to give the remaining seats to those parties or states with the highest fractions. For the U.S. House of Representatives, of course, an additional rule is that each state receives at least one seat. In the list P.R. systems, this method is known as the *largest remainders method*. In the apportionment literature, it is called the Hamilton or Vinton method; it was used for the apportionments in the second half of the nineteenth century.

Although the largest remainders and Hamilton methods are simple and straightforward, they have a number of grave deficiencies. The largest remainders method tends to encourage party splits: Two small parties with the same combined vote total as one single larger party may be entitled to more seats than the large party. For the purpose of apportionment, the Hamilton method may lead to the so-called Alabama paradox, discovered in 1881. The Alabama paradox is the phenomenon that a state may lose a seat when the total membership of the House increases by one seat.

These defects are avoided by the somewhat more complicated d'Hondt method of list P.R. and the equivalent Jefferson method of apportionment. The distinctive feature of d'Hondt is that, while it is a proportional method, it has a consistent bias in favor of the larger and against the smaller parties—which is also one of the reasons why it is the most frequently used list P.R. method. Similarly, the Jefferson method, used for the apportionments of the House based on the censuses of 1790 through 1830, favored the large states and discriminated against the smaller ones.

Balinski and Young (1980) have proved that the only nondiscriminatory method is the Sainte-Lague method of list P.R. and the equivalent Webster method of apportionment, used for the House apportionments following the censuses of 1840, 1900, 1910, and 1930. The Sainte-Lague method has only been used in a modified form—modified in such a way as to reintroduce an element of discrimination against the smallest parties—in the Scandinavian countries. The current method of apportionment for the House of Representatives, applied since the 1940 census, is the Huntington method. It yields results that are close to those of the Webster method, but it tends to discriminate slightly against the larger states.

12

Alternatives to Single-Member Plurality Districts: Legal and Empirical Issues

Bernard Grofman

In 1968, Paul A. Freund wrote that:

> While the major outlines of the reapportionment doctrine may be settled, there remain a host of questions still unresolved: its application to local government, the legal status of gerrymandering, the limits on multimember districts, the use of weighted or fractional voting in the legislature. (Freund, foreword to Dixon 1968, p. vi)

The latter three of these issues remain largely unresolved, and it is the last two issues on which this chapter will focus.

While single-member districting (smd) is the most common form of representation in the United States, apportionment schemes at the state and local level often make use of multimember districts (Klain 1955; Jewell 1971), the polar type of which is, of course, the at-large election;[1] and in one state (New York) weighted voting is the most common of the various systems in use for county government.[2] In the late 1960s and 1970s such non-smd systems have come under increasing challenge as violating Fourteenth Amendment equal protection standards.

Of the justifications advanced for deviations from the equal population rule, the desire to preserve local political boundaries is the most commonly voiced and the most frequently accepted. However, if the desire to preserve political boundaries is made a major concern, then this leads to consideration of systems of representation other than simple single-member districting and raises real constitutional issues as to what equal representation consists of. (See Grofman and Scarrow, 1981a.) If political subunits are of discrepant sizes, in a single-member districting system some small units will be denied their "own" representatives, while some larger units will be divided up. Political boundaries can be fully preserved only by (1) allowing for multiple-member districts (which may use plurality voting, or some form of

This research was supported by NSF Grant #SOC 77-24474, Political Science Program. I am indebted to the staff of the Word Processing Center, School of Social Sciences, University of California, Irvine, for turning my handwritten scribbles into finished copy; to Sue Pursche for bibliographic assistance; and to Howard Scarrow for helpful discussion of a number of the issues considered in this chapter.

A related article reviewing in detail twenty-one recent empirical studies of at-large versus ward districting is available upon request from the author.

proportional representation), or (2) using weighted voting to compensate for population differences across political subunits.

A Review of Recent Court Cases on Multimember Districts and At-Large Elections

Although multimember plans typically allocate the number of representatives to a district in direct proportion to that district's population, in the aftermath of the Supreme Court's entrance into the political thicket of reapportionment, the constitutionality of multimember districts and at-large elections has recently been challenged on several grounds related to one-man, one-vote issues.

First, multimember districts are said to submerge political, especially racial, minorities.

> The "winner-take-all" character of the typical election scheme creates the possibility that a specific majority will elect all the representatives from a multimember district whereas the outvoted minority might have been able to elect some representatives if the multimember district had been broken down into several single-member districts (Tribe 1978:750).

A second accusation against multimember districts is based on a mathematical argument advanced by Banzhaf (1966), which shows that residents of smaller districts are being denied equal representation because residents in the larger districts who are electing representatives proportional to their numbers have a more than proportionate chance of affecting election outcomes.[3]

A third and related challenge against multimember districts is based on the alleged propensity of representatives from such districts to act as a bloc. Chosen from the same constituency, almost certainly of the same party, the identity of interests among such representatives could be expected to be greater than those chosen from the same population divided up into plural distinct districts.

A fourth claim is that as the number of legislative seats within the district increases, the difficulty for the voter in making intelligent choices among candidates also increases. Ballots tend to become unwieldy, confusing, and too lengthy to allow thoughtful consideration.

A final charge brought against at-large elections is that, when candidates are elected at large, residents of particular districts may feel that they have no representative especially responsible to them (see *Chapman* v. *Meier*).[4]

Multimember districts have, however, not been without their defenders. Around the turn of the century replacing district systems with at-large elections was the goal of municipal reformers anxious to break the power of ward politicians. Similarly, Bryce (1889:463-64; cited in Klain, 1955:1118) deplored the spread of single-member districts, holding them responsible for the decline in quality of state legislatures. "The area of choice being smaller, inferior men are chosen." This charge has been endorsed by both politicians and political scientists (see Klain, 1955:1118, n. 30). The claim has also been made by some political scientists that "equal representation is technically more feasible with multiple districts" (Klain, 1955:1117; and see references cited in Klain, 1955:1117, n. 26; also see citations in *Whitcomb* v. *Chavis*),[5] by which is meant the statistical observation that the fewer the districts the easier it is to design districts so as to obtain exact population equality among them.

In the first of the post-*Baker* cases challenging multimember districts (*Fortson* v. *Dorsey*)[6] the complaint was that voters in the Georgia legislature's single-member districts could elect their own representatives; while voters in the multimember districts (who elected representatives at large but with the candidates required to be residents of a subdistrict, with each subdistrict allocated exactly one representative) were, it was proposed, being denied their own representative, since voters from outside the subdistrict helped to choose the subdistrict's representative. "The Court upheld Georgia's districting system, concluding that voters in multimember districts did indeed elect their own representatives—the representatives of the *county*, rather than of the subdistrict in which they happened to reside" (Tribe, 1978:752, emphasis added). In *Fortson* the Supreme Court held (as it had in *Reynolds* v. *Sims*)[7] that "equal protection does not necessarily require formation of all single-member districts in a state's legislative apportionment scheme." However, the Court had not yet been confronted with the full range of arguments against multimember districting. In particular, it had not yet been confronted with an alternative way of measuring citizen *weight* in an apportionment system involving districts of different sizes.

In the next case to come up on this issue, *Burns* v. *Richardson*, the Court reiterated[8] the standard advanced in *Fortson*[9] that "the legislative choice of multimember districts is subject to constitutional challenge only upon a showing that the plan was designed to or would operate to minimize or cancel out the voting strength of racial or political groups." In *Burns, Kilgarlin et al.* v. *Hill*[10] and in *Whitcomb* v. *Chavis* the court majority held no such showing was made. However, the holding in *Whitcomb* asserted that "the validity of multimember districts is justiciable"[11] and it "left open the possibility not only that a particular multimember district might be shown to cancel out the voting power of a minority group but also that multimember districts might eventually be declared illegal per se *if some of the indictments leveled at such districts generally could be established by more persuasive evidence"* (Tribe, 1978:753, n. 18, emphasis added).

In *Whitcomb* the Court squarely confronted for the first time the issue of the alleged overrepresentation of residents of the larger multimember districts as measured by their ability to affect election outcomes. In *Whitcomb*[12] the Court reiterated its views in *Reynolds* v. *Sims* on what is required for full and effective participation in the political process, to wit:

> Full and effective participation by all citizens in state government requires, therefore, that each citizen have *an equally effective voice* in the election of members of his . . . legislature (emphasis added).[13]

The challenge to the multimember apportionment scheme in *Whitcomb* rested on two quite distinct bases. The first was the assertion that the Marion County district "illegally minimizes and cancels out the voting power of a cognizable racial minority in Marion county."[14] This claim, as we noted above, was rejected by the Court on the grounds of an inadequate showing as to the facts. The second was the claim (based on the argument in Banzhaf, 1966) that "voting power does not vary inversely with the size of the district and that to increase legislative seats in proportion to increased population gives undue voting power to the voter in the multimember district since he has more chances to determine election outcomes than does the voter in the single-member district."[15] This claim was also rejected by the Court. (See note 3.)

If minority votes are not needed to win elections and there are no districts in which minorities predominate, minorities may be frozen out completely. The Supreme Court held this to have occurred for blacks in Dallas County, Texas, and Mexican-Americans in Bexar County, Texas (*White* v. *Regester*).[16] In *White* the Court found the Democratic party organization in Dallas County "did not need the support of the Negro community to win elections in the county, and it did not therefore exhibit good faith concern for the political and other needs and aspirations of the Negro community." Also, the court in *White* upheld the lower court findings that "the black community had been effectively excluded from participation in the Democratic primary selection process."[17] The Supreme Court in *White* similarly upheld district court findings that Bexar County's "multimember districts invidiously excluded Mexican-Americans from political participation" and that single-member districts were "required to remedy the effects of past and present discrimination against Mexican-Americans."[18]

In *White* the Court revealed that the hints, offered in *Fortson* and *Whitcomb,* that a properly mounted challenge to multimember districts (mmds), when sustained by a *historical* record of discrimination, could in fact succeed, were not idle ones. Other mmd schemes have subsequently been struck down by the federal courts. For example, in *Kruidenir* v. *McCulloch*[19] an eleven-member district was held unconstitutional; while in two important parallel cases, *Graves* v. *Barnes*[20] and *Graves* v. *Barnes,*[21] mixed single- and multimember districting for the Texas state legislature was repudiated as discriminatory against Mexican-Americans and blacks in a number of the most populous Texas counties. Moreover, in *Connor* v. *Johnson*[22] and *Chapman* v. *Meier*, the Supreme Court struck down judicially created apportionment schemes involving multimember districts, "creating a virtually *per se* rule against court-ordered multimember district plans in the absence of exigent circumstances" (Tribe, 1978:755, emphasis added).[23] Furthermore, the Justice Department, under the Voting Rights Act of 1965, has, in effect, prevented any jurisdiction covered by that act from *changing* to a pure at-large system.

As of 1970 "more than 60 percent of the cities (and one third of the counties) in this country elect their legislative bodies at-large rather than by districts, and the proportion of those has been growing" (Jewell, 1970). At the municipal level, it has been argued that at-large elections have acted to discriminate against racial and other minorities (Washington, 1971; Karnig and Welch, 1978; Heilig, 1978; Jones, 1976). With increasing frequency since the mid 1970s federal courts have been hearing cases challenging local electoral structure—cases often arising out of the Voting Rights Act. Until the 1980 ruling in *City of Mobile, Alabama* v. *Bolden*[24] (see discussion below) it had appeared that the major arena of apportionment challenges in the 1980s would have been with respect to at-large elections.[25]

That the Supreme Court would eventually declare at-large districting unconstitutional on its face was in our view never at all likely, since the Court had proceeded quite cautiously with respect to multimember districts, and in an aside in *Lucas* v. *Colorado General Assembly*[26] the Court asserted that, despite certain undesirable features of multimember elections, apportionment schemes that provide for the at-large election of a number of legislators from a county, or any political subdivision, are not "presumptively constitutionally defective." (See also *Beer* v. *United States.*[27]) Nonetheless, where a substantial racial minority exists and where there is a clear-cut history of past discrimination, at-large elections had successfully been challenged under standards enunciated in 1973 by the Federal Court of Appeal, Fifth Circuit in *Zimmer* v. *McKeithen.*[28]

In *Zimmer* it was held that unconstitutional discrimination could be demonstrated through a preponderance of evidence including (1) lack of access of minorities to the nomination process, (2) the unresponsiveness of legislators to the particularized interests of minorities, (3) a tenuous state policy underlying the preference for multimember or at-large districting, and (4) the existence of past discrimination precluding effective minority participation in the election system. In *Zimmer,* the Fifth Circuit Court also enunciated criteria that would provide indirect evidence of discrimination—including large districts, a majority vote requirement, provisions prohibiting bullet (single-shot) voting, and the lack of geographically linked posts. However, the sufficiency of these standards has now (1980) been repudiated by the Supreme Court in the *Mobile* case.

In *Mobile,* the Supreme Court enunciated a new and much stronger requirement. It is no longer enough to demonstrate that a given at-large districting is discriminatory in its *effects,* but rather one must also show that it is discriminatory in *intent.* [29] The discriminatory purpose doctrine in *Mobile* was derived from two earlier decisions, *Washington* v. *Davis* [30] and *Arlington Heights v. Metropolitan Housing Development Corporation.* [31, 32, 33]

In *Mobile,* a decision marked by the absence of a majority opinion and a plethora of competing views, the only thing that is sure is that the court no longer acknowledges the dual standard enunciated in *Fortson* that a plan is subject to constitutional challenge upon a showing that the plan *"was designed to or would operate to* minimize or cancel out the voting strength of racial or political groups" [34] (emphasis added). Indeed, quite remarkably, Justices Stewart, Burger, Powell, and Rehnquist argue in *Mobile* [35] that the Court has *never* had such a dual standard of intent *or* impact and that the language in *Fortson* (repeated in *Burns*) doesn't mean what it obviously says. For an instructive example of legal doublethink, note 13 in *Mobile* can hardly be bettered. (See, in this context, Marshall's stinging dissenting opinion in *Mobile*).

The principal consequence of the *Mobile* decision is that it will be extremely difficult to mount a successful challenge to an at-large election system, no matter how invidious may be its discriminatory impact on the representation of racial or linguistic minorities. The only optimistic note that can be sounded in the light of *Mobile* is that the *Mobile* decision does not (directly) affect the constitutional legitimacy of Justice Department action (under the Voting Rights Act) to forestall *changes* to at-large districting.

At-Large Elections and Minority Representation: A Brief Overview of the Empirical Evidence

The Supreme Court has been presented with a number of different challenges to the constitutionality of multimember districts and of at-large elections, including ones based on game-theoretic arguments (see Grofman and Scarrow, 1981a, for details). However, the only challenge that the Court has accepted as legitimate grounds for overturning an apportionment scheme is evidence that the plan "was designed to or would operate to minimize or cancel out the strength of racial or political groups" (*Fortson*). [36]

Confining ourselves to the issue of at-large versus ward elections (the analysis for multimember versus single-member districting is analogous), there are four different ways the question of impact on racial representation has been approached.

First, a priori theoretical arguments have been advanced to show why minorities are less likely to be successful in at-large rather than district-level competitions. Second, historical evidence has been amassed for a particular unit of government to demonstrate that blacks (or Mexican-Americans), although a substantial minority, have not been proportionally successful in electing representatives of their own kind—evidence that seems particularly telling when coupled with a historical record of racially polarized voting. Third, before-and-after case studies have been done of cities that switched from at-large to ward elections or vice versa. Fourth, cross-sectional analysis has been done comparing proportionality of racial and Hispanic representation in cities with various types of electoral systems.

Let us first examine the theoretical arguments on the relationship between election system and equity of minority representation: According to Tribe (1978:755, n. 26):

> (W)ell-established mathematical principles make clear that the likelihood of a minority's being able to elect a representative decreases as district size increases. Since the use of multimember districts leads, for any given size of the . . . legislature, to a higher average population per district, it exacerbates the always present likelihood that a minority will be left completely without representation.

We would wish to qualify Tribe's assessment because, as suggested by our discussion below, it leaves out the politics of the situation. Following Grofman and Scarrow (1978), we can, however, make Tribe's statement above (and analogous remarks in Comment (1970:1587-1588) and elsewhere) considerably more precise by looking at the notion of thresholds of representation and exclusion. The *threshold of representation, T_R* (Rokkan, 1968; Rae, Hanby, and Loosemore, 1971; Grofman, 1975) is the minimum support necessary to earn a group its first legislative seat. The *threshold of exclusion, T_E* (Loosemore and Hanby, 1971; Grofman, 1975), on the other hand, is the maximum support that can be attained by a group and nonetheless fail to win it even one seat. Both those indexes are rooted in the notion of an election as an n-person game.

If we let m be the number of representatives elected from the district and l the number of candidates contesting the race, and posit the minority group to run one candidate, then if all voters cast all the votes to which they are entitled, the thresholds of representation and exclusion become as in equation 14.1:

$$T_E = \frac{m}{m + 1} \, , \, T_R = \frac{m}{l} \tag{14.1}$$

Hence, for a single-member-district plurality elections $T_E = \frac{1}{2}$ and $T_R = \frac{1}{l}$.

Clearly $\frac{m}{m+1}$ $\geq$ ½ for $m \geq 1$; and $\frac{m}{t} \geq \frac{1}{t}$ for $m \geq 1$. Hence, for a minority constituting a fixed percentage of the population in each district, the maximum strength (under the worst of circumstances) that a minority group (fielding one candidate) can have and still be excluded from representation is higher under mmd plurality (bloc) voting than under smd plurality voting; and the minimum strength (under the most favorable of circumstances = all groups other than your own being of the same size) needed to gain a first seat is also higher under mmd bloc voting than under smd plurality. Thus, whether the best of circumstances or the worst, under the specified assumption as to distribution of minority strength across districts and as to voter behavior, for plurality election, smds are always better for minority representation than mmds.

In addition to these purely analytic arguments, it has also been noted that: in district races, white voters are less inclined to vote for black candidates than are black voters. Moreover, at-large contests allegedly increase campaign costs, tend to require endorsement by civic associations and the media, and are based often on name recognition—all elements which putatively reduce the chances of black electoral success (Karnig and Welch, 1978:2).

Turning now to the empirical approaches, we find a pattern of markedly contradicting claims.[37] At the municipal level, it has been argued that at-large elections have traditionally been used to discriminate against racial and other minorities (Karnig and Welch, 1978; Heilig, 1978; Jones, 1976; Washington, 1971). It should also be noted that, although many "at-large systems may not have been adopted with the specific intent of weakening black political influence, there are documented instances where cities have changed to at-large systems as tactics to dilute black political influence" (Jones, 1976:346; see also Heilig, 1978; Sloan and French, 1971).

While we find intuitively plausible Malcolm Jewell's view that "it is difficult to see how any local legislative body—city, county, or metropolitan—can be perceived as giving adequate voice and vote to minorites if it is elected in at-large elections without any form of districting or proportional representation" (Jewell, 1970; cf. Dixon, 1971:33-34), the empirical evidence on this point is, on the surface, far from clear.

On the negative side:

1. In Lakeland (a pseudonymous satellite city near Detroit), which shifted from ward to at-large elections with designated representatives, Sloan (1969) found no change in black representation.[38]
2. Using cross-sectional methods, Cole (1974) has shown that in sixteen New Jersey cities black representation is not significantly affected by the presence of at-large elections.

3. MacManus (1978), in looking at 243 central cities, has argued that once controls are introduced for socioeconomic and other factors, the impact of district elections on black city council representation vanishes. Moreover, MacManus (1978) singles out those cities that experienced a change in election system during the past decade and finds no significant difference in the proportionality of black representation between those cities that shifted from ward to at-large and those that shifted the other way, although the meaningfulness of this cross-sectional comparison is vitiated by the strong ceteris paribus assumption implicitly required.

4. Welch and Karnig (1978:2) provide evidence indicating that school districts with at-large contests actually have greater black representation in school board elections, though their limited sample of cities with district-based representation makes confident generalization impossible.

On the positive side:

1. Raleigh, North Carolina, and Charlotte, North Carolina, recently, via referendum, shifted from at-large to ward elections; and Mundt (1979) finds that in Charlotte, blacks now hold 27.3 percent of council seats as compared to 5.4 percent between 1945-1975 (see also Heilig, 1978), although in Raleigh, black representation remains unchanged.[39]

2. In Fort Worth and San Antonio the 1977 change from at-large to ward elections lead to a "dramatic increase" in Mexican-American representation in both cities (Cotrell and Fleischman, 1979).

3. Using the same cross-sectional data base of 273 central cities as MacManus (1978), Robinson and Dye (1978) come to quite different conclusions.[40] They assert (1978:137) that "black representation is significantly greater in cities with ward elections than in cities with at-large elections" and further assert (1978:139, 140) that "at-large election is the single most influential independent variable" and that "reformed government structures significantly and *independently* contribute to black underrepresentation" (emphasis added).

4. Using the same data base as both MacManus (1978) and Robinson and Dye (1978), Taebel (1978), who challenges the suitability of the ratio measure of inequity used by Robinson and Dye (1978) and uses instead the difference measure of MacManus (1978), nonetheless finds that both for blacks and Hispanics there is a relationship between at-large elections and inequity of minority representation, although this relationship is stronger for blacks than for Hispanics (especially when controlled for size of city council).[41]

5. In the study we believe to be the most impressive in its methodological rigor, which looks at the 264 American cities with population over 25,000 and with at least 10 percent black population, and which focuses

on the 66 cities that combine district with at-large representation, Karnig and Welch (1978) show that in cities with a mixed system, the district component is almost perfectly proportional in its racial representation while the at-large component is far from equitable ($N = 66$); and that in cities using district systems black representation is nearly proportional to black population (.92 on the difference measure, -1.3 percent on the ratio measure, ($N = 62$)); while in pure at-large cities representation is quite inequitable (.62 on the ratio measure, -9.6 percent on the difference measure, ($N = 111$)).[42]

The nine studies we have cited above (and other studies in this area) suffer from a variety of methodological flaws or limitations.

Although the case studies are longitudinal, in none of the case studies are there any control groups, so that we can't be sure that changes in patterns of minority representation are *causally* linked to changes in type of electoral system—minority representation may be changing due to other factors. In the cross-sectional studies (with the exception of the within-city comparisons for mixed systems in Karnig and Welch (1978)), we have the usual difficulty of causal inference. If cities with at-large elections differ in systematic ways from those with ward elections (not captured by the control variables used), then differences (or absence of differences) in equity of minority representation may be artifactual. Moreover, the cross-sectional studies differ in their operationalization of equity of representation, some using a ratio measure (Robinson and Dye, 1978; Welch and Karnig, 1978), some a difference measure (Cole, 1974; McManus, 1978; Taebel, 1978). These differences in operationalization can lead to differences in result. (See note 41.) Only Karnig and Welch (1978) and Grofman (in an unpublished retabulation of data in Sloan (1969)) make use of both the ratio and the difference measures.

The cross-sectional studies also differ in which other variables (for example, city council, council size, percent black population, city population, city median income level, city manager versus mayor versus commission, and so forth) are controlled for and in the fineness of categorization of type of electoral system used, with most authors using a trichotomous classification (ward, mixed, at-large) but some studies (MacManus, 1978; Karnig and Welch, 1978) introducing other potentially significant distinctions, for example, as between at-large elections with and without designated representatives. Also, the cross-sectional studies vary tremendously in the data being examined, with sample bases ranging from cities over 25,000, to central cities exclusively, to central cities excluding those with minimal black populations, to very large cities (populations over 250,000).

One omission common to all the cross-sectional studies is that (for those cities with explicit *or* implicit partisan contests) they do not differentiate between cities under Republican control and those under Democratic control. This is an important omission because we would anticipate that black representation would be comparatively lower in Republican-controlled areas because blacks are customarily part of the Democratic party constituency. Finally, and we believe most importantly, the cross-sectional studies do not (MacManus (1978) and Taebel (1978) are partial exceptions) look at geographic concentration of minorities in the cities they investigate. Clearly, the nature of political and demographic realities will determine the extent to which single-member or multimember districting will help or hinder particular minorities. If a minority is reasonably large and geographically concentrated, it may expect to get its own representative(s) in a single-member district but might be swamped by other groups if forced to compete for representation in a very large multimember district. On the other hand, if a minority is not geographically concentrated and if it has some political clout, it may be far more effective in a larger multimember unit, where it may be granted some representation, perhaps even representation proportional to its numbers, than engaged in fighting *and losing* a number of struggles for control of single-member districts. (See discussion in Carpenetti, 1972.)

Nonetheless, if we look to the representation not of any particular minority group but of minorities in general, then an argument can be made on behalf of single-member districts as opposed to at-large elections that we find to be compelling. At-large elections put minority representation at the discretion of the majority. In polarized situations, this is likely to leave minorities completely unrepresented.

Weighted Voting

By 1960, most New York counties used a unit-voting system for their county boards of supervisors in which each town/city ward was given one representative. This scheme was, not surprisingly, struck down in *Graham v. Board of Supervisors of Erie County*.[43] In the 1960s, in response to the voiding of unit-voting systems, nearly half of New York's fifty-seven counties sought to preserve township-based representation while still complying with Court directives on one-man, one-vote by shifting to weighted voting schemes similar to that in use in Nassau County (a county that, since 1917, has used weighted voting). Two cases involving such counties (Saratoga County and Washington County) were combined and decided by the New York Court of Appeals in an important decision, *Iannucci v. Board of Supervisors of the County of Washington*. In that case, the court held that weighted voting was permissible only if the weights led to Banzhaf power values for each legislator proprotional to the population he/she represented.

(See Banzhaf, 1965, 1966; Brams, 1975; Lucas, 1974; Grofman and Scarrow, 1980.)[44,45] We shall quote the court's opinion at some length:

> Although the small towns in a county would be separately represented on the board, each might actually be less able to affect the passage of legislation than if the county were divided into districts of equal population with equal representation on the board and several of the smaller towns were joined together in a single district (see Banzhaf 1965:317) . . . *The significant standard for measuring a legislator's voting power, as Mr. Banzhaf points out, is not the number or fraction of votes which he may cast but, rather his ability* . . . And he goes on to demonstrate that a weighted voting plan, while apparently distributing this voting power in proportion to population, may actually operate to deprive the smaller towns of what little voting power they possess, to such an extent that some of them might be completely disenfranchised and rendered incapable of affecting any legislation (*Iannucci,* emphasis added). [46]

> The principle of one-man, one-vote is violated, however, when the power of a representative to affect the passage of legislation by his vote, rather than by influencing his colleagues, does not roughly correspond to the proportion of the population in his constituency. Thus, for example, a particular weighted voting scheme would be invalid if 60 percent of the population were represented by a single legislator who was entitled to cast 60 percent of the votes. Although his vote would apparently be weighted only in proportion to the population he represented, he would actually possess 100 percent of the voting power whenever a simple majority was all that was necessary to enact legislation. Similarly a plan would be invalid if it was *mathematically impossible* for a particular legislator representing, say, 5 percent of the population to ever cast a decisive vote. Ideally, in any weighted voting plan, it should be mathematically possible for every member of the legislative body to cast the decisive vote on legislation in the same ratio which the population of his constituency bears to the total population. Only then would a member representing 5 percent of the population have, at least in theory, the same voting power (5 percent) under a weighted voting plan as he would have in a legislative body which did not use weighted voting—for example, as a member of a twenty-member body with each member entitled to cast a single vote. This is what is meant by the one-man, one-vote principle as applied to weighted voting plans for municipal governments. A legislator's voting power, *measured by the mathematical possibility of his casting a decisive vote,* must approximate the power he would have in a legislature which did not employ weighted voting (*Iannucci,* emphasis added). [47]

The Court then went on to confess itself unable to determine whether the plans before it met the criterion proposed and asserted that the boards are not entitled to rely on the presumption that their legislative apportionments are constitutional. Rather:

(W)ith respect to weighted voting . . . a considered judgment is impossible without computer analyses and, accordingly, if the boards choose to reapportion themselves by the use of weighted voting, *there is no alternative but to require them to come forward with such analyses and demonstrate the validity of their reapportionment plans (Iannucci, emphasis added).*[48]

With these words the court ushered in the age of computerized weighted voting in New York county government. The experiences of the twenty-four New York counties that have used weighted voting offer a number of useful lessons to legislatures considering options other than simple single-member districting and a number of lessons in terms of evaluating the ability of lawyers and judges to understand sophisticated mathematical arguments in the one-man, one-vote area.

First, in many counties weighted voting has given rise to situations in which a coalition of a very few of the larger political units can wield majority control. Second, by allowing modified weighted voting, without recognizing that representatives from the same district elected by the same constituency are likely to vote as a bloc, the courts have inadvertently allowed the largest unit in one New York county a disproportionate share of the power (Grofman and Scarrow, 1981b). Third, in general, weighted voting systems fail to satisfy the criterion of equalizing person power; that is, they do not allocate a number of representatives proportional to the population represented, thus failing to recognize that legislators perform services that have nothing to do with voting and that require personal attention. (See Grofman and Scarrow, 1981a.) Fourth, New York courts have unknowingly shifted the method of measurement used to measure the fairness of power apportionments in weighted voting schemes, so as to apply an extremely weak standard that is at variance with that used by the U.S. Supreme Court for judging single-member district schemes. Fifth, the court-imposed requirement of computer calculations to obtain optimal weight assignments for weighted voting systems has proven largely unnecessary; that is, the assignment of weights according to simple population proportions would have produced power scores that matched population proportions almost exactly. (For extended discussion, see Grofman and Scarrow, 1979, 1980, 1981a, 1981b.)[49]

In sum, it does not appear to me that weighted voting ought to be looked to as a means of providing particular geographic units (or geographically concentrated racial or linguistic minorities) a means of representation proportional to population. While weighted voting can be used to accomplish this end, I believe that its drawbacks more than outweigh its benefits, especially as its constitutionality has never yet been subject to Supreme Court test. Nonetheless, if district sizes are permitted to vary only slightly from equipopulation, weighted voting might be a useful way of reconciling one-person, one-vote standards with maintenance of political subunit boundaries and without requiring much if any decennial shifting of district boundaries (Lee Popayanopoulos, personal communication, June 14, 1980).

Proportional Representation

The Hare System

Slightly over two dozen U.S. cities have made use of proportional representation (in the form of the Hare single transferable vote) for their city council elections at some time during this century, primarily during the period 1915-1946 (Hoag and Hallett, 1926; Hallett, 1940). Most of these cities used PR for only a few elections, but seven cities (Ashtabula, Boulder, Cincinnati, Lowell, New York, Toledo, Wheeling), used PR for at least a decade, and one city (Cambridge) is still using PR and has done so since shortly after World War II, while New York began in the 1970s to use PR for school board elections. Until the early 60s, the National Municipal League had PR as one of the components of its model city charter.

The chief objections to PR have been that (1) the Hare system is too complicated for voters to understand; (2) the Hare system is too complicated for voters to use, leading to lower turnout and a high proportion of spoiled ballots; (3) PR makes stable majority rule government impossible; and (4) PR makes it possible for "undesirables" (for example, kooks, communists, Negroes) to be elected.

The first charge is partly true but largely false. Certainly the Hare vote transfer procedure is rather complicated to explain, but most voters can readily grasp the basic idea that any group that composes a certain proportion of the electorate is able under the Hare system to elect a representative of its choice. Moreover, it seems unlikely that Americans who can tell you how many games the Phillies are out of third in their division are really unable to comprehend the idea of rank-ordering their candidate preferences.

There is no evidence to support the second charge and little evidence to support the third charge, either (see esp. Dodd, 1976). Nonetheless, horror stories about the instability of European countries that used (party list) PR are used by PR opponents to attack the Hare system as malefic and unAmerican.

The fourth assertion, that PR leads to the election of "undesirables," has been responsible for the demise of PR in a number of instances. The election of alleged "irresponsibles" in Ashtabula, the election of communists in New York City, and the threatened election of a black mayor in Cincinnati were key factors in the referendum repeals of PR in those cities.

The repudiation of PR by all but one of the American cities that have used it has often been alleged to demonstrate its unsuitability for use in the United States. Actually, as far as we are aware, in those cities where the Hare system was used it worked well, and its undesirable consequences were mostly in the eyes of the previously impregnably entrenched majority beholders. Whether the present-day context of concern for effective minority representation can allow PR to make a comeback is an open question. There are a few signs of its present-day resuscitation, for example, use of the Hare System in the 1970s for school board elections in New York City and the replacement of winner-take-all primaries with a form of proportional representation in the Democratic party nominating process. (See Lengle, chapter 17, this volume.)

Cumulative Voting

Voting for the Illinois General Assembly has, for most of Illinois' period of statehood, made use of cumulative voting. Cumulative voting in Illinois takes place in three-member districts, in which voters may cast three votes for a single candidate or one-and-a-half votes for each of two candidates or one vote apiece for three candidates.

One consequence of cumulative voting as it has been practiced in Illinois is that virtually all districts have elected one minority-party and two majority-party representatives, since (for a two-party contest) only where the majority party has 75 percent or more of the voting strength (and can expect its loyalists to vote a straight party ticket) can that party capture all three seats in a district. Thus, the Republican downstate rural districts elect some Democratic representatives to the Illinois House and the Chicago Democratic districts elect some Republican representatives. This crossover prevents the urban-rural split in Illinois from being defined in purely partisan terms.

A proposal for the repeal of cumulative voting was made as part of a referendum to reduce the size of the Illinois Assembly. This referendum carried overwhelmingly in 1980 for reasons that had little or nothing to do with support/opposition to cumulative voting.

In our view, the Illinois experience demonstrates conclusively that the effect of a particular voting system can be understood only in the context of the politics in which it is embedded. In Illinois, cumulative voting has operated within the context of a rather strong two-party system. In Illinois, cumulative voting has not led to a proliferation of single-issue candidates or parties. Moreover, in Illinois, for a variety of reasons, the political parties have not run what (in retrospect) can be shown to be the optimal number of candidates. In particular, the majority party in each district plays it very safe. Even in cases where the majority party received over 60 percent of the vote—cases where it can be shown that it could not hurt for it to have run three candidates—over 80 percent of the time only two candidates were run (Brams, 1975:120).[50]

In Illinois, cumulative voting has certainly not destroyed two-party government nor has it been accompanied by an unusual proliferation of special interest representatives—charges often leveled against PR systems. Furthermore, it has usually given rise to a *very* good fit between a party's vote share and its share of legislative seats. On balance, the cumulative voting record in Illinois was a quite favorable one (Sawyer and MacRae, 1962; Blair, 1973; Epstein and Grofman, work in progress).[51]

Notes

1. For example, at present (according to the Council of State Governments) the upper house in thirteen states and the lower house in twenty-two states utilize some multimember districts.

2. New York has twenty-four of its sixty-two counties using some form of weighted voting within the county legislature and twelve electing representatives from a combination of single- and multiple-member districts or multiple-member districts of various sizes.

3. In two articles that appeared in American law journals in the mid-1960s, a lawyer named John Banzhaf III (Banzhaf, 1965, 1966) proposed to evaluate representation systems in terms of the extent to which they allocated "power" fairly. Banzhaf's analysis makes use of game-theoretic notions in which power is equated with the ability to affect outcomes.

Consider a group of citizens choosing between two opposing candidates. To calculate the power of the individual voter, we generate the set of all possible voting coalitions among the district's electorate. If there are N voters in the district, then there will be 2^N possible coalitions. Then we ask, for each of these possible coalitions, whether a change in an individual voter's choice from Candidate A to Candidate B (or from Candidate B to Candidate A) would alter the electoral outcome. If so, that voter's ballot is said to be *decisive*. A voter's power is defined as the number of times, in all possible coalitions, that his vote could be decisive, and can best be expressed as a percentage—that is, the number of his decisive votes divided by the total number of all the decisive votes of all the voters (including himself). The higher the percentage of voter coalitions in which *his* vote is *decisive*, the higher a voter's power score. The Banzhaf index has considerable intuitive appeal; power is based on ability to affect outcome. However, the Banzhaf calculations also rest on the not so reasonable proposition that all voting combinations are equally likely.

For single-member district systems, each district having equal populations, all voters have identical power; the ability of the voter in one district
to affect his district's electoral outcome is identical with the ability of
another voter in a neighboring district to affect the outcome there. But what
about the case of multiple-member districts, with some districts of one size
and others of another size? Here, since the voters who elect k representatives have k times as much importance as voters who can elect only one
representative, we might expect that to equalize voter power we should
assign the districts with k representatives k times as many voters as well,
since with all votes of equal weight, intuitively, we would expect that a
voter's ability to decisively affect outcomes would be inversely proportional
to district size. Banzhaf (1966) pointed out that this argument is
mathematically incorrect and that actually the voters have decisive power
proportional to the *square root* of district size.

This issue and the mathematics underlying this argument are discussed
at length in Lucas (1974) and Grofman and Scarrow (1981a).

4. Chapman v. Meier (1975) 420 U.S. at 15-16.

5. Whitcomb v. Chavis (1971) 403 U.S. 124 at 157-158, n. 38.

6. Fortson v. Dorsey (1965) 379 U.S. 433.

7. Reynolds v. Sims (1964) 377 U.S. 533 at 57.

8. Burns v. Richardson (1965) 384 U.S. 73, at 74.

9. Fortson v. Dorsey (1965) 379 U.S. at 439.

10. Burns, Kilgarlin et al. v. Hill (1964) 386 U.S. 120.

11. Whitcomb v. Chavis (1971) 403 U.S. 124 at 125.

12. Whitcomb v. Chavis (1971) 403 U.S. 124 at 141.

13. Reynolds v. Sims (1964) 377 U.S. 533 at 565.

14. Whitcomb v. Chavis (1971) 403 U.S. at 144.

15. Whitcomb v. Chavis (1971) 403 U.S. at 144-145.

16. White v. Regester (1973) 412 U.S. at 767.

17. White v. Regester (1973) 412 U.S. at 767.

18. White v. Regester (1973) 412 U.S. at 769.

19. Kruidenir v. McCulloch (1966) 142 N.W. 2d 355.

20. Graves v. Barnes (1972) 373 F. Supp. 704 (W.D., Texas)

21. Graves v. Barnes (1974) 378 F. Supp. 640 (W.D., Texas)

22. Connor v. Johnson (1971) 402 U.S. 690.

23. In *East Carroll Parish School Board* v. *Marshall* (1976) 424 U.S.
636 the Court held that single-member districting is the appropriate remedy
for federal courts to impose where at-large election schemes have been
found to unconstitutionally dilute the voting strength of black minorities.
In jurisdictions covered under the Voting Rights Act of 1965 (with powers
held legitimate by the U.S. Supreme Court in the *Petersburg* and *Richmond*
cases (see below)), since 1973 the Justice Department has had a virtual ban
on changes from ward to pure at-large districting.

24. City of Mobile, Alabama v. Bolden (1980) 48 L.W. 4436.

25. It appears as if a new wave of reformers has taken up district elections as a "reform" to replace the at-large elections that were a reform of an earlier generation of reformers. In addition to court challenge to at-large elections, referenda to replace at-large with district elections have taken place in a number of cities; and faced with the prospect of court challenge, a number of cities had voluntarily shifted from at-large to district elections. By one or the other of those mechanisms, at-large elections have been replaced with district systems in such cities as Albany, Georgia; Charleston, South Carolina; Fort Worth, Texas; Mobile, Alabama; Aberdeen, Mississippi; Raleigh, Virginia; San Antonio, Texas; San Francisco, California; and Waco, Texas (Heilig, 1978; Cotrell and Fleischman, 1979; Mundt, 1979). Neither political nor legal challenges against at-large elections or systems which mix district and at-large elections have, however, been uniformly successful. (See Karnig and Welch, 1978:2; Cotrell and Fleischman, 1979, note 8.)

26. Lucas v. 44th General Assembly of the State of Colorado (1964) 377 U.S. 713, n. 2.

27. Beer v. United States (1976) S. Ct. 1357.

28. *Zimmer* v. *McKeithan* (1973) 485 F.2d 1297. At-large elections for school board and police juries in Louisiana Parish (County) were repudiated in *Zimmer*, despite the fact that 46 percent of the registered voters in the parish were black and some black candidates had been elected in the previous at-large elections—including one candidate who had been defeated when running in his own ward when ward-based elections were in effect. (This case was affirmed, albeit on other grounds, as *East Carroll Parish School Board* v. *Marshall* (1976) 424 U.S. 636. See discussion in Dolgow, 1977, 173-475.) In *Wallace* v. *House* (1975) 515 F.2d 619 5th Cir, at-large municipal elections were invalidated in Ferriday, Louisiana, although a plan combining mixed single-member districts and at-large elections was upheld. (In that city, although blacks constituted nearly 50 percent of the voters, under the at-large scheme they had controlled not one of its aldermanic seats.) A number of other at-large elections have been struck down, but in other jurisdictions at-large elections were sustained against legal challenge. (See for example, *Hendrix* v. *Joseph* (1977) 559 F.2d 1265 and *David* v. *Gamson* (1977) 553 F. 2d 923.)

In Richmond, Virginia, a shift from at-large to ward elections for city council was the price the city was required (by the Justice Department) to pay if it wished to annex a suburban area that was predominantly white—an annexation that would have kept the city population majority white. The Justice Department's authority to impose such a requirement under the Voting Rights Act of 1965 and 1975 was sustained by the U.S. Supreme Court in *City of Richmond, Virginia* v. *United States* (1975) 422 U.S. 358.

(See also *City of Petersburg, Virginia* v. *United States* (1973) 410 U.S. 926.) See also *Beer* v. *United States* (1976) 76 S. Ct. 1357, in which the at-large component of a proposed change in election procedures for the New Orleans City Council election was exempted from Justice Department scrutiny because the at-large features remained unchanged from earlier election laws and thus were not held to be subject to review under the Voting Rights Act of 1965.

29. This result was anticipated in an earlier case before Fifth Circuit, *Nevitt* v. *Sides* (1978) 571 F.2d 209, in which the claim was rejected that at-large districting for a city council in a racially polarized city was per se discriminatory, and a showing of "intentional" discrimination found to be necessary. In *Nevitt* the court referred to at-large districting as "racially neutral, on its face," and the court asserted that "absent other evidence indicating the existence of intentional discrimination, state laws providing for at-large districting are entitled to the deference accorded any other statute; their means need only be reasonably related to ends properly within state cognizance." However, in *Nevitt* (at 221) the Court held that a plan, "racially neutral at its adoption" may be unconstitutional if it furthers "preexisting discrimination" or is used to "maintain" it. Moreover, and *most importantly,* in *Nevitt* the Fifth Circuit court majority was able, albeit through what we regard as ingenious logic chopping, to reconcile the proof of intent requirement enunciated by the U.S. Supreme Court in *Washington* v. *Davis* (1976) 426 U.S. 229 as being fully compatible with its own previous ruling in *Zimmer* v. *McKeithen.*

30. Washington v. Davis (1976) 426 U.S. 229.

31. *Arlington Heights* v. *Metropolitan Housing Development Corporation* (1977) 429 U.S. 252. Arlington Heights involved a zoning ordinance prohibiting multifamily dwellings, which was challenged on the ground that the ordinance had a racially discriminatory effect. *Washington* v. *Davis* involved the constitutionality of a written personnel test that blacks were four times more likely to fail than whites. Both the ordinance and the test were found to be devoid of any racial overtones that would require Court intervention on constitutional grounds, since in neither case was there found any *intent* to engage in racial discrimination.

32. The difference between the purpose doctrine and earlier rulings can be shown with a quote from the holdings in *Graves* v. *Barnes* (1974) 378 F. Supp. 640:

> Given general conditions indicating racial discrimination that has stunted the participation of blacks and Mexican-Americans in life of state, plaintiffs who claim that multimember legislative districts discriminated against such minority *need only prove an aggregate of factors* including restricted access of minority groups to slating of candidates for particular party nominations, consistent use of racial campaign tactics to defeat minority

candidates or those championing minority concerns, indifference or hostility of district-wide representatives to particularized minority interests, and *inability of minority groups to obtain representation in proportion to their percentage of district's population* (emphasis added).

33. We might also note that in *Kirksey* v. *Board of Supervisors of Hind County, Mississippi* (1977) 544 F. 2d 139, a 1977 case that also reached the U.S. Court of Appeals, Fifth Circuit, wedge-shaped single-member districts that cut up the Black population so as to deprive them of majority control of any district were rejected as discriminatory even though direct discriminatory intent was not proved; while in *City of Rome, Georgia* v. *United States* (August 9, 1979) 472 F.Supp. 221 (U.S. District Court, District of Columbia), a change of election system that introduced runoffs, numbered posts, and staggered elections was held to violate the Voting Rights Act even though no intent to discriminate was proved. In *Kirksey* there was an established history of previous discrimination and a holding that inequality of access to the political process was an inference that flowed from existence of economic and educational inequalities suffered by minority inhabitants of the county. In the words of Judge Godbold in that opinion, "nothing suggests that where purposeful and intentional discrimination already exists it can be constitutionally perpetuated into the future by neutral official action."

34. Fortson v. Dorsey (1965) 379 U.S. 433 at 439.

39. City of Mobile, Alabama v. Bolden (1980) 48 LW 4436, n. 13.

36. Fortson v. Dorsey (1965) 379 U.S. 433 at 439.

37. Karnig and Welch (1978:2-4) review a number of these studies and the reasons why findings differ. We draw upon their analysis in our discussion below. A detailed discussion of over a dozen studies (including all those cited below) is available upon request from the author.

38. Sloan (1969; table 3, 1967) does find that, under at-large elections with designated representatives, when two blacks run against each other, the black preferred by other blacks is *defeated* in the city-balloting. Thus, while the *percentage* of black representation may remain unchanged, the *nature* of that representation may have changed dramatically. We regard this as an extremely important point. A number of minority *representatives* proportional to minority population is not a *sufficient* condition for proportionate *representation* of minority interests; and indeed it may not even be a *necessary* one. We share the view of Tribe (1978:658-659) that:

> To speak of a group's electing *its* representative is, after all, an over-simplification. Various candidates appeal in varying degrees to all population groups. Thus a minority might insure some representation even in a district where it could not come close to electing a candidate who espoused its views without reservation; the minority could help elect the candidate

whose views were least obnoxious to its members. Of course, if there were clearly dichotomized minorities and majorities—and if voters never cast wayward ballots—the minority might still be completely denied representation. But these factual assumptions defy the facts of political life; there are many types of interests and many gradations of opinion, with the result that a process of accommodation is generally undertaken in which even small minorities can successfully vie for influence.

39. MacManus (1978), Taebel (1978), and Robinson and Dye (1978) look at the same cities. However, the exact data each look at are slightly different. See MacManus (1979).

40. Mundt (1979) has looked at Richmond. In response to legal challenge to a proposed annexation of white suburbs that have reduced the percentage of black population below 50 percent, there was a Justice Department-imposed shift from at-large to district elections in which four districts were created with a clear black majority, four with a clear white majority, and one district that was a swing district. The swing district has been won by a black candidate, creating black majority control.

41. All but two of the (cross-sectional) studies concluding that at-large elections impede black representation have employed the ratio approach (exceptions are Taebel, 1978, and Karnig and Welch, 1978), and both of the cross-sectional examinations uncovering no relationship between black electability and electoral form have utilized the difference approach (Cole, 1974; MacManus, 1978).

42. Karnig and Welch find the most inequitable black representation in cities using at-large elections with designated representatives (.44 on the ratio measure, -14.0 percent on the difference measure, $N = 27$).

43. Graham v. Board of Supervisors of Erie County, New York (1967) 267 N.Y.S. 2d 383.

44. Iannucci v. Board of Supervisors of Washington Country, New York (1967) 282 N.Y. 2d 502. See note 3 for a definition of the Banzhaf Index.

45. So long as each legislator has a single *yea* or *nay* vote on issues coming before the legislature, the question of legislative power does not have to be explicitly addressed. Thus, in the leading apportionment cases that have come before the U.S. Supreme Court, all of which have involved single- or multiple-member districts with each elected representative eligible to cast a single vote, it seems to be simply *assumed* that the justification for examining the number of persons contained within each district is the fact that their elected representatives by their vote wield equal decision-making power in the affairs of the polity; and that equality of apportionment thus indirectly results in equality of policy-making power among citizens.

But what about weighted voting schemes (also fractional voting schemes) where, say, a legislator from a district with 20,000 population casts two votes, while a legislator from a district with 10,000 population casts only one vote? Again, it was John Banzhaf III who pointed out the fallacy of such "common sense" apportionment schemes. Consider, for example, a three-member committee, with members *A* and *B* with two votes, and member *C* with only one vote. Despite the fact that *vote* shares (weights) are not equal, from the standpoint of Banzhaf's concept of decisive votes all committee members have equal *power* (⅓, ⅓, ⅓) when a majority (3 of 5 votes) is needed. When a two-thirds vote is necessary for passage, the power scores change. Now member *C* has no power at all (in the language of game theory, he is a *dummy*), while the other two members each hold 50 percent of the power. Banzhaf's argument is simply that when weighted voting schemes are designed, weights should be assigned in such a way that a legislator's *power* (as contrasted with the number of votes he wields) should be made proportional to the number of citizens in his district.

46. Iannucci v. Board of Supervisors of Washington County, New York (1967) 282 N.Y.S. 2d 502 at 507.

47. Iannucci v. Board of Supervisors of Washington County, New York (1967) 282 N.Y.S. 2d 502 at 508.

48. Iannucci v. Board of Supervisors of Washington County, New York (1967) 282 N.Y.S. 2d 502 at 510.

49. New York courts have also failed to recognize the mathematical identity between weighted voting systems and multimember district systems in which district representatives vote as a bloc. This is an important omission because partisan politics in New York makes bloc voting at the district level the reality in most New York political units with multimember districts.

50. Among the reasons why parties did not pursue an "optimal" strategy are (a) electoral uncertainties with them that prevent the clear identification of an optimal strategy (Brams, 1975: 120); (b) understanding opposite numbers in the other party—sweetheart deals that preserve incumbents and eliminate two-party competition (Sawyer and MacRae, 1962: 939-945); (c) control by the party's incumbents in the district of the number of candidates to be slated. Incumbents are reluctant to see additional candidates on the ballot. Candidates who aren't certain of election may act as individuals rather than as part of a party slate, thus potentially jeopardizing the electoral success of the party's other candidate(s). In particular, they may jeopardize the electoral success of the incumbent(s) running for reelection (David Epstein, parliamentarian, Illinois House of Representatives, personal communication, July 11, 1980); and (d) since the early 70s, a clause in the Illinois constitution compels political parties to run no fewer than two candidates in each district. With a handful of exceptions, this provision has been complied with throughout the state.

51. In November 1980 cumulative voting for the Illinois House was abolished as part of a referendum to reduce the size of the legislature.

13

The Consequences of Single- and Multimember Districting

Malcolm E. Jewell

As we enter the period of post-1980 reapportionments, one of the questions that remains uncertain is whether the trend toward single-member districting in state legislatures and city councils will continue, or whether some state legislatures will retain multimember districts and whether some city councils will continue to be elected at large. One cause of this uncertainty, of course, is the confusing and contradictory decisions that come from the courts. At the same time, not enough is known about the consequences of various types of districting. The courts have wrestled with the question of whether multimember districts discriminate against minorities, particularly racial minorities; they have also been concerned about the discriminatory intent of such districts. But, if the courts turn to political science literature for evidence about the consequences of various districting patterns, they will find relatively little evidence, most of which deals with the narrow question of the impact of districting on numerical representation of racial and partisan minorities. I suggest that we need to broaden the scope of our inquiry into the consequences of districting.

There are more than two possible districting patterns. At one extreme are single-member districts; at the other is the at-large election of all members of a city council or all state legislators in a metropolitan county. In between these extremes are several patterns: the combination of single-member and at-large districts in a city council; small multimember districts (two or three members) in a legislature; and at-large city council elections with members either residing in districts or elected in primaries by districts. The effects of multimember districting are also different depending on whether or not each candidate runs for a specific post or place.

The consequences of districting patterns are basically the same whether the unit of analysis is a city council or a state legislature, although the effects on minorities may be more severe in a city council. At the state legislative level there is always a possibility that a partisan or racial group that is a minority in one county may be a majority in the other. Another difference is that state legislatures often combine single- and multimember districts, while city councils may combine single-member and at-large districts. My remarks are related specifically to state legislatures, because my research has been focused on them, but I believe most of them are pertinent to city councils as well. (A year ago I conducted 220 interviews with legislators in nine states on various aspects of district representation.) I will look at the consequences of districting for elections, campaign techniques, communications with constituents, the service role of legislators, and policy.

Elections and Campaigns

The studies cited by Grofman (chapter 12, this volume) that are the most comprehensive and rigorous confirm that racial minorities are much more likely to be proportionately represented in city councils when single-member districts are used. A review of southern state legislatures (Jewell, 1980) shows that those lower houses having a substantial minority of black legislators are ones that use single-member districts exclusively (or like Georgia use them in the counties with the greatest black political strength): Alabama, Georgia, Louisiana, South Carolina, Tennessee, and Texas. The states with very few black representatives are all ones using large multimember districts in metropolitan areas: Arkansas, Florida, Mississippi, Virginia, and North Carolina. Moreover, in such states as Texas, Tennessee, Georgia, and Louisiana, there is evidence of a sharp increase in black representation (and of Mexican-American representation in Texas) following the shift to single-member districts.

Several factors affect the impact of districting on minority representation. Racial minorities must be large enough and concentrated enough to benefit from single-member districts—and what is large enough depends of course on the number of districts in a city or county. Obviously what counts is not the minority's proportion of the population, but its proportion of the voting population, and this depends on the level of political organization of the minority. In partisan elections, the crucial factor may be the strength of the minority bloc in the party primary (usually the Democratic one). We also need to consider the impact that party organizations and leaders may have on primaries and elections. In cities or counties with at-large elections and with strong organizations, leaders of minority groups have sometimes been able to win places on a winning slate for their group's candidates. This means, of course, that minority candidates can be elected only if they are acceptable to the slate makers. Leaders of minority groups can sometimes elect their candidates in at-large elections (without places or positions) if they can mobilize their members to engage in single-shot voting, but this tactic sacrifices their influence over the selection of the other candidates.

Studies of electoral effects have been devoted more to racial than to partisan minorities, but in partisan city council and legislative races the effects of multimember districts on partisan minorities may be important. One significant consequence of single-member districting in southern state legislatures has been to elect more Republicans in the higher-income sections of metropolitan counties. It is probable that the development of single-member districts has accelerated the growth of southern metropolitan Republican parties and enhanced their ability to recruit candidates. The impact of districting on the partisan balance in a legislature depends on the strength of partisan voting patterns. In Indiana, for example, there is an unusually strong tradition of straight-ticket voting. When all state legislators were elected at large in Marion County (Indianapolis), it was normal for the Marion County delegation to shift from being all-Democratic to all-Republican. Now that county is divided into five three-member House districts, and straight-ticket voting prevails in each district. In North Carolina, however, there is less straight-ticket voting; in the at-large legislative races in metropolitan counties it is common to have members of both parties elected from a county.

The tactics and costs of state legislative campaigns are quite different in single-member and in large multimember districts. In single-member districts most legislative candidates run their own campaigns. They raise their own funds and build small organizations of volunteers. They run personal campaigns, going door-to-door, frequenting the shopping centers and other gathering places, and speaking to neighborhood groups. There is a maximum of personal contact, and a minimum of emphasis on issues. Candidates may seek the support of organized groups and may get some help in the general election from the party organization, but their success does not depend heavily on such groups. Except in the larger, more populous districts (such as those in California, New York, or Ohio), the cost of such campaigns is relatively low.

The pattern is different in large multimember and at-large districts, particularly in metropolitan areas. In such districts it is impractical for candidates to campaign door-to-door or to concentrate on neighborhood gatherings and meetings. Instead it is necessary to speak at group meetings around the district and attend rallies if they can be organized. It is also more necessary to use media advertising, though television may be prohibitively expensive. In such districts assistance of the party organization becomes more important, and group endorsements assume higher priority. Newspaper endorsements may also be significant. Candidates of the same party often campaign as a team, and sometimes a slate of candidates will work together in a primary. The costs of campaigns are almost inevitably higher in a multimember district (controlling for other variables), although a candidate who runs as part of a team may be able to limit those costs.

Which type of district is more conducive to the reelection of incumbents? It is generally assumed that name recognition is more important in large multimember districts, where the voters have trouble keeping track of many candidates and the incumbent normally has a headstart in name recognition. To win reelection, however, the incumbent may have to retain the support of the party organization and/or interest groups. In a single-member district the incumbent probably has a better opportunity to build and maintain a political base and to maintain contacts with and provide services for constituents, thereby becoming difficult to beat. Legislators generally seem to believe that their prospects for reelection are better in single-member districts.

Communicating with and Serving Constituents

The relationships between legislators and constituents are fundamentally different in single-member and in large multimember districts. In the single-member district, there is more direct personal contact with constituents and less reliance on the media and on organized groups. Legislators who originally campaigned door-to-door sometimes go back to the precincts to talk with voters in between elections. Most of them find plenty of opportunities to talk to neighborhood groups and to attend local functions (even if they are not invited to speak) to maintain visibility and accessibility. A few legislators (as in California and Texas) maintain district offices that are regularly staffed.

Although the job of maintaining contacts is generally easier in single-member districts, there are sometimes problems that occur when district lines do not follow natural community boundaries. Some legislative districts in metropolitan counties do not incorporate existing communities and do not have many organized groups; some districts include bits and pieces of different counties; some in rural areas are so vast geographically as to make personal contact difficult. To the extent that boundary lines cut across the communities that form the basis for organizations and communications patterns (such as newspapers), single-member districts may create more difficulties for representation than do multimember districts.

In a multimember district, particularly a countywide metropolitan one, it is impractical for a legislator to try to maintain close personal contacts with constituents or attend neighborhood meetings scattered across the district. The advantage of representing a larger district, particularly one encompassing a whole county, is that many groups are organized at the city or county level. In other words, the legislator can reach constituents through groups, or at least to reach those who are interested enough in public affairs to attend group meetings. If several legislators represent a countywide district, they may try to divide up the workload and the invitations to speak at meetings. Those who are the most aggressive and effective speakers, however, may get the most opportunities to develop visibility and contacts through organized groups.

In rural parts of a state, most legislators find it easy to get space in newspapers to publicize their viewpoints and activities because there are usually only one or two legislators representing any county. In a large metropolitan area, however, all legislators must compete for attention in the press. It is the legislators who understand public relations best and those who most often become involved in controversial issues who are most likely to get media attention. In metropolitan areas the problem of getting media access is essentially the same for legislators whether they represent single- or multimember districts. One difference is those representing multimember districts are more dependent on the media because they lack the opportunities for personal contacts. Some single-member district legislators also find that they can utilize local or suburban (usually weekly) newspapers that have circulation areas roughly coinciding with or including their district. In a number of states, legislators from single-member districts are using newsletters to reach constituents. Some of these are quite professionally done, and some include questionnaires on issues. These are mailed to constituents in states where the legislature has authorized funds for postage, and are distributed door-to-door where funds are lacking. But this method of communication is used almost entirely in single-member districts. Legislators in large multi-districts consider it not to be feasible.

A significant trend in recent years has been the growing service role of legislators. As legislators become more visible and their staff resources increase, constituents are increasingly turning to them for help in dealing with state agencies or even for help with federal or local officials. These demands from constituents occur where legislators are visible, and particularly where legislators have advertised their willingness to perform services and have made themselves and their staffs available. While these demands are greater, and are different in character, in lower-income districts, they are present in other types of districts as well—if the legislator encourages them. But the constituency-service role is important only for those legislators who represent single-member districts.

It is clear that legislators representing large multimember districts seldom get requests from constituents for individual assistance. They lack the visibility and personal contact that are necessary, and for the most part they do not believe that this is a legitimate part of their job. In fact, some of them believe that one advantage of multimember districting is that legislators do not get service requests. More research is needed on city councils to find out how or whether constituents get help in dealing with local officials from members of councils elected at-large. It is clear from a few examples that when state legislators elected from single-member districts represent parts of cities that use at-large elections, the state legislators are more likely to be asked to help constituents with purely local problems.

In addition to dealing with individual problems, the single-member district legislator is likely to become much more involved in very local problems: helping citizens get a stoplight installed, intervening in zoning questions, getting state funds to repair a local road or improve a local park. In other words, the state legislator from a single district is more parochial in his concerns. Moreover, the legislator who is conscientious and effective in handling these local problems, and who handles individual problems well, can build a favorable image that will be valuable in winning reelection.

This brief summary of communications and service patterns is based on interviews with legislators in a number of states with different, sometimes changing, districting systems. If we are to understand more fully the consequences of districting, we need surveys of constituents to find out their awareness and perceptions of legislators; we also need more detailed examinations of the service role performed by state legislators—how many constituents are served in what ways and with what results. There are obviously some normative questions involved as well. Should state legislators be devoting much of their time (and that of their staff) to individual requests, and should they be focusing attention on parochial projects and problems? Would the needs of metropolitan communities be better served if state legislators shared a broader viewpoint? Does at-large representation actually mean that broader interests are served or only that conservative business interests get more attention and more direct representation? However important these normative questions, they cannot be posed accurately—or answered intelligently—until we have better empirical answers to these questions about the consequences of alternative districting systems.

Consequences for Policy

Probably the most difficult question to answer about districting is the consequences for policy. We may assume that if single-member districts provide more representation for either racial or partisan minorities, there will be some effects on policy, but measuring these effects is more difficult. We need to examine how effective such minority representatives are in the legislature. If representatives from single-member districts are less dependent on either party organizations or interest groups for campaign support, we need to study whether they act independently.

There is some evidence, from roll call data, that voting cohesion in state legislative delegations has usually declined when there has been as shift from multi- to single-member districts (Jewell, 1969; Hamm, Harmel, and Thompson, 1979). This is especially likely to occur when the change in districting has affected either the partisan or the racial balance of the districts. When I interviewed North Carolina legislators, chosen at-large in metropolitan counties, they asserted that this districting system assured more cohesion among the county delegations on bills and projects affecting the county. In both Texas and Tennessee, legislators agreed that districting had reduced the amount of cohesion on local bills and projects, but there was considerably more disunity in some metropolitan delegations than in others. Divisions within metropolitan delegations resulted from partisan, racial, and ideological differences, and also from personality conflicts and political rivalries among the legislators. There was also disagreement about whether the decline in legislative delegation harmony that follows single-member districting is a serious problem or not. Those legislators who shared the conservative, business-oriented philosophy that used to dominate the delegations in states like Texas and Tennessee tended to be critical. Those who represented more liberal viewpoints and racial minorities were not unhappy about disunity, because they considered it inevitable if the viewpoints and interests they represented were to be heard in the legislature. Now that reapportionment has forced state legislatures to pay attention to metropolitan problems, it seems inevitable that if all the major interests in the metropolis are going to be represented in the legislature, through districting, it is going to be more difficult to reach agreement on solving those problems.

The effects of districting on policy making are complex, and they are not easily measured through aggregate analysis of legislative or budgetary outputs. What are needed are more detailed studies of the decision-making process in legislatures. We need to know how a variety of organized groups and less organized citizens make their views known to legislators who represent different kinds of districts, and how legislators resolve the conflicting pressures they are subjected to. Is the at-large legislator more vulnerable to organized group pressures, while the single-member district legislator is more visible to and thus more sensitive to pressures from individuals and small groups? We need to know more about how recruitment patterns differ in various districting situations and what effects, if any, this has on policy. Although it may be difficult to measure policy consequences, it seems clear that districting changes the political environment in which a legislator operates, the character of policy demands that are made on him, and the roles that he must play in responding to those demands.

14 Approval Voting: One Candidate, One Vote

Steven J. Brams

In this chapter I shall discuss an election reform called *approval voting*. It appeared *de novo* about three years ago and has rapidly achieved considerable prominence. It now is the subject of over twenty scholarly works and has also been discussed by the media. I shall begin by examining the problem posed by elections involving more than two candidates, suggest how approval voting would ameliorate this and related problems of elections, show, as an illustration of its effects, how the results of New Hampshire's 1980 presidential primaries probably would have changed under approval voting, and, finally, indicate the reform's prospects for adoption (Brams, 1980a, 1980b).

The Problem

It is a sad fact that elections today are often rigged against majority candidates. For example, James Buckley was elected a U.S. Senator from New York in 1970 with only 39 percent of the vote. Buckley, a conservative, was probably no more representative of New York state voters than John Lindsay, a liberal, was representative of New York City voters when he was reelected to a second term as mayor of New York in 1969 with 42 percent of the vote. The 61-percent majority that voted for Buckley's two opponents, and the 58-percent majority that voted for Lindsay's two opponents, were effectively denied representation, at least in terms of their apparent ideological preferences, for six and four years, respectively.

One can think of many examples in which three or more candidates in a plurality contest divided the total vote such that no candidate received a majority. A dramatic recent example is the 1977 New York City mayoral election, in which six candidates got between 10 and 20 percent of the vote in the Democratic primary. This contest was followed by a runoff between the two top vote-getters, Edward Koch (19.8 percent in the plurality election) and Mario Cuomo (18.6 percent), which Koch won.

The runoff, however, offered no assurance that one of the four other candidates in the 10-20 percent range couldn't have beaten Koch. Koch may well have been the strongest candidate in the Democratic field, but the plurality election, even followed by a runoff, did not offer incontrovertible evidence that he indeed was.

137

The problem in all these cases is that a candidate, with support from a relatively small percentage of the electorate, can either win a plurality election outright or qualify for a runoff. When four-fifths of the electorate vote for other candidates, as happened in 1977, the winner can hardly claim a great popular mandate. Worse, if there is another candidate whom a majority would actually prefer, the election system, in my opinion, is working perniciously.

This situation was probably the case in the Buckley and Lindsay elections. If either candidate had been in a head-to-head contest with just one of his opponents, he almost surely would have lost to him.

What a shame for the voters when a winner in an election is in fact a weaker candidate than one or more of the losers! This paradoxical result most often occurs when two or more moderate candidates split the centrist vote, allowing a more extremist candidate to eke out a victory with only minority support. It is precisely this perversity of our system that seems in part responsible for the nomination of Barry Goldwater by the Republican party in 1964 and the nomination of George McGovern by the Democratic party in 1972. Although each nominee had vociferous minority support within his party, each was a disaster to his party in the general election.

A Solution

I think there is a simple, practicable solution to this defect in our election system. It is a new voting system called approval voting, which allows a voter to vote for, or approve of, as many candidates as he or she wishes in a multicandidate race (one with more than two candidates).

Thus, if there were five candidates, voters would not be restricted to voting for just one candidate. They could vote for two or more candidates if they had no clear favorite. However, only one vote could be cast for every approved candidate—that is, votes could not be cumulated and several cast for one candidate. The candidate with the most approval votes would win.

Approval voting has several compelling advantages over plurality voting, or plurality voting with a runoff (for a more detailed summary of its features, see Brams, 1979):

1. *It gives voters more flexible options.* They can do everything they can under the present system—vote for a single favorite—but if they have no strong preference for one candidate, they can express this fact by voting for all candidates they find acceptable. For instance, if a voter most preferred a candidate who had little chance of winning, that voter could vote for both a first choice *and* a more viable candidate without worrying about wasting his or her vote on the less popular candidate.

2. *It could increase voter turnout.* By being better able to express their

preferences, voters would more likely go to the polls in the first place. Voters who think they might be wasting their votes, or who cannot decide which of several candidates best reflects their views, would not have to despair about making a choice. By not being forced to make a single—perhaps arbitrary—choice, they would feel that the election system allows them to be more honest, which I believe would make voting more meaningful and encourage greater participation in elections.

3. *It would help elect the strongest candidate.* Today, as the previous examples illustrate, the candidate supported by the largest minority wins, or at least makes the runoff. Under approval voting, by contrast, it would be the candidate with the greatest overall support—the one most approved of—who would win. An additional benefit is that approval voting would induce candidates to try to mirror the views of a majority of voters, not just cater to minorities whose votes could give them a slight edge in a crowded plurality contest—wherein a candidate with only 20 to 30 percent of the vote can win. The fact that Jimmy Carter won the 1976 Democratic primary in New Hampshire with only 28 percent of the vote, and Henry Jackson won the primary in Massachusetts one week later with only 23 percent of the vote, says nothing about how acceptable either candidate was to the approximately three-quarters of the voters in each primary who *didn't* vote for them.

4. *It would give minority candidates their proper due.* Minority candidates would not suffer under approval voting: Their supporters wouldn't be torn away simply because there was another candidate who, though less appealing to them, was generally considered a stronger contender. Because approval voting would allow these supporters to vote for both candidates, they would not be tempted to desert the one who was weak in the polls, as under plurality voting. Hence, minority candidates would receive their true level of support under approval voting, even if they could not win.

5. *It is eminently practicable.* Approval voting can readily be implemented on existing voting machines. With paper ballots, the counting of votes would be somewhat more tedious, but this should not, in my view, be a major barrier to implementation.

To enact approval voting would require a statutory, not a constitutional, change in most jurisdictions. Consider the statute in New Hampshire for voting in the presidential primaries. To enact approval voting in these elections would require only the substitution of the words in parentheses for the words that precede them:

> Every qualified voter . . . shall have opportunity . . . to vote his preference (*preferences*), on the ballot of his party, for his choice (*choices*) for one person (*any persons*) to be the candidate (*candidates*) of his political party for president of the United States and one person (*any persons*) to be the candidate (*candidates*) of his political party for vice president of the United States.

The common-sense reasons I have outlined for adopting approval voting are supported by a number of technical arguments, which I shall touch on now for those who want to pursue the burgeoning mathematical and empirical literature on this reform. Among all nonranked voting systems, approval voting is more sincere, strategyproof, and has the greatest propensity to elect so-called Condorcet candidates—those who, if they exist, would defeat all others in a series of pairwise contests (Brams and Fishburn, 1978; Brams, 1976a, 1978a, 1978b)—and these results carry over to the election of committees (Fishburn, 1982). It maximizes the efficacy of voters and is, in a particular sense, more equitable than other nonranked systems (Fishburn and Brams, 1981a, 1981b). Approval voting has several advantages over preference, or ranking, systems, including a safeguard against the premature elimination of Condorcet candidates (Fishburn and Gehrlein, 1979; Brams and Fishburn, 1979; Fishburn, 1980; Fishburn and Brams, 1981b, 1981d). Finally, computer simulations, based on thermometer-scale ratings of real candidates by respondents in voter surveys (Kiewiet, 1979), experiments (Kellett and Mott, 1977), reconstructed ballot data (Brams and Fishburn, 1981, 1982; Fishburn and Brams, 1981d), and pilot survey data (Brams and Sharrard, 1979) lend empirical support to several of the postulated and derived theoretical effects—including those of Hoffman (1982, 1979a, 1979b); Merrill (1979a, 1981); and Weber (1978a, 1978b, 1978c).

A Case in Point: The 1980 New Hampshire Primaries under Approval Voting

The results from New Hampshire's 1980 presidential primaries are now familiar: On the Republican side, Ronald Reagan was the big winner with 50 percent of the vote, with George Bush and Howard Baker trailing far behind with 23 and 13 percent, respectively. No other Republican candidate received more than 10 percent of the vote.

Would these results have changed significantly under approval voting? To approximate approval voting, "ABC News" asked voters as they were leaving the polls in New Hampshire to indicate *all* the candidates they considered acceptable, and presumably would have voted for, if they could have cast more than one vote. The responses indicated that Reagan would have increased his total by 8-percentage points to 58 percent and Bush by 16-percentage points to 39 percent, but by far the biggest gainer would have been Baker: He would have climbed a dramatic 28-percentage points to finish in second place, behind Reagan, with 41 percent of the vote.

In other words, under approval voting Howard Baker would have more than tripled his plurality vote total and wound up a very creditable second-place candidate instead of finishing a dismal third. Although not the first choice of most Republicans, he had greater residual support than his closest rival, George Bush, on election day in New Hampshire. Unfortunately for Baker, the returns never revealed this fact, and he dropped out after second poor showings in the Massachusetts and Vermont primaries one week after the New Hampshire primary.

On the Democratic side, the order of finish probably would not have changed under approval voting. Even if Edward Kennedy had been approved by all Jerry Brown's supporters (10 percent), this still would not have been sufficient to wipe out Jimmy Carter's 11-percent lead (49 to 38 percent). To be sure, some of Carter's supporters would also have approved of Kennedy, and vice versa, but it seems very unlikely that Kennedy would have defeated Carter under approval voting. In fact, the "ABC News" approval voting figures confirm this proposition: Carter would have received 60-percent approval, Kennedy, 48 percent, and Brown, 36 percent.

In sum, the results reveal a more tightly packed race in the Republican primary, with one candidate displacing another, but no displacement would have occurred in the Democratic primary. To me the most important finding is that the race in both parties would have been more competitive and, in the Republican party, also looked significantly different for one candidate (Baker), generally considered a moderate, coming out of New Hampshire (Brams, 1980b).

Prospects for Adoption

I believe that approval voting may well become the election reform of the twentieth century, just as the Australian, or secret, ballot—printed by the government with the names of all authorized candidates—was the election reform of the nineteenth century. In effect, the principle of one-man, one-vote under plurality voting becomes the principle of one-candidate, one-vote under approval voting. That is, each voter makes judgments about every candidate under approval voting, so the tie-in of a vote is not to the voter but rather to the candidates.

As an avowed advocate of approval voting, I have campaigned for the adoption of this reform in the presidential primaries of New Hampshire and other states. (It was not used in any 1980 primaries, but it now seems likely to be tried in state and local elections in New Hampshire or other states in the not-too-distant future.) This campaign has received coverage in the *New York Times* (1979, 1980)—wherein an Op-Ed essay also appeared (Merrill, 1979b)—*Los Angeles Times* (1979), and several other newspapers, as well as on radio and television. Over the past year, I have had voluminous correspondence from presidential candidates, secretaries of state, state legislators, state chairs of the Democratic and Republican parties, major public interest organizations such as the League of Women Voters and Common Cause, and others about the adoption of approval voting. Approval voting is receiving serious consideration in about a dozen states now; besides New Hampshire, where I visited twice in 1979 and testified before both House and Senate committees on this reform (Brams, 1980b), legislators from Texas, Wisconsin, and other states have indicated a strong interest in introducing bills to implement approval voting in their state elections, especially party primaries, which usually attract large fields of candidates. At the local level, a University of Pennsylvania group recommended, in a recently commissioned study, that approval voting be used in nonpartisan elections in Atlantic City, New Jersey, in a proposed charter revision for that city (*A New Government for Atlantic City: A Strong Mayor—Strong Council Plan*, 1979).

Many voters are cynical today. Their choices are artificially limited. Approval voting could go a long way to defusing their anger and frustration at a system that has nominated patently unrepresentative candidates like Barry Goldwater and George McGovern, who decimated their parties' presidential hopes in the years in which they ran and gave many voters no viable alternative to their opponents. By averting the nomination of such candidates, approval voting would strengthen the parties by tending to elect their strongest nominees and increasing competition in the general election. Moreover, by letting voters express themselves better at the polls, approval voting would greatly enhance democratic choice. This essentially costless reform thus seems well suited for voters, parties, and the heightening of competition among candidates that maximizes a voter's viable options.

15 Comparative Perspectives on Fair Representation: The Plurality-Majority Rule, Geographical Districting, and Alternative Electoral Arrangements

Arend Lijphart

Fair Representation and Descriptive Representation

Direct democracy being impractical in large countries, democracy is necessarily representative democracy: government by elected representatives. Hence there is no more basic issue in democratic theory and practice than the question of how to organize a system of fair election and representation.

What does *fair representation* mean? Probably the oldest theory of democratic representation states that elected representatives should reflect the interests, opinions, and characteristics of their electors as much as possible. For instance, John Adams argued in the American Revolutionary period that a representative legislature "should be an exact portrait, in miniature, of the people at-large, as it should think, feel, reason and act like them," and Edmund Burke maintained that "the virtue, spirit, and essence" of a representative body depended on "its being the express image of the feelings of the nation" (cited in Pitkin, 1967:60-61). This theory has been called the *correspondence theory* of representation (Eulau and Wahlke, 1978: 17), the theory of *descriptive representation* (Pitkin, 1967:60-981), or the theory of *microcosmic representation* (Birch, 1971:16-17).

Heinz Eulau and John C. Wahlke (1978:17) criticize the concept of descriptive representation as especially naive when it holds that "if only representatives were facsimiles of their constituents' demographic characteristics (age, sex, race, residence, and so on), they would be more representative than if they possessed noncorresponding traits." When the correspondence between representative and represented refers not to demographic characteristics but to similar opinions, attitudes, and interests—*issue congruence* (Miller and Stokes, 1963) or *policy concurrence* (Verba and Nie, 1972)—a more creditable version of the descriptive representation theory emerges.

Even so, the latter more sophisticated concept offers only a partial view of representation. A more complete view also includes the ideas that the representative acts for, or on behalf of, the represented and is accountable to the represented. Accountability is a crucial element of democratic representation and is effected by means of periodic elections. As Hanna Pitkin (1967: 89-90) points out, elections may also have the function of enhancing descriptive representation: "In a practical way, perhaps one can assure accurate correspondence between representative and constituents if the former is elected by the latter." But, she adds, "voters often prefer to elect men who are not representative (typical) of the district, and that may be a good thing."

A crucial threefold distinction is implied by Pitkin's statement when we think in terms of the representativeness of a legislature rather than that of the individual representative: (1) A legislature may be actually representative (typical) of the voters' views and interests; (2) a legislature may be potentially but not actually representative because voters choose candidates that are atypical; (3) a legislature may be unrepresentative (atypical) because the representative-electoral system does not permit descriptive representation and because the legislature is therefore not even potentially representative. It seems to me that what is usually meant by fair representation hinges on the distinction between the potential representativeness of the election system rather than its actual representativeness. In other words, the fairness of the electoral method depends on whether substantial numbers of voters who wish to elect one of their own members or a person with their particular political outlook can, in fact, do so.

The above formulation of what fair representation means is a very general principal (and begs the question of exactly how many voters constitute a substantial number), but the specific criteria of fair representation for the American political system that have been suggested, demanded, or imposed—by, respectively, academic observers, interest groups, and the courts—can all be considered to be derived from it. At least sixteen specific criteria can be distinguished; these will be discussed in the next section of this chapter.

My main thesis is that many of these criteria are inconsistent with each other and lead to contradictory recommendations, and that these incompatibilities are caused by the fact that two basic and virtually unalterable rules impose severe constraints on fair representation: the plurality-majority rule and geographically defined electoral districts. The plurality rule is the norm in the United States, but a two-ballot majority system (with a runoff election if no candidate wins 50-percent-plus-one of the votes on the first ballot) also occurs frequently. The usual form of electoral district is the single-member district, but multimember districts and at-large elections are also common, especially below the national and state levels, and weighted voting is common in New York.

I argue that if these constraints are relaxed—according to the examples of several democratic states with electoral systems that differ more or less radically from that of the United States—the chances of satisfying the criteria of fair representation can be improved significantly. The final question to which I try to give at least a tentative answer is whether the benefits of such a relaxation of the plurality-majority rule and geographical districts outweigh the costs and the risks of making these changes.

Criteria of Fair Representation

The following list of criteria of fair representation is not exhaustive, but it does include the criteria—some of which are widely accepted while others are more controversial—that are most frequently mentioned (see Grofman, 1981e; Grofman and Scarrow, 1981a; Niemi and Deegan, 1978):

1. Representation must be equal for each citizen. This is the basic one-person, one-vote, one-value principle. For single-member district systems, it means that the districts must contain equal numbers of citizens, in line with the *Westberry* v. *Sanders*[1] and *Reynolds* v. *Sims*[2] decisions of the U.S. Supreme Court (Tribe, 1978:739-741). For non-single-member districts, the criterion calls for representation that is equal per capita. The number of representatives in multimember districts must be proportional to the population being represented, or the number of votes cast by representatives elected from districts of unequal sizes must be weighted according to the population being represented (Grofman and Scarrow, 1981a:2-3).

2. The boundaries dividing the electoral districts must coincide with local political boundaries as much as possible.

3. Electoral districts must be compact and contiguous in territory.

4. The boundaries of electoral districts should be drawn in such a way as to provide representation for political minorities (*sophisticated gerrymandering*).

5. The boundaries of electoral districts should be drawn in such a way as to provide representation for ethnic and racial minorities (*affirmative gerrymandering*).

6. The electoral system should not be biased in favor of any political party in awarding seats for a certain percentage of the total vote. This is the criterion of *neutrality,* the first of the four criteria of fair districting suggested by Richard G. Niemi and John Deegan, Jr. (1978:1304): "A districting plan which treats all parties alike in allocating seats per given vote totals is said to be neutral."

7. The electoral system should not be biased in favor of any racial or ethnic group in awarding seats for a certain percentage of the total vote. This is the Niemi-Deegan criterion of neutrality, extended to groups other than political parties.

8. The electoral system should have a wide range of responsiveness to changes in the electorate's party preferences. Niemi and Deegan (1978: 1304-1305) define the range of responsiveness as "the percentage range of the total popular vote (for the entire political unit) over which seats change from one party to the other. Specifically, the low end of the [range] is the minimum percentage of the total vote required for a party to win at least one seat . . . , while the upper end is the minimum percentage of the total vote required to win all of the seats."

9. The electoral system should have a "constant swing ratio;" that is, the rate at which a party wins seats per unit gain in the percentage of its vote should be constant (Niemi and Deegan, 1978:1306). The principle that a party's share of the seats should be proportional to its vote share is a special case of this criterion.

10. There should be proportionality between the share of the seats won by any particular ethnic or racial group and its vote share. This criterion extends the above proportionality principle to groups other than political parties.

11. The system should be competitive in the sense that each party should have a chance of election in each district. Niemi and Deegan (1978: 1309-1311) operationally define this criterion as requiring each party's vote to be in the 45- to 55-percent range in each district.

12. Each citizen should have equal power to affect the outcome of elections by casting the decisive vote (Grofman and Scarrow, 1981a:3-4). This voting power varies inversely with the square roots of the sizes of the district populations (Banzhaf, 1966).

13. Each citizen's vote should be "used" as much as possible toward the election of a candidate and the "wasted" vote should be minimized. The used vote is "the number of votes required by the winning party to attain a plurality and . . . represents the votes that are actually used to elect its candidate to office." It can therefore also be defined as "the size of the vote received by the party polling the second highest vote plus one." All other votes—the votes received by the winner that exceed the plurality and the votes of all losing parties—are wasted (Cohan, McKinlay, and Mughan, 1975:365). This criterion is similar to criterion 11 (competitiveness) in the case of a two-party system.

14. Each legislator's power in the legislature should be proportionate to the number of citizens he represents. Banzhaf (1966) argues that not only the citizen's power to affect election outcomes (criterion 12) but also his influence on legislation varies inversely with the square roots of the district populations.

15. There should be equal numbers of representatives working on behalf of equal numbers of citizens. As Bernard Grofman and Howard A. Scarrow (1981a:18-19) point out, representatives have many functions in

addition to voting on proposed legislation, such as performing various services for their constituents: "Any system of representation, such as adoption of the square root principle or weighted voting in any form, which results in some citizens having a proportionately greater access to these personal services because it does not apportion equal numbers of representatives to equal numbers of citizens, would therefore be unfair."

16. A majority of citizens should be able to control legislative outcomes through their representatives (Grofman and Scarrow, 1981a:19-21). In other words, minorities of citizens should not be able to elect majorities of legislators. This is the basic majoritarian principle.

Incompatibilities between Criteria

Although each of the above sixteen criteria of fair representation can be satisfied individually (with one exception, to be discussed below), they cannot all be satisfied to their full extent simultaneously within the constraints of a plurality-majority system and geographically defined districts. Maximizing the value of one criterion will often require deviating from one or more other criteria. Moreover, the different criteria lead to different recommendations with regard to whether a plurality or majority rule should be adopted and with regard to the kind of electoral districts that should be instituted.

The one exception to the statement that each individual criterion can be fully satisfied is the criterion of minority group representation by means of affirmative gerrymandering. The problem is that drawing district boundaries in such a way as to achieve representation for one minority may affect adversely the chances that another minority living in the same general area will be represented. This was the dilemma facing the Supreme Court in *United Jewish Organizations of Williamsburg* v. *Carey*[3] when a choice had to be made between the right to minority representation of blacks and Puerto Ricans on the one hand and Hasidic Jews on the other (Wells, 1978a). As Pitkin (1967:87) points out, the problem of choosing which groups deserve representation is a general problem that is inherent in the norms of descriptive representation: "representation as *standing for* by resemblance, as being a copy of an original, is always a question of which characteristics are politically relevant for reproduction."

The conflicts between pairs of criteria are indicated in table 15-1. Four clusters of conflicts can be distinguished. The first is the well-known tension between the requirement of absolute per-capita population equality (criterion 1) and districts that follow local political subdivisions and that are compact and contiguous (criteria 2 and 3). The Supreme Court has recognized, and solved, this incompatibility by assigning a higher priority to the equal-population rule than to the secondary criteria of local boundaries,

Table 15-1

Conflicts among Sixteen Criteria of Fair Representation under the Plurality-Majority Rule and Geographical Districts

(Criteria, by number—see text)

	16	15	14	13	12	11	10	9	8	7	6	5	4	3	2	1
1	—	—	X	—	X	—	—	—	—	—	—	—	—	X	X	—
2	—	X	—	X	—	X	X	X	X	X	X	X	X	X	—	—
3	—	X	—	X	—	X	X	X	X	X	X	X	X	—	—	—
4	—	—	—	—	—	—	—	—	—	—	—	—	—	—	—	—
5	—	—	—	—	—	—	—	—	—	—	—	—	—	—	—	—
6	—	—	—	X	—	X	—	—	—	—	—	—	—	—	—	—
7	—	—	—	—	—	—	—	—	—	—	—	—	—	—	—	—
8	—	—	—	X	—	X	—	—	—	—	—	—	—	—	—	—
9	—	—	—	X	—	X	—	—	—	—	—	—	—	—	—	—
10	—	—	—	—	—	—	—	—	—	—	—	—	—	—	—	—
11	—	X	—	—	—	—	—	—	—	—	—	—	—	—	—	—
12	X	—	—	—	—	—	—	—	—	—	—	—	—	—	—	—
13	—	X	—	—	—	—	—	—	—	—	—	—	—	—	—	—
14	X	—	—	—	—	—	—	—	—	—	—	—	—	—	—	—
15	—	—	—	—	—	—	—	—	—	—	—	—	—	—	—	—
16	—	—	—	—	—	—	—	—	—	—	—	—	—	—	—	—

compactness, and contiguity (Tribe, 1978:746-747). Because the requirement that there should be equal numbers of representatives working on behalf of equal numbers of citizens (criterion 15) largely coincides with the criterion of per-capita equal representation, it is also in conflict with criteria 2 and 3. Finally, there may be a conflict between the latter two criteria if the local political subdivisions deviate significantly from compactness and contiguity. All of these conflicts may be alleviated by moving from single-member districts to multimember districts or weighted voting. At-large elections eliminate the problem by eliminating districts and district boundaries altogether.

The second cluster includes the conflicts between the local boundary, compactness, and contiguity criteria (criteria 2 and 3) on the one hand and the series of criteria that call for electoral districts that will serve political purposes such as minority representation, responsiveness, and competitiveness (criteria 4 through 11). To achieve these objectives, the criteria of congruence with local subdivisions, compactness, and contiguity will almost always have to be violated. The criterion of minimizing the wasted vote (criterion 13) is, in a two-party system, similar to the competitiveness criterion (criterion 11). Hence it, too, conflicts with criteria 2 and 3.

The third cluster includes the incompatibilities among the Niemi-Deegan criteria (criteria 6, 8, 9, and 11; see Niemi and Deegan, 1978: 1311-1312). In particular, the competitiveness and responsiveness criteria call for very different districts. Here again, the criterion of minimizing the wasted vote behaves like the competitiveness criterion.

The fourth cluster consists of conflicts between the four criteria of equality (criteria 1, 12, 14 and 15). These occur only when there is a system of mixed single-member and multimember districts, a system of multimember districts with different numbers of representatives per districts, or a weighted voting system. In these situations, criteria 1 and 15 demand the numbers of representatives per district (or the numbers of legislative votes cast by the representatives) be proportional to the district populations, instead of proportional to the population square roots as demanded by criteria 12 and 14. The latter two criteria also violate the principle of majoritarianism because the square-root rule would lead to an overrepresentation of smaller districts, which together may contain only a minority of the population but may be able to elect a majority of legislators.

Of the sixteen criteria of fair representation, eleven are neutral with regard to the choice between the plurality and majority rules, but the remaining five lead to different recommendations. The basic majoritarian principle (criterion 16) obviously favors majority rule. Minimizing the wasted vote (criterion 13) is also more easily achieved when majorities rather than pluralities are necessary for election, and competitiveness (criterion 11) is similarly enhanced when the electoral contest is reduced to two candidates in a runoff election. On the other hand, it can be argued that the plurality rule favors cohesive minorities, which may be able to elect their candidates when the majorities are divided (criterion 4 and 5).

The divergent recommendations with regard to the type of districting that are implied by the sixteen criteria are of greater significance. These are outlined in table 15-2. Rather surprisingly, a majority of the criteria (1, 2, 3, 6, 7, 12, 14, 15, and 16) favor at-large elections and clearly do not favor single-member districts. The reason is that by eliminating districts, the equality, neutrality, and majoritarianism criteria are satisfied completely, and the problem of congruence with local boundaries, compactness, and contiguity disappears. The second most desirable type of districting according to these criteria are districts other than single-member districts because they offer more flexibility to achieve equality, compactness, and so on and because there is less risk of a deliberate bias against particular parties or groups.

A second cluster of criteria leads to the completely opposite advice of adopting single-member districts (criteria 8, 9, and 10). There is a well-known empirical relationship between the magnitude of electoral districts (that is, the number of representatives elected per district) and the degree of proportionality of the election results: In systems of proportional representation, proportionality increases as the district magnitude increases, but in plurality and majority systems, proportionality decreases with increasing district magnitude (Blondel, 1969:194-200). Hence the highest degree of proportionality—or the smallest deviation from proportional results—in a plurality-majority system is achieved when the districts are as small as possible. Criteria 9 and 10 are therefore satisfied optimally by single-member districts. Similarly, the range of responsiveness (criterion 8) is maximized by a high degree of proportionality and consequently also by single-member districting.

Two criteria (4 and 5) are maximized by weighted voting. The reason is that it is easier to gerrymander a district for the purpose of minority representation if the district can be small. One of the main advantages of weighted voting is to give representation to small districts without violating equal per-capita representation and without making the legislature too large and unwieldy. If weighted voting is not used, the second most desirable system from the point of view of minority representation is a system with single-member districts—either an exclusively single-member district system or a mixed single-member and multimember district arrangement.

The last two criteria, competitiveness and minimizing the wasted vote (criteria 11 and 13), similarly favor weighted voting. To devise districts in which the votes received by the two major parties are in the 45- to 55-percent range—assuming that the total vote of the parties falls outside this range—it is obviously an advantage to have as much flexibility as

Table 15-2
Optimal and Second-Best Types of Districting According to Sixteen Criteria of Fair Representation

Types	Single-Member Districting	Mixed Single-Member Multimember Districting	Multimember Districting	At-Large	Weighted Voting
1. Per-capital equality	—	X	X	XX	X
2. Local boundary fit	—	X	X	XX	X
3. Compact/contiguous districts	X	X	X	XX	X
4. Sophisticated gerrymander	X	X	—	—	XX
5. Affirmative gerrymander	—	X	—	—	XX
6. Unbiased toward parties	—	X	X	XX	X
7. Unbiased toward groups	—	X	X	XX	X
8. Responsiveness	XX	X	—	—	—
9. Constant swing ratio	XX	X	—	—	—
10. Proportional representation for groups	XX	X	—	—	XX
11. Competitiveness	—	X	X	XX	X
12. Equal voting power	—	X	X	—	XX
13. Minimizing wasted vote	—	X	X	XX	X
14. Equal legislator power	—	X	X	XX	X
15. Equal representative power	—	X	X	XX	X
16. Majoritarianism	—	X	X	XX	X

Note: XX = optimal; X = second best.

possible as far as district size is concerned. The second best situation, however, differs from that called for by criteria 4 and 5: Multimember districts or mixed multimember and single-member districts offer better opportunities for drawing the largest possible number of competitive districts than single-member districts. There is one important qualification to the above conclusions: If the over-all vote for each of the two parties is in the 45- to 55-percent range, at-large elections would be completely competitive and would therefore be the optimal method.

Three other patterns in table 15-2 deserve special attention. First, although at-large elections are the ideal districting method according to nine of the sixteen criteria, they are not the second best method according to any of the other criteria. Secondly, mixed single-member and multimember districts are not optimal according to any of the criteria but they are among the second best methods according to all of the criteria. Thirdly, multimember districts are never optimal either, but they are also frequently, in eleven of the sixteen cases, among the second best solutions.

Nongeographical Districts and Minority Representation

All of the conflicts and incompatibilities between the criteria of fair representation and between the electoral and districting methods that they call for occur when we try to find the optimal electoral system within the constraints of the plurality-majority rule and geographically defined districts. This raises the question of whether the conflicts can be said to be the inevitable result of these constraints. If the constraints are relaxed, do the conflicts disappear?

In this section, I shall explore the consequences of relaxing the rule that districts must be defined exclusively in geographical terms. In particular, I shall examine a number of examples of using nongeographical districts to guarantee the representation of ethnic and racial minorities: Cyprus, New Zealand, Belgium, and Lebanon. These examples constitute nongeographical alternatives to geographically oriented affirmative gerrymandering (see criterion 5 above).

The most straightforward and direct method to secure ethnic minority representation is to establish separate nongeographical districts for each ethnic group. A good example is the first election held in independent Cyprus in 1960. Of the fifty parliamentary seats, thirty-five were assigned to the Greek majority and fifteen to the Turkish minority. The country was divided into six geographical areas, and each area was further divided into a Greek electoral district and a Turkish electoral district. Table 15-3 shows the numbers of seats at stake in the twelve mainly multimember districts.

Table 15-3
Numbers of Representatives Elected in Twelve Ethnic Electoral Districts in Cyprus, 1960

Geographical Areas	Greek Ethnic Districts	Turkish Ethnic Districts
Nicosia	12	5
Limassol	7	2
Famagusta	7	3
Larnaca	3	2
Paphos	4	2
Kyrenia	2	1
Total	35	15

Source: Adapted from Nohlen, 1978: 154.

The winning candidates in each district were determined by the plurality rule (Nohlen, 1978: 153-155).

A major disadvantage of nongeographical ethnic districts like those of Cyprus is that they require separate ethnic voter registers. This was not a problem in Cyprus with its clear-cut cleavages between the ethnic communities, but it is likely to be controversial or even unacceptable elsewhere. For instance, one of the strongly criticized features of the South African government's proposals for constitutional reform is that it calls for separate white, colored, and Asian single-member districts (Lijphart, 1980:67-68).

New Zealand's system for giving parliamentary representation to the small Maori minority suggests a solution to the problem of requiring voters to register under an ethnic label. The country is divided into eighty-eight regular, relatively small single-member districts, but also into four special large districts that are reserved for the Maoris. However, each Maori voter has the option to register and vote either in the special Maori district or in the regular district in which he or she resides (McRobie, 1978).

A similar solution is suggested by the electoral system adopted by Belgium for the election of the twenty-four Belgian members of the European Parliament in 1979. Two nongeographical, or only partly geographical, ethnic districts were established; a Flemish district, comprising Flanders and the Flemings living in Brussels, with thirteen representatives; and a French-speaking district, consisting of Wallonia and the Francophones in Brussels, with eleven representatives. In Flanders and Wallonia, the voters could only vote for Flemish and French-speaking candidates respectively, but residents of Brussels received a ballot with both sets of candidates printed on it and could use either the Flemings' or the French-speakers' part of the ballot without having to register in advance on an ethnic basis (Neels, 1979:246). It should be pointed out that this example is instructive but imperfect because proportional representation instead of the plurality or majority rule was used in each of the two districts; however, the principle of giving voters a free choice of nongeographical districts in which to cast their ballots is equally applicable to nonproportional election systems.

A final example of guaranteeing representation to minorities without requiring separate voter registers is the Lebanese electoral system. The number of seats in the Lebanese parliament has changed a great deal over the years, but the seats have always been allocated in advance to the sects roughly according to the sectarian composition of the population (see table 15-4). The 1960 electoral law divides the country into twenty-six multimember districts, in each of which candidates can only be elected according to a predetermined sectarian ratio. For instance, a hypothetical four-member district may have to elect two Maronites, one Sunnite, and one Shiite. The ballot will contain both balanced tickets of four candidates—two Maronites, one Sunnite, and one Shiite per ticket—and independent candidates. The voter will normally vote for one of the tickets, but he may also pick four candidates from different tickets and from the independents as long as he respects the sectarian ratio for the district. It should be noted that the Lebanese system is a plurality and multimember district system in which the districts are basically geographical; the unusual feature from the American point of view is that the voters are prevented from casting all of their votes for members of their own group.

Table 15-4
Predetermined Sectarian Composition of the Lebanese Parliament, 1947-1960

Sects	1947	1951	1953	1957	1960
Christian					
Maronite	18	23	13	20	30
Greek Orthodox	6	8	5	7	11
Greek Catholic	3	5	3	4	6
Armenian Orthodox	2	3	1	3	4
Armenian Catholic	0	1	1	1	1
Protestant	0	1	0	0	1
Moslem					
Sunnite	11	16	9	14	20
Shiite	10	14	8	12	19
Druze	4	5	3	4	6
Other minorities	1	1	1	1	1
Total	55	77	44	66	99

Source: Adapted from Koury, 1976: 6.

The Cypriot, New Zealand, Brussels, and Lebanese examples are superior to the affirmative gerrymandering of geographical districts in two respects: they guarantee minority representation instead of merely making it more likely, and they can provide representation to two or more minorities living in the same area so that a discriminatory choice favoring one minority over another, as in the *United Jewish Organizations of Williamsburg* v. *Carey* case, can be avoided. On the other hand, they share with affirmative gerrymandering the drawback that an ethnic or other group categorization, to which many voters may be indifferent or hostile, is imposed on the electoral process. One of the great advantages of proportional representation—the subject of the next section—is that it permits and encourages the representation of minorities that wish to be represented without any need for a prior authoritative decision as to which minorities deserve special treatment and without forcing any minority into a pattern of representation that it may not wish.

Fair Representation Equals
Proportional Representation

The conflicts and incompatibilities between the sixteen criteria of fair representation are resolved almost entirely when we relax the constraint of the plurality-majority rule and consider the effects of proportional representation. In fact, most of the sixteen criteria require or favor proportionality. As Robert G. Dixon, Jr. (1971:13) states: "A paradox of the one-man, one-vote revolution is that we now perceive our goal to be something approaching a proportional result, in terms of group access to the legislative process, while retaining the district method of election. But the district method itself, when combined with straight plurality election, is the source of many problems." Conversely, as Dixon (1968:525) argues elsewhere, proportional representation "may be the only way of making good on one-man, one-vote if that is interpreted: one-man, one-vote, each vote to be as *effective* a vote as possible." Similarly, J. Roland Pennock (1979:358) calls proportional representation "the logical extension of the one-person, one-vote ideal."

There are two basic types of proportional representation: the list system (used in all Continental European democracies except France and also in Israel) in which the voter chooses among different party lists, sometimes also indicating a preference among the candidates within the list that is chosen, and the single transferable vote (used in Irish, Maltese, Australian Senate, Tasmanian, and Northern Ireland elections) in which the voter places individual candidates in order of preference. The different kinds of list PR systems—d'Hondt, largest remainders, and modified Sainte-

Lagüe—differ only slightly with regard to the degree of proportionality in the seats-votes relationship (see Lijphart and Gibberd, 1977). The more important difference between PR systems is that in practice the single transferable vote requires relatively small districts; the constituencies in Ireland elect between three and five representatives each. The districts in list PR systems tend to be considerably larger. In Israel and the Netherlands, the entire country serves as a single electoral district.

The different criteria of fair representation are satisfied almost perfectly by proportional representation systems using large districts. PR maximizes the four dimensions of voter equality (criteria 1, 12, 14, and 15), party and ethnic minority representation (criteria 4 and 5), neutrality toward parties and other groups (criteria 6 and 7), proportional results for parties and other groups (criteria 9 and 10), responsiveness (criterion 8), and the used vote (criterion 13). Especially if the districts are large, they can easily be drawn in such a way as to respect local boundaries as well as the compactness and contiguity principles (criteria 2 and 3).

Only two of the criteria are not satisfied optimally by large-district PR. The criterion of competitiveness (criterion 11) presupposes party competition to win seats by a plurality or majority, and it is therefore irrelevant in judging PR systems. The ideal of majoritarianism (criterion 16) is usually respected by proportional representation, but it is quite possible that a party's vote of close to but not quite 50 percent of the total vote is translated by PR formulas into a majority of the seats. Among the 121 elections in twenty countries from 1945 to 1965 analyzed by Rae (1967:74-75), there are ten cases of PR systems in which a party received only a minority of the votes but a majority of the seats.

Since proportional representation approximates the ideal of fair representation, are there any reasons why the plurality-majority system and geographical districts should be retained? Dixon (1979:5-6) argues that the system prevailing in U.S. elections "accomplishes the ideal (or strongly tends to) of preserving a two-party system. A two-party system operates to produce such coordinate goals as a clear governing majority, governmental stability, and pinpointing of governing responsibility."

This justification is far from convincing. First of all, plurality elections do not invariably produce two-party systems, and proportional representation does not always lead to a proliferation of parties. For instance, Canada has a three-party or four-party system in spite of its plurality elections, and Austria enjoys an almost pure two-party system in spite of PR. Other countries with PR, such as Germany and Sweden, do not have two-party systems, but they do have competition between two strong alliances of parties.

In the British two-party system, in which a solid majority party in the House of Commons strongly supports the executive, it makes sense to speak of both a clear governing majority and a clear governing responsibility, but especially at the national level the American parties are so weak, undisciplined, and uncohesive that they cannot be said to provide either. In fact, it is difficult to regard the fragmented American party system as a true two-party system. The U.S. presidential system and the bicameral Congress with its two co-equal houses may lead to even more diffusion of power when the presidency, the Senate, and the House are not controlled by the same party. The assignment of responsibility for governmental actions becomes highly problematic under such circumstances.

It seems to me that a much stronger argument in favor of the plurality and single-member district system is that it provides a clear link between representative and represented. In PR systems, this link tends to be very weak, especially if the electoral districts are large. Does this advantage outweigh the many advantages of proportionality?

Combining Proportional Representation and Single-Member Districts

The last question assumes that a choice has to be made between single-member districts and proportional representation. This is not necessarily the case. The West German electoral system attempts to combine the advantages of both, and the recent report of the Hansard Society's Commission on Electoral Reform in Britain proposes a similar combination of single-member districts and proportionality. These two systems provide instructive examples because they approach the problem of combining PR and single-member districts from different directions. The German method is to achieve proportional results and to accommodate district elections within the overall proportional scheme. The Hansard Commission gives first priority to the elections in single-member districts and proposes a method to increase proportionality as a second step.

The most important features of the West German system are: (1) Each voter has a first vote to be cast in one of the 248 single-member constituencies and a second vote to be cast for a party list. (2) The second votes are counted on a national basis and all 496 Bundestag seats are allocated to the parties that have won a minimum of 5 percent of the total vote or three district seats, by PR according to the second vote totals. (3) The seats won by pluralities in the 248 districts are subtracted from the seat totals assigned according to PR. (4) The remaining seats to which the parties are entitled are filled from the party lists. The popular term *personalized PR* is an accurate description of the system (Urwin, 1974: 136).

The Hansard Commission recommends the following system for Britain: (1) Four hundred eighty members of the House of Commons will be elected directly in single-member constituencies by plurality vote. (2) An additional 160 seats will be divided among twelve large regions. (3) In each region, the parties with at least 5 percent of the total regional vote will participate in the allocation of the additional seats in such a way as to maximize proportionality. (4) The additional seats won by a party will be assigned to its candidates who have not been directly elected but who have won the highest percentages of the vote in their districts (Hansard Society Commission, 1976: 37-40; Roberts, 1977). It should be noted, of course, that neither this proposal nor the German system is perfectly proportional because both contain a 5-percent threshold that constitutes a considerable barrier to very small minorities.

Conclusion: Proportional Representation for the United States?

Most of the debate about electoral reform in the United States is still taking place within the confining parameters of the plurality and majority rules and geographical districts. In this chapter, I have tried to prove that these constraints give rise to serious conflicts and inconsistencies among objectives and among districting plans and that their alleged contribution to governmental efficiency, stability, and responsibility is questionable. Consequently, alternative electoral arrangements deserve a serious and thorough discussion. In particular, the examples that go halfway in the direction of proportionality, such as the German system and the Hansard Commission proposal, should be considered very carefully.

Many people are likely to object that any reform in the direction of PR would entail such a drastic change in the American political system that it is both *unlikely* to be adopted because of the system's basic conservatism and *undesirable* because it has too many unknown, unpredictable, and potentially dangerous consequences. Although there are undoubtedly some uncertainties, risks, and obstacles to change, these should not be exaggerated:

1. A great deal is known about the operation of PR because most of the world's democracies already use it and have been using it for many years—generally without dire consequences.
2. The change to PR is indeed a major but not an impossible innovation. Most of the countries that now have PR originally had plurality or majority systems and abolished these in favor of PR.
3. The trend is still toward the adoption of PR. For instance, France uses the two-ballot majority method for electing its National Assembly, but it changed to the list PR system for the election of the French represen-

tatives to the European Parliament in 1979. In the United Kingdom, the single-member-district plurality system was retained for the election of the British representatives in the European Parliament, but the three Northern Ireland representatives were elected by PR (Huber, 1979).

4. Even in the United States, PR is not completely unknown. Approximately twenty-five American cities have experimented with it, and Illinois had used the cumulative vote, a semi-proportional system, for the election of its lower house from 1870 to 1980.

5. Recent experience shows that the American political system is by no means completely resistant to change. A particularly clear example is the rapid and almost complete shift from the winner-take-all rule in presidential primaries to a more proportional division of delegates among the presidential candidates according to their share of primary votes.

To be sure, a shift from the familiar American electoral methods to PR would indeed be a drastic change. But there are many precedents, both in the United States and abroad, and it is therefore not so drastic as to be unthinkable.

Notes

1. Wesberry v. Sanders (1964) 376 U.S. 1.
2. Reynolds v. Sims (1964) 377 U.S. 533.
3. United Jewish Organizations of Williamsburg v. Carey (1977) 430 U.S. 144.

16 Logic and Politics in Electoral Engineering

John C. Wahlke

Critical observers of the American political scene have often noted Americans' cultural proclivity for converting political debates over policy, constitutional change, administrative procedure, or anything else having to do with the process of government into legalistic arguments about the logical implications of abstract principles. The proclivity is as readily observable in the politics of representation as in other arenas of American politics. Consider, for example, the hope often heard expressed of "eliminating politics" from the redrawing of boundaries of legislative districts by feeding abstract principles and logical requirements into computers in the expectation that its outputs will be decisions resulting from pure logical reasoning, untainted by human political motives. Professor Lijphart's work (chapter 15, this volume) is an excellent starting point for helping us keep logical and political considerations in proper perspective when dealing with questions about the structure of electoral systems.

Political problems arise immediately, of course, out of the normative character of the concept of fair representation, a standard and goal virtually all students of the subject probably accept as valid and important for any system of apportioning and electing representatives. Despite such probable unanimity on the abstract principle, the theoretical literature amply documents the lack of consensus on more concrete aspects of meaning of both the basic concept, *representation* itself, and the qualifier, *fairness* in it.

Meanings given the term *representation* range from the simple notion of descriptive representation (Pitkin, 1967:60-91)—the degree to which a representative body matches the general population in the distribution of demographic, political, or other characteristics deemed relevant and important—to Edmund Burke's notion of virtual representation (Pitkin, 1967: 170-185)—the spokesmanship of an elite body for the best interests of a whole nation or an individual member for a whole constituency, even though the spokespersons be not elected by, and even though they be not reflective of, demographic, attitudinal, or any other characteristics of those people they virtually represent. Without minimizing the importance of the conceptual and theoretical problems surrounding the principle of representation, we can accept Lijphart's formulation as a baseline here: Whether or not a system is representative "depends on whether substantial numbers of voters who wish to elect one of their own members or a person with their particular outlook can in fact do so" (Lijphart, chapter 15, this volume).[1]

This formulation has the virtue of emphasizing that the conceptual choice is a basically political decision, made in an explicitly political way, namely, choice by the represented themselves as to which normative meaning should guide structuring and evaluation of their representative system. If, for example, being represented means to them being able to elect members of their own race, and racial membership in the representative body proportionate to their ratio in the general population, then a system must be judged representative to the extent that it promotes such a distribution and such a statistical relationship. If instead they want representatives who guide their constituents' thinking about policy and public issues rather than letting constituents' views determine their actions as representatives, then that must be the normative conception against which the system is judged. Leaving practical definition of the basic normative conception up to the people is, of course, thoroughly consistent with the principle of popular sovereignty on which doctrines of representative government ultimately rest. The more important point for us here is that the choice is unavoidably a political one, that is, a determination as to whose conceptions shall prevail. Logic can (must) guide the deduction of operating principles from those basic premises once determined. But logic alone can never dictate whose conception of representation is right.

Whatever conception of representation prevails, fairness is an additional standard that the system will be expected to meet. Although there might seem at first glance to be less room for political controversy here than there is over the supposedly more basic issues of representation, Lijphart's examination of the sixteen criteria comprising the standard of fairness shows clearly that is not the case. Several of them—for example, criterion (4), sophisticated gerrymandering, and criterion (5), affirmative gerrymandering—clearly pose the same kind of normative problems as the more general concept of representation itself. Several others—for example, criterion (2), coincidence of electoral and political boundaries, and criterion (3), compactness and contiguity of geographical districts—seem so indirectly related to the concept of fairness as possibly to raise similar questions, although they may seem unobjectionable enough per se to most people. Still, most of the criteria Lijphart elucidates would probably be accepted with scant dissent as valid standards for judging the fairness of any representative system.

The important point, however, is the one Lijphart makes very effectively: Particularly in American contexts, it is logically impossible to satisfy all these criteria simultaneously; each one is in logical contradiction with at least one other and most conflict logically with several. An electoral system designed to meet or maximize any given one of them will inevitably violate or fail to meet some other(s). Logic alone, therefore, will not make the numerous design decisions necessary to construct an electoral system—

geographical-district or at-large election? single- or multimember districts? majority or plurality rule? and with or without runoffs? As Lijphart points out, some criteria are neutral with respect to any given one of these engineering choices, but others clearly call for one rather than another choice under one or another of these and similar headings. The choice of which standards of fairness will govern electoral arrangements is again political, not logical, at bottom.

In sum, every decision about electoral mechanics is essentially a political decision as to whose ideas shall prevail. Collectively those decisions have the political effect of determining "which groups deserve representation" (Lijphart, chapter 15, this volume). The ultimate criterion for evaluating a representative system and its working is thus necessarily the political one— the practical effects of the institutions and processes in question on the distribution of political power.

Here again more than simple logical deduction is required. Determining the power implications of any given or proposed electoral arrangements requires empirical analysis of their probable effects and consequences.

The first and most obvious step in such analysis is to find out what groups, in fact, require representation, that is, which groups, for whatever reasons, "wish to elect one of their own members or a person with their particular political outlook" (Lijphart, chapter 15, this volume). Since we have no dependable theory about the dynamics of political interest formation or political group alignment, the answer cannot be deduced from any set of demographic or other facts about the society. It can be found only from observation. All the evidence from history, anthropology, and comparative politics suggests that the diversity of possible claimants to representation is much broader than we generally admit. As James Madison asserted in the tenth Federalist Paper (1911:4), even though "the various and unequal distribution of property" may be "the most common and durable source" of political cleavage, it is far from being the only or the controlling one. "A zeal for different opinions concerning religion, concerning government, and many other points . . . ; an attachment to different leaders ambitiously contending for preeminence and power; . . ." and, indeed, "the most frivolous and fanciful distinctions have been sufficient to kindle [people's] unfriendly passions and excite their most violent conflicts."

The four systems providing minority representation through nongeographic districts, described by Lijphart, exemplify other kinds of self-identified groups that may or may not be observed in other specific times and places: linguistic groups (Belgium), ethnic groups (New Zealand, Lebanon, Cyprus), and religio-ethnic groups (Belgium, Lebanon, Cyprus). How diverse the patterns of social cleavage and the corresponding political alignments and pressures for political representation can be is also suggested by a recent study of seventy-six political parties in twenty-eight

Western European and Anglo-American countries that found that religion and not social class is the most common basis of party cohesion and inter-party conflict in those cases. Urban-rural, linguistic, communal, and regional group bases for conflict were also found to be not uncommon in this study (Rose and Urwin, 1969).

Whatever the character of the claimants for representation, the basic principle of representation stated above legitimizes all of them. While they may contest politically to assert their claims, the analysts' task at this point is to identify claimant groups as precisely as possible and to see that they are fairly represented (according to the criteria of fairness otherwise established). There is no need, nor any justification, for political choice among claimants, favoring some and disfavoring others. Assuming the claimants accept the objective recommendations of analysts, practical decisions about electoral mechanics can be relatively politics-free in the sense that they are not influenced by political considerations beyond those dictating the standards of fair representation that are being applied.

But such decisions may rapidly become obsolescent. Social and political processes, whose workings we by no means fully understand, inevitably produce changes in the structure of groups and the group alignments on which the decisions were based, so that a new round of all the decisions and choices described above is in order. As Lijphart notes, however, there is a way to avoid this cycle of disproportionate representation, and, indeed, to simplify greatly, if not eliminate altogether, the need for the kind of empirical group analysis described above. That is by the single-transferable-vote system of PR, which has the unique property of facilitating the formation of *self-defined constituencies*. That is (Lijphart, chapter 15, this volume), "it permits and encourages the representation of minorities that wish to be represented without any need for a prior authoritative decision as to which minorities deserve special treatment and without forcing any minority into a pattern of representation that it may not wish." By thus eliminating the need for sophisticated or affirmative ger-rymandering, and by avoiding the constraints of the plurality-majority rule and geographically defined districts, proportional representation (but not necessarily the list variety of it) can, as Lijphart says, forestall the logical contradictions that pose varying degrees of political problem in other systems.

At this point, however, we encounter a set of political considerations that lies beyond Lijphart's discussion. The power of any group will depend on much more than the bare arithmetic of its representation. It will depend on organization, management, leadership, resources, and many other factors. It can be maintained that such considerations need not enter into the analysts' calculation of representational fairness, that fair representation means only giving claimants a fair chance at getting their fair share of power, according to the doctrine of equal opportunity. It can also be maintained that other kinds of political engineering (for example, regulation of campaign financing and campaign practices) can be brought into play along with the calculation of fair representation. But it is safe to say that practical decisions about such matters would clearly entail conflict in the political arena settled on political grounds and not on the basis of objective analysts' recommendations.

The principal difficulty raised here, however, is that we can offer analysts no reliable and valid way of measuring political power, or any way that is sufficiently general to permit them to map the distribution of power among the disparate groups composing any modern society. Analysts are thus severely handicapped in their ability to make the objective analysis required of them in terms other than simple numerical ratios of representatives to represented. The power over which claimants to representation are contending may be distributed quite differently than indicated by representational figures. Decisions about electoral mechanics may therefore in some cases be objective and logical so far as purely representational criteria are concerned, yet be quite irrelevant to the political function of representation.

Just as the political function of representation involves more than simple arithmetic, so the business of government involves more than just the distribution of power. It involves also, for example, processes of management and leadership, intelligent policy making, and values of accountability and responsibility. Many of the more important arguments for and against different features of electoral mechanics depend heavily on assumptions about how they would affect such functions and values. It has been alleged by both advocates and opponents of PR, for example, that its adoption would weaken a two-party system. Defenders of the two-party system have maintained, in turn, that only a strong two-party system can provide clear governing majorities, identify and elevate competent political leaders, establish governmental accountability and responsibility, and thus generally promote strong, effective, and stable government.

While most people might agree that stability, responsibility, and effectiveness are desirable properties of government, there would be disagreement about the value of strong leadership, highly competitive two-party politics, and some of the other goals and properties of government mentioned. In other words, even if all analysts and political actors agreed about the virtues of PR in purely representational terms, this would not forestall political disagreements about its value based on other, more fundamental grounds.

But that is the least of the problems. Most of the propositions mentioned above concerning the effects of PR and other sorts of electoral engineering on governmental processes, functions, and values beyond the purely representational aspects represent not hard empirical knowledge but political science folklore. The sad fact is, we have even less solid knowledge about how the dynamics of governmental structure and process, including its electoral parts, will affect broad governmental goals and values than we have about the dynamics of human behavior that affect the formation, disappearance, or changing political relevance of political and social groups. However we resolve the political choices among conflicting goals and values to be served by government, we lack, at least for the present, the empirical causal knowledge essential to our choosing logically those electoral arrangements most likely to achieve the goals and values chosen.

Lacking adequate grasp of the facts, and lacking the kind of empirical knowledge necessary to interpret them, analysts' generalizations about this important set of political consequences can only be determined by a variety of "political" considerations. Whose theory will prevail will inevitably depend on who mobilizes some kind of superior force or power more than on the weight of objective evidence and logical reasoning.

The general conclusions to which this brings us will in some respects be mildly disconcerting to some academic students of representation. From the analysts' standpoint, certain basic questions are above all political questions, questions that can be answered not by scientific, logical, objective analysis, but only by the thoughts, attitudes, and actions of citizens. These include such normative matters as the fundamental meaning of representation, the criteria of fairness, and the basis of people's right to choose "their own" representative(s). Such questions can be decided only in the political (and constitution-making) arena, not at the analysts' desks.

Given those fundamental decisions, analysts can supply recommendations about proposed elements of electoral mechanics based on logic and objective analysis of their effects on the representation of whatever groups claim representation. If some of those groups try to circumvent or twist those recommendations to their own advantage, such action can readily be labeled political efforts that are improper according to the fundamental political agreements supporting the system. If analysts' recommendations are based on political preferences or otherwise flawed analysis, other analysts can point out and help rectify such violations of objectivity and logic. Thus it is not unreasonable to hope that such electoral engineering decisions can effectively be made by analysts' logic rather than in the political arena, although it is there, of course, that they must be formalized and legitimized.

But political controversy is bound to surround the making of many, if not most, decisions of electoral engineering, not because normative elements are involved in them but because analysts lack the essential tools for making recommendations on any other grounds. They may well strive for and attain objectivity and impartiality in their analysis of the effects of electoral mechanics on the distribution of power, but their conclusions can be no more reliable and valid than the empirical theory of cause and effect on which they base their study. In all matters where conclusions depend on present social and political science knowledge about macropolitical dynamics concerning the distribution of power in society, those conclusions will inevitably reflect some kind of balance of power among weakly grounded opinions, not intellectual consensus on logically defensible and empirically demonstrable propositions. In such circumstances, the practical decisions in the political arena are more than ever likely to be governed by the political interests of the contenders for political power, who can cloak those interests in appropriate arguments chosen from the conflicting impartial and objective, but equally unreliable and invalid, expert analyses.

Note

1. This is Lijphart's definition of *fair representation*, but it is really the central concept that is at issue here. The standard of fairness seems rather to be an additional norm applicable to whatever conception of representation one seeks to institutionalize.

Part III
Representation within the
Political Party System

Introduction to Part III

Howard A. Scarrow

As its title indicates, the unifying theme of this book is the theory and practice of democratic representation.

The complexity of that topic—the several (and sometimes contradictory) normative goals that representation systems might seek to realize, and the difficulty of designing rules that will achieve the goals selected—has been amply demonstrated in the issues that have surrounded the reapportionments of American legislatures since *Baker* v. *Carr*. No less dramatically, however, the complexity of democratic representation has been demonstrated by the issues that have surrounded the changes in the processes by which American presidential candidates are nominated, especially within the Democratic party. Indeed, as Austin Ranney notes in chapter 18, the apportionment reforms and the nomination reforms were both part of a movement that might be termed *born-again progressivism*. That is, those who urged apportionment reforms shared with those who urged nomination reforms the belief that American institutions were not written on stone, but were subject to change by reform-minded critics; and that democratic values are more fully realized when each individual citizen is treated equally and given the maximum opportunity to affect political outcomes through his participation in the selection (election, nomination) process. One group had as its charter Supreme Court decisions (*Baker, Reynolds, Wesberry*), while the other derived legitimacy from reports of study commissions (McGovern-Fraser, Mikulski, Winograd).

Within both reform movements, however, the initial victories opened up troublesome questions of democratic theory. Are elections (to legislative bodies or to nomination conventions) the means of individual representation or group representation? Can only a black represent a black? Does a black Ph.D. represent an unemployed black worker? Should elections be winner-take-all, or should they try to yield results proportional to group strength? Should the elected official (legislator, delegate) think only of his own district, or should he consider the welfare of the entire community? Should he be bound by "instructions" given to him by the voters? Within both reform movements, moreover, initial principles were pushed to what seemed to be self-defeating extremes. By insisting on minute precision of population equality in congressional districts, the Supreme Court ran roughshod over many other legitimate principles of fair representation. Similarly, by its quota rules, the Democratic party ended up with conventions that were representative in only one narrow sense of the term.

Finally, for both reforms, political scientists have been divided in assessing their impact. Regarding the change in nomination procedures, all sides seem to agree that the changes have had a profound impact on the outcome of the nomination process, but they are divided as to whether the results have been good or bad. Regarding the apportionment changes, political scientists cannot agree whether there has been any significant impact at all. (The latter question will be more fully examined in the last part of this book.)

17 Participation, Representation, and Democratic Party Reform

James I. Lengle

In 1972, George McGovern stood at the podium of the Democratic National Convention as the party's nominee and proclaimed that his nomination was all the more precious because it was a product of the most *open* presidential nomination process and the most *representative* national convention in this country's history. Less than six months later George McGovern suffered one of the worst defeats in Democratic party history. How can McGovern's acceptance by Democratic primary and caucus participants and by a majority of popularly elected Democratic National Convention delegates be reconciled with his rejection by an overwhelming majority of general election voters, most of whom were Democrats? Much of the answer lies in the rules changes adopted by the Democratic party between 1968 and 1972 and the effect they had in determining to whom the process was opened and of what the national convention was representative.

The Call for Reform

The 1968 Democratic National Convention marked the beginning of the reform movement. Eugene McCarthy arrived at the convention as the only contender with a number of primary victories to his credit, and as such, laid claim to the title "voice of the party rank and file." Hubert Humphrey's support, on the other hand, was based among party professionals (national, state, and local party officeholders and officials). Since most delegates in 1968 were chosen by state and local conventions and caucuses, and since these mechanisms were controlled by party organizations in most localities, Humphrey easily defeated McCarthy on the first ballot.

McCarthy supporters both inside and outside the convention hall were outraged. To them, the entire delegate selection process had been a sham, and the national convention was just another example of bossism run rampant and of smoke-filled-room politics. They charged that delegate selection procedures in most states violated basic standards of fair play, that participation in delegate selection was restricted to party regulars, and that both of these factors produced a national convention that was top heavy with party professionals, and hence, demographically, attitudinally, and preferentially unrepresentative of the party rank and file.

In a spirit of compromise, and with an eye toward a unified party for the general election, the 1968 convention adopted a resolution recommending that the chairman of the Democratic National Committee establish a special committee to study state delegate procedures and recommend such improvements as can assure even broader citizen participation in the delegate selection process. Out of that directive, the Commission on Party Structure and Delegate Selection, or as it has been more commonly called, the McGovern-Fraser Commission, was born.

The McGovern-Fraser Commission took its responsibility seriously. After holding seventeen public hearings in all regions of the country, the twenty-eight-member committee issued a set of eighteen guidelines (Commission on Party Structure and Delegate Selection, 1970) that would govern delegate selection to the 1972 Democratic convention. The eighteen guidelines (see appendix 17-1) can be divided into two broad categories: those opening access to, and facilitating participation in, the delegate selection process and those providing for a more representative national convention. The guidelines that fell into the first category included A-3 (urging the reform of registration procedures), A-4 (reducing costs, fees, and petition requirements), A-5 (requiring state primaries to have written rules covering delegate selection), B-2 (separating delegate selection from all other state party business), C-1 (requiring adequate public notice of all delegate selection meetings), C-3 (urging the banning of open primaries), and C-6 (requiring open slate-making processes.)

Accurate demographic and preferential representation were provided for by guidelines A-1 and A-2 (the *quota guidelines*—requiring minorities, women, and young people to be included on delegations in reasonable relationship to the group's presence in the population of the state), B-1 (prohibiting proxy voting), B-3 (setting 40 percent quorum requirements for party meetings involved in delegate selection), B-4 (requiring same procedures for choice of alternate and original delegates), B-5 (banning unit rule), B-6 (urging proportional representation at each level of delegate selection), B-7 (requiring 75 percent of all delegates to be chosen from units no larger than congressional districts), C-2 (prohibiting ex-officio delegates), C-4 (requiring delegates to be selected in calendar year of national convention), and C-5 (limiting proportion of a state's delegation that could be appointed by a party committee to 10 percent).

From the start, none of the state parties had rules or procedures that met the guidelines and many faced a complete restructuring of their rules to comply. But by July 7, 1972, the day when the final report of the McGovern-Fraser was filed, forty state parties, the territories, and the District of Columbia were in full compliance and the remaining ten were in substantial compliance (Commission on Party Structure and Delegate Selection, 1972:2). In less than four years, the Democratic party overhauled a 135-year-old nomination process, and now all eyes turned to the national convention to see how the reforms would work.

Compared to 1968, the 1972 nomination process and national convention were judged to a huge success. Participation in 1972 primaries exceeded participation in 1968 primaries by over 9 million voters. Caucus attendance also jumped and newspapers reported a qualitative change in the nature of caucus participants—grass-roots Democrats were outnumbering party professionals in many of the caucus and convention states.

Demographic representation at the national convention also increased. As table 17-1 shows, the percentage of black and women delegates in 1972 tripled and the percentage of young delegates increased fivefold. Although women and youth were still slightly underrepresented when compared to their percentage of the general population, they still made extraordinary gains. Blacks, on the other hand, were even slightly overrepresented, as their percentage of the convention delegates exceeded their percentage of the general population by four percentage points.

Thus the twin goals of an open process and a representative convention were thought to be met, and George McGovern was the product. But then came the shock—the nominee lost. And then came the important comparison between 1968 and 1972. The nominee of the closed process and the unrepresentative convention four years earlier lost to Richard Nixon by 0.7 percent, or 511,000 votes, or 110 electoral votes. In striking contrast, the nominee of the open process and representative convention of 1972 lost to

Table 17-1
Demographic Representation in Democratic National Conventions
(percents)

Categories	General Population (1970)	Convention Delegates (1968)	(1972)
Blacks	11	5	15
Whites	89	95	85
Total	100	100	100
Women	51	13	40
Men	49	87	60
Total	100	100	100
Age 18-30	27	4	21
Over 30	73	96	79
Total	100	100	100

Source Adapted from Ranney, 1975: 155.

the same candidate by 23 percent, or 18 million votes, or 503 electoral votes. And then came the question—why?

The answer is twofold. First, an open process does not automatically guarantee a representative convention. In an open system, convention delegates reflect the ideological dispositions, issue concerns, and candidate preferences of those Democrats who turn out in primaries and caucuses. If those who vote are significantly unrepresentative of the party membership or of the general election electorate, then an open process may create just the opposite effect: an unrepresentative convention, an unpopular nominee, and four years of a Republican administration.

Second, part of the answer is definitional. While the 1972 convention did mirror certain traits more accurately than the 1968 convention, it was also true it was demographically unrepresentative on other counts, and most importantly, it was significantly unrepresentative attitudinally. These two explanations are explored more fully in the next two sections.

Open to Whom?

All studies of primary voters and caucus participants seem to reach the same conclusion: voters and participants tend to be *demographically* unrepresentative of the party-following and of the party's general election electorate. In a comparison of the 1968 New Hampshire primary intenders and nonintenders and of 1968 Wisconsin primary voters and nonvoters, Austin Ranney (1972) found that those who voted (or intended to vote) were older, richer, more active in civic, religious, and political organizations, and more likely to hold stronger opinions about the issues of the day.

A study (Lengle, 1981) of 1968 and 1972 California Democratic presidential primary voters found both California electorates to be demographically unrepresentative of the party-following. Examining education, income, social class, occupation, and race, this study found that college-educated and advanced-degree Democrats, rich Democrats (over $20,000 income bracket), upper-middle- and upper-class Democrats, white-collar Democrats, and white Democrats comprised a much larger percentage of both primary electorates than they did of party membership. On the other hand, those groups who historically have formed the nucleus of the party and the core of its general election support (less-educated Democrats, poor Democrats, working-class Democrats, lower-middle- and lower-class Democrats, and black/Asian/Hispanic Democrats) were significantly underrepresented.

An upper socioeconomic bias was also present in 1976 (Commission on Presidential Nomination and Party Structure, 1978). Table 17-2 compares the percentage of less-educated and better-educated Democratic voters in thirteen Democratic primary electorates to their percentage in Democratic

Table 17-2

Percentage of Less-Educated and College-Educated Voters in Democratic Primary Electorates and in Democratic General-Election Electorates

State	Less Than High School		College Degree or More	
	Primary	General	Primary	General
California	11	27	34	17
Florida	13	30	28	17
Illinois	19	34	23	6
Indiana	21	40	13	6
Massachusetts	12	19	36	22
Michigan	20	30	20	10
New Hampshire	11	18	38	18
New Jersey	12	41	35	14
New York	15	31	32	19
Ohio	15	32	25	10
Oregon	19	18	23	20
Pennsylvania	17	32	23	15
Wisconsin	18	25	22	15

Source: Commission on Presidential Nomination and Party Structure, 1978:11-12.

general-election electorates. With the exception of the Oregon primary, Democrats with less than a high-school education were significantly underrepresented, ranging from 7 percent below parity in Massachusetts and Wisconsin to 19 percent below parity in Indiana and New Jersey. Democrats with a college degree or more were significantly overrepresented in all thirteen states with the greatest disproportion found in New Jersey, New Hampshire, Illinois, and California.

The explanation for a demographic bias in primary electorates is, of course, variation in turnout. If turnout among all groups were either 100 percent or proportionally equal, then the primary electorate would be a perfect demographic replica of the party membership. Primary turnout, however, just like general-election turnout, varies by socioeconomic status. In the 1972 California primary (Lengle, 1981), for instance, college-educated Democrats outvoted Democrats with an eighth-grade education or less by 38 percent, rich Democrats (over $20,000) outvoted poor Democrats (under $3,000) by 27 percent, white-collar Democrats outvoted blue-collar Democrats by 16 percent, upper-middle- and upper-class Democrats outvoted lower-middle- and lower-class Democrats by 20 percent, and white Democrats outvoted black/Asian/Hispanic Democrats by 18 percent. As a consequence, primary voters in both electorates were demographically unrepresentative of the party-faithful.

By itself, a consistent demographic bias is theoretically interesting but politically inconsequential. It becomes politically significant, however, if those groups who are overrepresented possess ideological perspectives and issue concerns different from those who are underrepresented because then the demographic bias produces an ideological or attitudinal bias.

To date, the results of studies on this question are mixed. The findings seem to vary by state and election year. For instance, Austin Ranney (1972) found that 1968 New Hampshire primary voters tended to be more hawkish on the Vietnam War than nonvoters. In California (Lengle, 1981) in 1968 and 1972 just the reverse was true. Those overrepresented in both primary electorates (upper SES Democrats) identified themselves as liberal and were more concerned about the Vietnam War, pollution, conservation, and education. Underrepresented Democrats (lower SES Democrats), on the other hand, were more middle-of-the-road to conservative, were less concerned about Vietnam, and were more concerned about social issues (crime, drugs), bread-and-butter issues (jobs, housing), and national defense.

Limited evidence (Commission on Presidential Nomination and Party Structure, 1978:14) on 1976 suggests that conservative Democrats were again underrepresented but not to the same degree as 1972.

The last and probably most politically significant way primaries can be unrepresentative is preferentially. That is, if groups who are overrepresented tend to possess candidate preferences different from those that are underrepresented, then primaries become institutional distorters rather than recorders of candidate popularity and strength. The evidence here is consistent within some states and within certain years but inconsistent across time. In the 1968 and 1972 California study (Lengle, 1981), both electorates were unrepresentative preferentially. Table 17-3 shows the consistency and selectivity with which overrepresentation and underrepresentation bestowed their advantages and disadvantages on certain California constituencies, and hence, on certain candidates, ideological perspectives, and issue concerns. Of the ten socioeconomic groups of Democrats who were underrepresented in both 1968 and 1972, and to whom disproportionate candidate preference can be attached, all ten were lower SES groups, and nine out of the ten preferred the two moderates in the two races (Kennedy, 1968; Humphrey, 1972). Of the six groups of Democrats who were overrepresented in both elections, and to whom disproportionate candidate choice can be attached, all six were upper SES groups, and all six preferred the two liberal ideologues in the two races (McCarthy, 1968; McGovern, 1972).

Preferential unrepresentativeness was found in four other primary states in 1972 (Lengle, 1981). In Florida, Wisconsin, Pennsylvania, and Michigan, McGovern was found to be the choice of upper SES Democrats and Humphrey was found to be the choice of lower SES Democrats.

In 1976, candidate preferences were not as strongly polarized along socioeconomic lines (Orren, 1976). Although Udall drew support consistently from professional, college-educated, and rich Democrats, Carter's support tended to be uniform across all status categories.

Table 17-3
Candidate Choice by Representation in California Presidential Primaries

Candidate Preferences	Representation	
	Democrats Under-represented in 1968 and 1972	Democrats Over-represented in 1968 and 1972
Kennedy/Humphrey (1968) (1972)	8th-grade and under education / 9th-11th-grade education / Under $3,000 yearly earnings / $3,000-$6,900 yearly earnings / Lower class / Lower middle class / Operative/Semiskilled / Service/Household / Asian/Hispanic	—
Kennedy/McGovern (1968) (1972)	—	—
McCarthy/Humphrey (1968) (1972)	High school education	1-4 years college / Advanced college degree
McCarthy/McGovern (1968) (1972)	—	$10,000-$14,999 yearly earnings / Over $15,000 yearly earnings / Upper middle class / Professional/Executive/Manager

Source: This table is used with permission of the publisher, Greenwood Press, a division of Congressional Information Service, Inc., Westport, Conn., and appears in *Representation and Presidential Primaries: The Democratic Party in the Post-Reform Era*, by James J. Lengle.

The socioeconomic bias found in primary states is probably even more pronounced in caucus states since turnout in caucuses (2 percent in 1976) is significantly lower than turnout in primaries (28 percent in 1976) (Ranney, 1977a:15, 20). A study (Marshall, 1976) of the 1972 Minnesota caucuses found a significant overrepresentation of professional Democrats, and this demographic bias also produced an ideological and preferential bias since caucus attendees were generally more liberal and less supportive of Humphrey than rank-and-file Democrats.

In summary, the effects of demographic unrepresentativeness on Democratic party politics depend on whether the class-related patterns of 1968 and 1972 or the more muted and random patterns of 1976 will predominate in the future. If the latter is the case, then a strong upper-socioeconomic bias is for the most part inconsequential since ideology, attitudes, and candidate preferences of participants and nonparticipants do not differ significantly. On the other hand, if the patterns of future campaigns resemble those of 1968 and 1972, then the effects of unrepresentativeness can be substantial. In the medium run, the effect may be to mold party candidates more and more toward the image, style, and issue-orientation of that sector of party stimulated by circumstances to participate in nomination campaigns. By the same token, party candidates may come less and less to take into account those elements of the party indisposed by circumstances to play a role in the primaries. In the long run, due to the perpetual and subtle conditioning of elite, masses, and issues, the structure, ideological thrust, and constituent base of both political parties could be substantially and permanently altered.

Representative of What?

From the outset, members of the McGovern-Fraser Commission faced a number of serious theoretical and political questions, and the answers that prevailed shaped the reforms they accepted. They were agreed that a national convention was preferable to a direct national primary and therefore that representative democracy was preferable to direct democracy. They disagreed, however, over what constituted representative democracy and how it was best achieved. A short review of various interpretations of the concept of representation provides a useful starting point in understanding the commission's view and the major issues surrounding—and the reforms that evolved from—that view.

The best analysis of the concept of representation is found in *The Concept of Representation* by Hannah Pitkin (1967). In her book, Pitkin discusses a number of variants of the concept of representation that have evolved over time. The first two views she presents are formalistic interpretations. One defines representation in terms of giving authority; the other, in terms of keeping accountable. The basic feature of the authorization view are these: A representtive is someone who has been authorized to act, the represented becomes responsible for the consequences of that action, and anything done after the right kind of authorization and within limits is by definition *representing*. For adherents of the accountability viewpoint, a representative is someone who is to be held to account, who will have to answer to another for what he does, and the men to whom he must eventually account are those whom he represents. As Pitkin (1967: 55-56) further explains, these two views are opposed in many other ways:

> For the [authorization theorist], being a representative means being freed from the usual responsibility for one's actions; for the accountability theorist, being a representative means precisely having new and special obligations. Whereas authorization theorists see the representative as free, the represented as bound; accountability theorists see precisely the converse. The authorization theorist defines representative democracy by equating elections with a grant of authority: a man represents because he has been elected at the outset of his term in office. The accountability theory, on the contrary, equates elections with a holding to account; an elected official is a representative because he will be subject to re-election or removal at the end of his term.

A third view of representation, and one that helps in understanding what the noun *representativeness* or the adjective *representative* means, is what Pitkin calls *descriptive representation*. This approach is very different from the authorization and accountability views. According to this view, representing is not acting with authority, acting before being held to account, or any kind of acting at all. Rather, says Pitkin (1967:61), "it depends on the representative's characteristics, on what he *is* or *is like*, on being something rather than doing something. The representative does not act for others; he *stands for* them by virtue of a correspondence between them, a resemblance or reflection. In political terms, what seems important is less what a political body does than how it is composed." And it is when this body is an exact miniature or condensation of the original that it is considered representative or we can speak of its representativeness.

It was the descriptive view of representation that prevailed in the McGovern-Fraser Commission and provided the model they followed in designing a representative national convention. But while this view seems simple enough to understand, implement, and measure, it does pose three important questions: Who should be represented? Who should be the representatives or delegates? What characteristic or trait should be reflected?

On the surface, the answer to the first question seems obvious—the party membership. But party membership can be defined in a number of different ways: (1) all registered Democrats, (2) all Democratic general-election voters, and (3) all Democratic nomination participants (primary voters and caucus participants).

Strong arguments can be made for each of these groups. All registered voters could be considered party members since they did take the time and make the effort to register and because their choice of the Democratic party does indicate a sense of belonging or feeling of attachment to the party. There are those who feel that only those who support the party's candidates in general elections are party members and that therefore the membership should be restricted to Democratic general-election electorates. Others feel that even more involvement is necessary and that only those who participate during the course of the nomination campaign are really true Democrats.

What is important here is not that there are three reasonable definitions of party membership but that these three definitions represent three different subpopulations and, hence, three different aggregations of attitudes, issues, and candidate preferences that could be reflected at national conventions. For instance, union members and Catholics would be much larger components of the party membership under definition 2 than under definition 3, since they both comprise a much larger proportion of Democratic general-election electorates than Democratic nomination electorates. On the other hand, the representation of better-educated, upper-income, and white-collar Democrats would increase under definition 3 and decrease under definitions 1 or 2 for the opposite reason. Thus different definitions of party membership in a descriptive system of representation could produce different national conventions, policy platforms, and presidential nominees.

In its guidelines, the McGovern-Fraser Commission implicitly defined the represented, or the party membership, as those who participate in the nomination process in a given year. Most of the eighteen guidelines have the effect of locking in candidate choices (and hence issue interests) of participants only or of excluding the possibility of nonparticipant candidate and issue representation by removing whatever flexibility or discretion the party once had in the process. Both of these in turn make the party more representative of, and responsive to, *nomination majorities* than *general-election majorities*, and the party's competitive edge suffers to the degree these majorities differ either ideologically, attitudinally, or preferentially.

The second question the McGovern-Fraser Commission had to address was "Who should be the delegates?" Opinion on the Commission was divided between those who favored the continued presence of party professionals and those who sought an increase in the number of grass-roots (issue- and candidate-activists) delegates.

The argument in favor of party professionals is persuasive because in a sense they are the party. Their lives have been devoted to party affairs and their continued commitment has maintained the party as an ongoing organization. In addition, since the individual and collective interests of party professionals depend largely on the party's electoral prospects and since this is integrally tied to nomination politics, organizational representation not only seems reasonable but legitimate and mandatory. Without some degree of self-determination, party organizations as we know them may disappear, and the important functions they serve in the political system would be lost.

If one views parties as programmatically rather than electorally oriented, then a case can be made for the presence of issue- or candidate-activists at conventions. Since activists view themselves as the party's conscience, their presence would inject a more moral and ideological tone to convention debate and would redirect the convention's focus (and hence, the party's focus) from choosing a winner to taking positions on the great issues of the day.

Since the McGovern-Fraser Commission was a by-product of the dissatisfaction over the "boss-run" convention of 1968, the proactivist position carried the day. Some of the guidelines that were intended to minimize the influence of party regulars and maximize the influence of issue activists were A-4 (removing costs and fees involved in delegate selection), A-5 (requiring state parties to adopt and make accessible all party rules governing delegate selection), B-1 (prohibiting proxy voting), C-2 (prohibiting ex-officio delegates and requiring all delegates to be chosen in the calendar year of the convention), C-5 (prohibiting state party committees from choosing more than 10 percent of any state's delegation), and C-6 (requiring open slate-making procedures).

As table 17-4 shows, the guidelines had their intended effects. Although the percentage of Democratic governors at the 1972 convention varied little from previous conventions, the percentage of Democratic senators in 1972 compared to 1968 dropped almost 50 percent and the percentage of Democratic congressmen dropped 60 percent. The effect on state party officials

Table 17-4
Percentage of Major Democratic Party Officeholders at National Conventions

Year	U.S. Senators[a]	U.S. Congressmen[b]	Governors[c]
1956	90%	33%	100%
1960	68	45	85
1964	72	46	61
1968	68	39	83
1972	36	15	80

Source: Commission on Presidential Nomination and Party Structure, 1978:18.
[a]Percentage of Democratic U.S. senators who were voting delegates or alternates.
[b]Percentage of Democratic U.S. congressmen who were voting delegates or alternates.
[c]Percentage of Democratic governors who were voting delegates or alternates.

was just as dramatic. In convention years prior to 1972, about 50 percent of the delegates had held, or held at the time of the convention, a major state party position. In 1972, the percentage of state party officials dropped to 33 percent (Commission on Presidential Nomination and Party Structure, 1978:19).

The last major question inherent in descriptive representation and one that the McGovern-Fraser Commission had to face was whether the convention should represent the rank-and-file demographically, attitudinally, or preferentially. The Commission opted for both proportional *demographic* and *preferential* representation.

Guidelines A-1 and A-2, which stated that minorities, young people, and women should be represented in state delegations in reasonable relationship to their presence in the population, established demographic representation. If a state's general population was 51 percent women, 13 percent black, and 20 percent young people, then the state's delegation should reflect these distributions as well. The assumption underlying these two guidelines was that group interests were best represented by group members.

At the 1972 convention, demographic representation was both a success and a failure. Although the convention was fairly representative of these three groups, it was far from a cross section of the party rank-and-file with respect to other demographic traits. For instance, only 22 percent of all Democratic party identifiers in 1972 had incomes over $15,000 but 62 percent of all Democratic delegates earned over $15,000. Or, to take another example, only 25 percent of the Democratic rank-and-file had a college education in 1972 and only 4 percent had postgraduate degrees. In contrast, 60 percent of the convention delegates were college educated and 30 percent had graduate degrees (Kirkpatrick, 1974:22-23).

Demographic representation as implemented by the McGovern-Fraser Commission also raised a number of interesting questions. First, why should state delegations only reflect young people, women, and minorities? A strong case could be made for blacks since their registration and vote is disproportionately Democratic. But if these are the criteria, then why not also include Catholics, blue-collar workers, and Jews? If the defense rests on overcoming past discrimination, then why not also include ethnics (southern and eastern Europeans) who are much more deserving on those grounds than young people?

Proportional preferential representation was provided for in guideline B-6, which urged state parties to ensure the fair representation of candidate preferences to the highest level of the nominating process. Thus, if the vote tally in a state primary or convention was 50 percent for Humphrey, 30 percent for McGovern, and 20 percent for Wallace, then the state's delegation had to reflect these distributions as well.

The advantage of a proportional preferential system of representation is that it does guarantee the accurate reflection of the candidate preferences of those who turn out. The drawback, however, is that those who turn out may be preferentially or attitudinally unrepresentative of the party following or the party's general-election electorate. The end result, of course, would be a convention like 1972, which was preferentially representative of the nomination majority but preferentially unrepresentative of the general-election majority.

The third type of representation, attitudinal, received much less attention from the commission than the other two. Yet in many respects, the essence of true convention representation lies, not in the correspondence of traits or preferences, but in the correspondence of the delegates' *attitudes* with those of the rank-and-file. Nothing in the guidelines was aimed directly or explicitly at this objective, but some commissioners (Ranney, 1977b:188) thought it would be achieved as an important by-product of the proportional representation of candidate preferences.

Table 17-5, which compares the attitudes of Democratic party identifiers, Democratic delegates, Republican party identifiers, and Republican delegates in seven important issue areas, shows that they were wrong. In five of the seven areas (welfare, busing, crime, demonstrations, and military) Republican national convention delegates better represented the positions of the Democratic rank-and-file than Democratic national convention delegates. The mean difference on all issues between the views of Democratic voters and Democratic delegates was 31-percentage points, while the corresponding difference between the views of Democratic voters and Republican delegates was 9-percentage points.

New Round of Reform—Same Old Questions

Since 1972, two new reform commissions (Mikulski and Winograd) have come and gone and in the process have had to tackle the same difficult questions that faced the McGovern-Fraser Commission. Partly as a result of the McGovern disaster and partly as a result of having different members, these commissions have arrived at slightly different answers and therefore have modified the rules of the game accordingly.

The Mikulski Commission (Commission on Party Structure and Delegate Selection, 1974), which was mandated by the 1972 Convention, weakened demographic representation by replacing quotas with affirmative action and strengthened preferential representaiton by defining a proportional system of representation with a 15 percent threshhold. In response to the party-professional-as-delegates-versus-issue-activists-as-delegates debate, the Mikulski Commission sided with the professionals by increasing

Table 17-5

Issue Positions of Party Identifiers and Convention Delegates, 1972

(percents)

Issue Positions	Democrats		Republicans	
	Rank and File	Delegates	Rank and File	Delegates
Welfare[a]				
Abolish poverty	22	57	13	10
Obligation to work	69	28	79	75
Busing[b]				
Bus to integrate	15	66	5	8
Keep children in neighbor-				
hood schools	82	25	93	84
Crime[c]				
Protect the accused	36	78	28	21
Stop crime regardless of				
rights of accused	50	13	56	56
Political Demonstrations				
Favorable attitude	14	59	8	14
Unfavorable attitude	67	22	76	72
The Military				
Favorable attitude	67	42	71	84
Unfavorable attitude	16	43	12	4
The Police				
Favorable attitude	81	71	84	94
Unfavorable attitude	7	13	5	2
Inflation				
Government action against	78	87	74	63
No government action against	9	4	6	14

Source: Adapted from Kirkpatrick, 1973:265-322.

[a]Respondents were asked whether in welfare policy the main stress should be on abolishing poverty or on the obligation to work.

[b]Respondents were asked whether in busing policy the main stress should be on busing to achieve racial integration or on keeping children in their neighborhood schools.

[c]Respondents were asked whether in policy on crime the main stress should be on protecting the rights of the accused or on stopping crime regardless of those rights.

from 10 to 25 the percentage of a state delegation that could be selected at-large by state committees. It was hoped by the commission that this guideline would encourage the selection of party and public officials.

The Winograd Commission (Commission on Party Structure and Delegate Selection, 1978), which was mandated after the 1976 Convention, went even further in reestablishing the presence of party professionals at national conventions by increasing state delegation size by 10 percent and reserving these slots for party and public officials. The commission in one sense also reendorsed demographic representation by reviving the quota for women and by maintaining affirmative action programs for blacks, Hispanics, and native Americans. In addition, the Winograd Commission tried to broaden the base of election-year participants (and hence broaden the base of the represented) by instituting outreach programs for persons over sixty-five, ethnics, young people, persons with a high school education or less, and the physically handicapped. Lastly, and in keeping with previous commissions, the commission pushed the party even further down the path of preferential representation by outlawing *loopholes primaries* (winner-take-all congressional district) and by requiring each step of the delegate-selection process to faithfully reflect the candidate preferences of the previous step.

What the future has in store for the Democratic party as a result of these reforms is unclear, and what future reform commissions may decide is equally unclear. What is certain is that the debate will revolve around the same three questions. Who are the represented? Who are the representatives? How should the convention represent?

Appendix 17A: Guidelines for the Selection of National Convention Delegates

Committee on Party Structure and
Delegate Selections

A. Guidelines prohibiting rules or practices which inhibit access to and full and meaningful participation in the delegate selection process. State parties are:
   1. *Required* to add to their rules and enforce all six basic elements of the Democratic National Convention's rules prohibiting discrimination against would-be participants on the basis of race, color, creed, or national origin.
   2. *Required* to overcome the effects of past discrimination by affirmative steps to encourage representation on the national convention delegation of young people—defined as people of not more than thirty nor less than eighteen years of age—and women in reasonable relationship to their presence in the population of the State. (Note: It is the understanding of the Commission that this is not to be accomplished by the mandatory imposition of quotas.)
   3. *Urged* to use their good offices to remove or alleviate any provisions in their states' registration laws, customs, and practices which inhibit effective participation in primaries, caucuses, conventions, and other party affairs.
   4. *Urged* to remove all costs, fees, and excessive petition requirements involved in delegate-selection processes.
   5. *Required* to adopt and make available readily accessible and explicit rules governing the delegate-selection process. These rules must facilitate maximum participation by interested Democrats in the delegate selection process.
B. Guidelines prohibiting rules or practices which dilute the influence of Democrats in the delegate selection process after they have exercised all available resources to exert such influence. State parties are:
   1. *Required* to add to their explicit written rules provisions which forbid the use of proxy voting in all procedures involved in the delegate selection process.
   2. *Required* to make it clear to voters how the selection of state party officials and other party business affects the process by which national convention delegates are selected.

3. *Required* to adopt rules setting quorums at not less than 40 percent for all party committees involved in the delegate-selection process.

4. *Required* to select alternates in the same manner as that prescribed for selecting delegates.

5. *Required* to include in their explicit written rules provisions which forbid the use of the unit rule or the practice of instructing delegates to vote against their stated preferences at any stage of the selection process.

6. *Urged* to adopt procedures which will provide fair representation of minority views on presidential candidates. The Commission also *recommends* that the 1972 National Convention adopt a rule requiring state parties to provide for the representation of minority views to the highest level of the nominating process.

7. State parties which apportion their delegations to the national convention are *required* to apportion them among substate units on a formula giving equal weight to total population and to the Democratic vote in the previous election of that substate unit. State parties with convention systems are *required* to select at least 75 percent of their national convention delegates at congressional district or smaller unit levels.

C. Guidelines prohibiting rules or practices combining attributes of the procedures disapproved in categories A and B. State parties are:

1. *Required* to ensure adequate public notice of all party meetings involved in the delegate-selection process and also of the presidential preferences of candidates or slates of candidate for delegates.

2. *Required* to repeal party rules or resolutions which call for any national convention delegates to be chosen ex-officio.

3. *Urged* to provide for party enrollment that (1) allows non-Democrats to become party members, and (2) provides easy access and frequent opportunities for unaffiliated voters to become Democrats.

4. *Required* to prohibit practices by which officials elected or appointed before the calendar year choose nominating committees or propose or endorse slates of delegates.

5. *Required* to limit national convention delegates chosen by the state committee to not more than 10 percent of the total number of delegates and alternates, and *urged* to eliminate all selection of delegates by the state committee.

6. *Required*, in states where entire slates are presented to caucuses, conventions, committees, or voters in a primary, to adopt procedures which ensure that (1) bodies making up the slates have been elected, assembled, or appointed for the slate-making task with adequate public notice that they would perform such task; (2) the

persons making up each slate have adopted procedures that will facilitate widespread participation in the slate-making process (which the proviso that any slate presented in the name of a presidential candidate in a primary state be assembled with due consultation with the presidential candidate or his representative); and (3) adequate procedural safeguards are provided to assure that the right to challenge the presented slate is more than perfunctory and places no undue burden on the challengers.

18

Comments on Representation within the Political Party System

Austin Ranney

Let me begin by making one small correction to James Lengle's explanation (chapter 17, this volume) regarding the origins of the Winograd Commission. The commission was originally established in 1975 by Robert Strauss, who was then Democratic National Chairman. The commission consisted mainly of scholars, although it was chaired by Morley Winograd, the Democratic chairman of Michigan, and it was charged with making a scholarly examination of the reasons for the proliferation of presidential primaries and of their impact upon the presidential nominating process. At the time of the 1976 Democratic National Convention it was the only national commission in being, and so the convention referred several rules matters to it for its consideration and thereby converted it into the party's third reform commission—which was not its original assignment. After it had been so converted, in early 1977 the new Democratic National Chairman, Kenneth Curtis, undoubtedly acting under President Carter's orders, doubled the size of the original commission and appointed to the new positions all Carter loyalists. So the Winograd Commission after the 1976 Convention was quite different in both purpose and personnel from what it had been originally.

Aside from this one small correction, I want to take my departure in this chapter from Lengle's conclusions in the previous chapter—with which I strongly agree. The kinds of issues that have been raised in the course of changing the presidential nominating system are very much like the issues that are involved in determining the apportionment of seats in Congress and the state legislatures. After all, national party conventions are also intended to be representative decision-making bodies, and the questions of how they should be apportioned and how their delegates are to be selected are very similar to the questions on representation and redistricting that are the focus of this book.

The reforms that have been made in the delegate selection process since 1968 constitute a more radical change in our presidential nominating process than any made in our history since the demise of the congressional caucus and the rise of the delegate convention in the period from 1824 to 1932. They show, just as the reapportionment revolution in our state legislatures since 1962 shows, that American institutions are *not* immutable, fixed forever in concrete. On the contrary, they are quite easily changed. So the question is not whether we can change an institution, rather, it is what kind of change do we want and what kind of result is any particular change likely to produce.

It seems to me that if you look at the changes in the presidential nominating process in general and the rules of the Democratic party in particular since 1969 you learn at least two things that are very relevant to the general question of representation and apportionment issues in the 1980s. One thing you learn is that our ability to predict the consequences of changes we make is very poor (and that lack of ability applies to lawyers and members of interest groups as well as political scientists).

The second thing you learn is that when people appraise and evaluate the changes that have been made in apportionment or delegate selection rules, they seem to fall into one of two camps, each of which can be characterized by an old proverb. One group might be called the "virtue is its own reward" group. Characteristically, this group is primarily concerned with whether the rules of the game have been made intrinsically more fair, more decent, more democratic and the process more open and participatory. The object is to get rules that are good *in themselves*, without much regard to the results they produce.

The other group might be called the "by their fruits ye shall know them" group. Characteristically, the members of this group focus mainly on the *results* the new rules produce—that is, the kinds of persons who become national convention delegates, the kinds of candidates they nominate, the health of the political parties, and so on. For example, Lengle (chapter 17, this volume) says that the 1972 Democratic convention was a disaster because it nominated George McGovern, a very poor candidate who lost by a landslide. But some other commentators, notably William Crotty at Northwestern University, say that the 1972 Democratic convention was a great success because there were far more blacks, women, and young people as delegates than ever before. So clearly Lengle is a member of the by-their-fruits-ye-shall-know-them school and Crotty is a member of the virtue-is-its-own-reward school.

Perhaps the most useful contribution I can make is to raise a few questions about the nature of political representation that have not yet received adequate attention. Again, let me use some examples from the Democratic reform commissions on which I served, including the McGovern-Fraser Commission and the Winograd Commission.

The McGovern-Fraser Commission, as Lengle noted, was trying to do several things, some of which turned out to be incompatible with each other (although we didn't know it at the time). We on the commission certainly wanted to make the delegate selection process more open, and, as Lengle quite correctly observed, we thought that every person who *wanted* to participate—anyone who had a favorite candidate or cause to support—should be allowed to participate. We did not think that past or future service to the party should be a criterion for participation. The rules we drew up were very effective in opening up participation to such people, and since 1972 previous party service has been of negligible importance in getting chosen as a delegate to a national convention.

In addition, the McGovern-Fraser Commission wanted to make the national conventions more representative, and we used the term *representative* in the two senses Lengle describes. We certainly wanted to make the conventions more *descriptively* representative. We wanted to have more blacks, we wanted to have more women, and we wanted to have more young people.

But we also wanted to make the conventions more representative in another sense, which has come to be known as *fair reflection* in the jargon of the party rules. It means that we wanted to have the distribution of presidential preferences among the delegates in each state delegation—and therefore in the convention as a whole—fairly reflect the distribution of the presidential preferences of the people who picked the delegates—the people who voted in the presidential primaries or participated in the caucuses and conventions of the nonprimary states. Thus if 52 percent of all the people who voted in the primaries preferred McGovern, then 52 percent of the delegates at the convention should also prefer McGovern. That was our goal.

So we wrote into the rules a whole series of procedures guaranteeing that the process of selecting national convention delegates would also be a process for registering the presidential preferences of persons who chose the delegates. One rule, for example, required that every person trying to become a delegate must make his or her presidential preference known in advance of the selection process so that in deciding whether or not to vote for that person for delegate the voters would ask not "Is he a nice guy?" or "Has he done good work for the party?" but rather "Is he for Humphrey or McGovern?" That way if the person choosing the delegates was for McGovern he would know which delegate to vote for. And as Lengle asserts, the rules worked very well. The delegates' presidential preferences did indeed fairly reflect the voters' preferences.

But the Democrats' rules reforms have had at least two major unanticipated consequences, neither of which is very pleasing to many of the people who wrote those reforms. One is the enormous proliferation of presidential primaries. Let me give you a few statistics. In 1968, before we applied our magic to the presidential nominating system, only sixteen states and the District of Columbia held presidential primaries, and about one-third of all the delegates were chosen or bound by primaries. In 1980 no fewer than thirty-seven states held presidential primaries, and about 80 percent of the delegates were chosen or bound by them. I do not think it is too strong to say that we have now made the national nominating conventions to the presidential nominating process what the electoral college is to the presidential election process. Our nominating conventions are no longer deliberating, decision-making bodies. They are bodies whose function is to register the preferences that are expressed by the voters in presidential primaries. And this is not by happenstance. It is by the rules of the party and the laws of the states. All those rules are intended to make the presidential nominating conventions agencies for registering decisions made by people before the conventions meet.

If that is the case, and I think it is, then it really doesn't matter very much who the delegates are. It doesn't matter whether 50 percent or 20 percent of them are women or blacks or Hispanics or young people or whatever. I have not heard anyone deplore the fact that most of the members of the Electoral College are white males and there aren't enough Hispanics, blacks, or women. Nobody cares because the Electoral College really doesn't do anything except automatically register the decisions made by others. I would argue that the same thing is now true of national party conventions. It no longer matters whether they are representative in the sense of their proportions of women, blacks, and other minority groups.

There is a lot of talk these days about what we ought to do about the presidential nominating process, and many different proposals are being put forward. There are proposals by David Broder and Morris Udall, for example, to have regional primaries, to restrict the number of states that can hold primaries, and so on. Donald Fraser would like to have a rule that the Democratic party convention would allow only fifteen states to select their delegates by direct primaries. But it seems to me that all of these proposals, whatever may be their merits, run sharply counter to a basic movement in American politics that has been very strong in the 1970s and is likely to be even stonger in the 1980s. It is what might be called *born-again progressivism*. It is a movement to abolish or weaken representative institutions of all kinds and replace or supplement them with various devices of direct democracy.

For example, take the institutions of the initiative and the referendum. In the past decade we have seen a greatly increased use of initiative and referendum by the states that already have them and a number of states that have never had them, such as Minnesota, are now considering adopting them. Also there is a bill before the Congress to establish a national initiative and referendum that has approximately twenty-five senators and representatives as sponsors. Although it is not likely to pass in the near future, I think we are going to hear more and more about it.

As for the presidential nominating process, the reform that in my judgment is most likely to be adopted within the next decade or so is a national one-day presidential primary and the abolition of the conventions altogether. There are a number of proposals for such changes before the Congress right now, and while none of them are likely to pass in the near future they do seem to me to be a logical extension of the past reforms and very much in keeping with the mood of the time.

In this regard, it's interesting to note that in 1979 George Gallup published an article entitled "The Six Reforms That Americans Want Most." Two of those reforms, each of which was getting about 70 percent approval in the Gallup polls, were (1) abolition of the national conventions and nomination of presidential candidates by a national one-day primary, and (2) the establishment of a national initiative and referendum.

Let me conclude by emphasizing two points. The first is that in my judgment one of the leading issues in the area of representation and apportionment with which we will be faced in the 1980s will continue to be the presidential nominating process—which indeed might receive more attention than the issues of apportionment and districting for Congress and the state legislatures will receive.

The second point is that much of the discussion of this issue is going to take place—not in a context such as the Conference on Representation and Redistricting Issues, in which everyone seems to believe in representative institutions and wants to perfect them, but in a context of great suspicion of all representative and intermediary institutions because they are seen as getting between the sovereign people and their government. I am not happy with these trends but I believe they are very strong and any discussion of improving representative institutions must take them into account.

**Part IV
Consequences of
Reapportionment**

Introduction to Part IV

Howard A. Scarrow

Within two subfields of political science—comparative national politics and comparative state politics—the 1960s were distinguished by research and writing that denied the primacy of politics and focused instead on the overriding importance of social and economic factors in explaining political outcomes. Perhaps inevitably, by 1970 the stirrings of reaction were clearly visible in both subfields: It was now argued that political variables *were* important.

Nowhere was this dialectic more pronounced than with regard to the question of what impact the Supreme Court's reapportionment decisions had on policy outputs in the American states. Indeed, so conspicuous was the debate that the respective labels *reformers* and *skeptics*, terms first used when the literature was comprehensively reviewed by Bicker (1971), have stuck: Reformers are those who think that reapportionment would (will) make a difference in policy outcomes in the American states, while skeptics are those who deny that such a structural change would make (has made) any difference.

In addition to the several studies that have found that reapportionment *has had* an impact (Saffell's chapter 19, this volume, identifies these), a number of criticisms have been levied at the early studies for their assumptions and their methodology, leading Bicker (1971) to levy the charge of mistrial. Several of these criticisms have been well summarized in a paper by Uslaner and Weber (1979). Drawing upon the writings and perspective of V.O. Key, Jr., Uslaner and Weber argue that the student of policy impact must initially determine what, if any, change reapportionment has made in a state's pattern of political party representation. Only then is he in a position to know whether or not the *potential* exists for policy changes to occur. Uslaner and Weber are also critical of cross-sectional analysis, as used in the early studies, arguing that "Mississippi is not likely to become similar in its policy decisions to Massachusetts even if the apportionment systems of the two states are made as identical as cartographers and politicians might be able to accomplish. Yet, cross-sectional designs require just such assumptions."

It is clear from these various literature reviews, as well as from the two chapters that follow, that the important question of policy impact has not yet been resolved.

19 Reapportionment and Public Policy: State Legislators' Perspectives

David C. Saffell

Since the mid-1960s there has been a continuing and often heated debate among political scientists regarding the question, "Does apportionment make a difference in the nature of public policy in the American states?" This chapter begins with a review of the apportionment literature.[1] In rough chronological order, the literature may be divided into five areas: (1) the reformers, (2) the skeptics,[2] (3) the counterskeptics, (4) case studies of individual states, and (5) a current assessment of the general consensus of thought on the effects of apportionment.

The remainder of the chapter examines the question of the policy impact of reapportionment from the perspective of state senators. This is done as another approach to test the proposition, as expounded by the skeptics, that reapportionment has *not* had a significant effect on the nature of state public policy.

A questionnaire (see appendix 19A) was sent to 224 state senators in the fall of 1979. This represented all the senators in forty-nine states[3] who were in office in 1979 and also were serving in their state's senate in 1967. State senators were selected for study because of the longer terms of senators, which yield more stability and perhaps more noticeable changes than in larger bodies. This, of course, makes them easier to analyze than houses of representatives. In many states both upper and lower houses of state legislatures were unrepresentative of their populations in 1962. The most severe malapportionment in state senates was in Nevada, California, Florida, Maryland, Montana, Idaho, Rhode Island, and New Jersey. The base period 1967 was selected because significant reapportionment in most states occurred after 1964 (*Reynolds* v. *Sims*).[4] Only a few states had reapportioned in the early 1960s. As a result, most changes in policy, especially in states where the typical term of office is four years, could not be expected to take effect until at least the late 1960s or early 1970s (Sokolow, 1976:26). Therefore, those senators in office since 1967 (some, of course were elected prior to 1966) had at least a twelve-year perspective by which to judge the

Much of the work on this chapter was completed while I was a participant in a N.E.H. Summer Seminar in 1979 held at the University of California, Santa Barbara, under the direction of Gordon E. Baker.

before-and-after effects of reapportionment. Moreover, each state senate was reapportioned again in the 1970s. Had the base period been extended prior to the 1966 election year, some states would not have had any senators represented in the sample.

Reformers have been criticized by skeptics because of the impressionistic nature of their speculation on the effects of malapportionment. Skeptics have concluded that when careful empirical study is done of the traditional beliefs that party competition, voter participation, and apportionment have a direct bearing on public policy, they will be seen as "mere strawmen erected for economic determinists to attack" (Dye, 1976:26). Later studies by empiricists have criticized both the skeptics' methods and their conclusions. Others believe that empiricists may overlook important historical, anecdotal, and impressionistic factors. This chapter is an attempt to see how the views of legislators mesh with the impressions of academics as well as with their empirical findings.

The Reapportionment Literature

Reformers

During the period immediately preceding and following the Supreme Court's historic decision in *Baker* v. *Carr*,[5] the "conventional wisdom" among political scientists held that malapportionment did have a significant effect on the substance of state policy (Bicker, 1971:52). Most political scientists believed that political factors, including apportionment, party competition, and voter turnout, had a strong impact on the nature of public policy.

These effects of malapportionment in the states seemed most striking in regard to rural-urban conflict. Gordon E. Baker (1966:61) noted that "Substantial disparities in the distribution of state tax funds frequently seemed directly traceable to the legislative underrepresentation of urban communities." Classic examples of such conflict were cited in such states as Florida and New York (Harvard and Beth, 1962; Baker, 1955). It was suggested that urban underrepresentation in state legislatures was a major factor causing cities to turn to the federal government for direct financial help.

In general, reformers believed that reapportionment would result in more liberal state policies, particularly as they affected cities and minorities (Jewell, 1962; Keefe and Ogul, 1964; Lockard, 1959; Sorauf, 1962). Reformers often assumed that coalitions of nonurban legislators in malapportioned states were acting to withhold liberal benefits in the areas of taxation, welfare, education, and transportation. It was assumed that the greatest impact would be on those states where malapportionment was greatest. Since two-party states were not severely malapportioned prior to 1962-64, it was expected that reapportionment would have a more direct effect in one-party or modified one-party states (Grumm, 1971; Francis, 1967).

In addition, V.O. Key (1956:52-84) contended that malapportionment contributed to divided party control of state legislatures. This was a particular problem for Democratic governors. In New York, for example, Republicans controlled both houses of the state legislature from 1938 to 1965 with at least a 55 percent majority even when Democrats won statewide office. Under this pattern of a Democratic governor and Republican legislature, it was believed that liberal policies suffered in northern states.

Skeptics

The beliefs of the reformers were strongly disputed in a quick succession of studies appearing in the mid-1960s. Done independently and with a common analytic framework of rank-order correlation and cross-tabulation, all of these empirical studies came to the general conclusion that apportionment does not make a significant difference in the substance of state policy. Instead, they concluded (Dye, 1966:293) that: "Differences in policy choices of states with different types of political systems turn out to be largely a product of different socioeconomic levels rather than a direct product of political variables." In approaching the subject of policy analysis, these political scientists were building on the work of economists such as Solomon Fabricant (1950) and a series of studies in the 1950s published in the *National Tax Journal*.

In 1963, Dawson and Robinson reported that political factors such as interparty competition and voter turnout did not have a significant influence on welfare policies (1963:265-289). Instead, as Fabricant had concluded, per-capita income correlated most positively with the liberalness of welfare programs. The following year Herbert Jacob (1964:260) found that: "Our data demonstrates that malapportionment in and of itself is not associated with some of the major ailments of the states." Jacob suggested that many state issues are not settled on the basis of urban-rural divisions, but by temporary coalitions molded by interest groups or strong governors. In the South, where malapportionment had been the worst, Jacob found no more of an effect on policy making than in the North.

Using increasingly sophisticated statistical techniques, Thomas Dye (1965:586-601), Richard Hofferbert (1966:73-82), David Brady, and Douglas Edmonds (1967:41-46) came to similar conclusions. Looking at data from 1952 to 1961, Hofferbert found no relationship between apportionment and levels of welfare, benefits, or state aid to large cities. He did, however, find a strong relationship (0.70) between levels of industrialization and welfare benefits. Dye's approach of examining broad expenditures and revenue variables (education, welfare, taxation) as measures to assess the effects of apportionment is common to the other studies. Also, each of the studies essentially relies on the same measurements of malapportionment (Shubert and Press, 1964). Dye (1971 and 1978) concludes that before *Baker v. Carr* there was no evidence that policy choices differed in well- and malapportioned legislatures and that there is little expectation of better aid to cities now that reapportionment has occurred.

In his examination of congressional redistricting, Edward Tufte (1973:553) found that incumbents became stronger and that party competition declined after reapportionment. There seems to be evidence that the rate of success for incumbents in state legislatures has at least remained equally high following reapportionment. If so, this may support Tufte's (1973:554) conclusion that: "Many redistrictings, although perfectly satisfactory by current legal standards, have produced quite biased and unresponsive electoral systems."

Writing in response to the findings of the counterskeptics, Dye speaks of a "near-panic" among some political scientists to counter the findings of economic determinants of public policy. While noting that governmental institutions and political processes may, in part, affect the content of public policy, Dye notes (1976:31) that "we should not insist that political variables influence policy outcomes simply because our traditional training and wisdom in political science tells us that political variables are important."

Counterskeptics

The conclusions of the skeptics have had a strong influence on subsequent research and writing in the area of reapportionment.[6] After an early period of general acceptance, additional research has led to criticism of both the methodology and conclusions of the skeptics.

In a skeptical study published in 1968, Pulsipher and Weatherby (1968: 1218) found a positive relationship (significant at the level equal to or greater than 80 percent) between malapportionment and total state expenditures, higher education, total public welfare, and housing and urban renewal (Dye and Dyson, 1969; Pulsipher and Weatherby, 1969). Also, contrary to the findings of Dye et al., Fry and Winters (1970:522) concluded that "politics plays a dominant role in the allocation of the burdens and benefits of public policy." In their examination of how state expenditures are distributed among income classes, apportionment was a more significant indicator than median income or levels of industrialization.

Robert B. McKay (1968:230-231) also found that reapportionment had a substantial effect on the nature of state policy. He believed that reapportionment had led to increased state aid for schools, stronger civil rights statutes, more effective pollution control, and stronger consumer protection laws.

The most impressive review of the skeptics' studies has been by William E. Bicker (1971). After examining the evidence they present, Bicker declares a mistrial, contending that the skeptics have failed to make their case. Writing in 1971, Bicker criticizes the skeptics' methods and advances a plan of how adequate tests of the reformers' arguments can be carried out. Briefly, as perceived by Bicker, the skeptics' problems center around (1) their use of measures of malapportionment; (2) their choice of broad expenditure and revenue variables to assess the impact of reapportionment on policy choices; and (3) their techniques of analysis. Bicker (1971:196) states that an adequate test of the reformers' position would be longitudinal, going back to the turn of this century. He suggests that policy analysis should shift from finance to state policy and regulatory powers. Bicker stresses that the choice of policy areas to be studied should be based largely on which interests have been under- and overrepresented.

Two studies completed in the 1970s have followed, at least in part, the Bicker suggestions and have come to conclusions that differ from those of the skeptics. Hanson and Crew (1973:86) studied policy making in fifteen states, comparing their expenditures before reapportionment with expenditures during the first legislative session after reapportionment. Using unstandardized regression coefficients, they found that in thirty-nine of seventy-five instances (52 percent) there was a policy change in those states that were reapportioned by 1965. In the nonreapportioned states there was a policy change in 62 of 165 instances (37 percent). Policy changes (that is, higher spending) in reapportioned states were most noticeable in the areas of highways and hospitals. State aid to cities increased in 10 of 29 instances (34 percent) in reapportioned states compared to 18 of 73 (23 percent) in nonreapportioned states. Hanson and Crew (1973:88) found the percentage of difference between the two groups of states in aid to cities discouraging. Their data suggest that one result of reapportionment was passage of policy favorable to suburban areas. This, of course, is where the greatest increase in numbers of legislators occurred.

Frederickson's and Cho's (1974:18) detailed study of the effects of reapportionment followed the Dye pattern of analyzing total state spending in reapportioned states while plugging in control variables for such factors as party participation, governor's power, economic development, and legislative professionalism. They found that reapportionment did not significantly alter spending patterns in the period 1957-1962. However, their later data showed that in 1969 the distribution of state funds was positively correlated with apportionment for eleven of fourteen functional items. Frederickson and Cho found that longer experience with reapportionment is associated with higher spending for education, public health, hospitals, and highways. They also found that there was a positive linkage between some nonfiscal policies and reapportionment. Reapportionment improved legislative responsiveness to the views of the majority of the electorate on civil rights, firearms control, and public employee labor rights (Rae, 1971). Frederickson and Cho conclude that reapportionment does result in changes in the direction of urban interests.[7]

Timothy O'Rourke (1980:151) comes to more modest conclusions regarding the impact of reapportionment. O'Rourke suggests that we should expect a substantial impact only in a few states where there was severe malapportionment and weak two-party systems. In his study of the Delaware, Kansas, New Jersey, Oregon, South Dakota, and Tennessee legislatures (based on the period 1962-1974), he found extensive change only in Kansas and Tennessee. He concludes that "reapportionment has affected selected policies in all sample states, but that the overall influence of reapportionment on policy has been rather limited and immeasurable." The O'Rourke study is referred to in more detail in the second section of this chapter.

Other studies of a different nature (not focusing on expenditure patterns) also have confirmed many of the predictions of the reformers. Robert Erikson's (1971:64-65) study of the partisan effect of reapportionment (1952-1968) in northern states found that, overall, Democrats gained 2.9 percent more seats. East of the Mississippi River the Democratic gain was 7.4 percent; in the West, Democrats lost 2.7 percent. Since Democrats gained most in urban states, Erickson predicts that more liberal policy should result and the frequency of divided government should decline.

In his study of the California senate (the worst apportioned legislative body before 1965), Bruce Robeck (1972:1254-1255) found that there was a significant increase in party voting cohesion after reapportionment. Robeck's findings support the earlier positions of Malcolm Jewell (1966:75) and Thomas Flinn (1964:71) who argued that reapportionment would stimulate changes in the nature of party competition and responsiveness. In his study of party politics in Ohio, Flinn (1964) concluded that increased party responsibility in the states was dependent "on the spread of party competition and upon a sorting out of legislative constituencies so that districts represented by the respective parties are homogeneous."

Studying innovation among the states, Jack Walker (1969:886) found a positive correlation between apportionment and willingness to innovate during the period 1930-1966. Walker notes that "those states which grant their urban areas full representation in the legislature seem to adopt new ideas more rapidly, on the average, than states which discriminate against their cities" (1969:887).

Individual State Studies

In general, the large number of single state studies conclude that reapportioned states became more responsive to urban needs and their spending patterns became more liberal. In California, Sokolow (1976) found that farm labor, metropolitan areas, civil rights, and consumers benefited from changes in legislative policy. Significantly, Sokolow concludes that it took two or three sessions after reapportionment in 1965 for legislative changes to occur. This is so because of the timelag for new legislators to gain power and for internal mechanisms to change. This suggests that studies based on data limited to the 1960s would invariably conclude that the impact of reapportionment was negligible.

Studies in southern, one-party states found significant changes after legislatures were reapportioned. For example, Hawkins' (1971) study of Georgia concluded that urban areas received more favorable treatment, that there was an increase in the number of black legislatures, and there was greater turnover after reapportionment. A similar situation occurred in Florida. Some research has shown a more modest impact in two-party states such as New York, Colorado, and Illinois (Lehne, 1972; Furness, 1973; Grove, 1973:105-113). However, David (1972) found that reapportionment in Connecticut helped Democrats gain control of the lower house for only the second time since 1900.

Clearly, it was urban areas that gained representation following reapportionment. In California, for example, Los Angeles County had one state senator in 1962 and by 1966 it had fifteen. Hartford, Connecticut, had two assemblymen in 1962 and ten in 1967. Policy changes in the direction of urban interests in reapportioned states included labor law reform in Iowa and Delaware, prison reform in Vermont, and tax reform in Florida. Although he cautions against overstating the effects of reapportionment, Duane Lockard (1969:293) states that:

> (T)here is no question that the atmosphere and operations of the New Jersey legislature were enormously different in the two years following reapportionment . . . reapportionment helped give Democrats overwhelming control of the Senate. The result was an avalanche of long-held-back legislation. While apportionment alone was not the cause of this it was a necessary contributing factor.

Current Assessment

Although reformers in the early 1960s may have overstated the anticipated benefits of reapportionment, much of what they predicted has occurred. Empirical studies in the 1970s consistently have concluded that state legislatures have become more responsive to majority will.

As Samuel Patterson (1976:155) notes, reapportionment has increased the number of younger, better educated, and ethnic minority members in state legislatures. In reviewing the literature, Patterson concludes that reapportionment has stimulated party competition and fostered a greater degree of party voting in state legislatures. Patterson finds a stronger incidence of rural versus urban voting in state legislatures. The increase in urban representatives has resulted in more liberal, urban-oriented policy.

Clearly reapportionment has not cured all the political ills that affected the states prior to 1962. Yet not even the most optimistic of the reformers suggested that it would. While it may not be the single most important influence on state policy, reapportionment has been shown to play a definite role in the substance of state legislation. Certainly more study remains to be done on the effects of both political (apportionment, party competition, voter turnout, gubernatorial powers, legislative professionalism) and economic factors on state policy making. Both skeptics and counterskeptics have realized, however, that even if one concludes that economic factors are more important than political factors, this does not mean that political factors are unimportant.

The Views of State Senators

In this survey, questionnaires were sent to 224 state senators. This represented all those persons serving in 1979 who had also been in office in 1967 (see table 19-1). The response rate was 64.7 percent.

Although state senates had been reapportioned several times by 1979 and gross malapportionment no longer existed, no senate except Iowa had reached perfect equality in the size of senate districts. For example, in Wyoming senate districts varied in percent deviation in actual versus average population per seat from + 27.9 to − 21.6 (*Book of the States 1978-79*, 1978:14). Senates varied in size from sixty-seven seats in Minnesota to twenty in Alaska and Nevada. In California, each senator represented 499,322 people; in Wyoming each senator represented 11,080 people. While most states had single-member districts, thirteen states had multimember senate districts.

The responses from senators in each of the states are summarized in table 19-1. Because there often was disagreement among senators from the same state, many of the responses are presented in percentage form. If all responding senators in a state were in agreement on a particular response (for example, partisan benefits), the state score was 1.00. If there were differences of opinion, the state score might be .33 Democratic, .33 Republican, and .33 no change. Averages were based on the percentage scores for states, not on the responses of individual senators.

While it was expected that senators would differ on their evaluation of policy impact, it is curious that their perceptions of the partisan impact of reapportionment often are contradictory. Other inconsistencies can be seen in the areas of urban-rural benefits and liberal-conservative direction. For example, Indiana senators indicated that policy had become more conservative and benefits were increased to urban areas. In Vermont, survey data showed that senators believed policy had become more liberal and aid to rural areas was increased.

Policy Impact: More Liberal or More Conservative

The survey data, based on state responses, revealed the following distribution of attitudes concerning the direction of state policy after reapportionment:

More liberal	51.75 percent of the states
More conservative	14.5 percent of the states
No difference	33.8 percent of the states

Clearly, policies were perceived to have become more liberal. In only nine states (Alaska, Arizona, Arkansas, Delaware, Hawaii, Indiana, Missouri, New Mexico, and South Carolina) did any of the respondents indicate that policy had become more conservative. O'Rourke (1980:132) also found that legislators in each of the six states he studied believed that more liberal legislation was introduced and adopted after reapportionment. The O'Rourke (1980:163-168) questionnaire was sent out in 1973 to all legislators in his six sample states. His overall rate of return was 43 percent.

O'Rourke cautions that in this area legislators are being asked to identify changes in policy and recognize the causes of change. Moreover, as noted by several respondents, there may have been any number of intervening factors that affected the nature of state policy. It is very difficult to separate the effects of reapportionment from other factors such as national political trends or changes in patterns of federal aid. Still, most senators were willing to say that they believed state policy had become more liberal.

In this survey, one senator from Arkansas noted that voting in his state has been confusing since reapportionment. He commented that: "The state is very conservative, but elected liberal governors after Faubus. People wanted to get rid of liberal Fulbright, but replaced him with even more liberal former governor Bumpers." A senator from Pennsylvania believed that greater representation given to suburban areas (at the expense of rural areas) had resulted in more liberal legislation in "moral" fields such as authorized gambling, a state lottery, and relaxed liquor laws. In Ohio, the reapportioned legislature passed a state income tax.

An interesting situation occurred in Hawaii. There the senator responding believed that rural areas have been more liberal because of the strong

Table 19-1
Response from State Senators

State	Difference in Policy: More Liberal or More Conservative	Urban-Rural Benefits	Democratic or Republican Gains	Effects on Tenure	Number of Senators in office, 1967-1979	Number of Respondents
Alabama	1.0 no difference	1.0 no difference	1.0 no change	1.0 no change	1	1
Alaska	1.0 more conservative	1.0 more rural	1.0 no change	1.0 no change	1	1
Arizona	1.0 more conservative	1.0 more urban	1.0 Republicans	1.0 no change	1	1
Arkansas	.60 more liberal / .40 more conservative	.60 more urban / .40 more rural	1.0 no change	1.0 no change	11	5
California	1.0 more liberal	1.0 more urban	.67 no change / .33 Democrats	.67 shorter / .33 longer	9	4[a]
Colorado	1.0 no difference	1.0 more urban	1.0 no change	1.0 shorter	2	1
Connecticut	1.0 no difference	1.0 more urban	1.0 Democrats	1.0 no change	2	2
Delaware	1.0 more conservative	1.0 more urban	1.0 no change	1.0 no change	2	1
Florida	1.0 more liberal	1.0 more urban	1.0 Republicans	1.0 shorter	1	1
Georgia	.50 more liberal	.75 no difference	.37 Democrats / .37 no change / .26 Republicans	.62 no change / .38 longer	10	8
Hawaii	1.0 more conservative	1.0 more urban	1.0 Republicans	1.0 shorter	3	1
Idaho	.50 more liberal / .50 no change	1.0 more urban	.50 Republicans / .50 no change	.67 no change / .33 shorter	6	6
Illinois	.67 more liberal / .33 no change	.67 urban up / .33 rural up	.67 Democrats / .33 no change	1.0 no change	4	3
Indiana	1.0 more conservative	1.0 more urban	1.0 no change	1.0 no change	2	1
Iowa	1.0 no difference	1.0 no difference	1.0 Democrats	1.0 no change	1	1
Kansas	.75 more liberal / .25 no change	1.0 urban up	1.0 Democrats	.50 no change / .50 shorter	4	4
Kentucky	1.0 more liberal	1.0 no difference	1.0 no change	1.0 no change	2	1
Louisiana	1.0 more liberal	1.0 more urban	1.0 no change	1.0 no change	7	4
Maine	.50 more liberal / .50 no difference	.50 more urban / .50 no difference	.50 Democrats / .50 no change	1.0 no change	2	2

State						
Massachusetts	1.0 more liberal	1.0 more urban	1.0 Democrats	.50 no change / .50 longer	4	2
Michigan	.75 more liberal / .25 no change	.75 more urban / .25 more rural	1.0 Democrats	1.0 no change	6	4
Minnesota	1.0 more liberal	.50 more urban / .50 more rural	.50 Democrats / .50 Republicans	1.0 shortened	3	2
Mississippi	.86 more liberal / .14 no change	.57 more urban / .43 no change	.57 Republicans / .43 no change	1.0 shortened	11	7
Missouri	.67 liberal / .33 conservative	.67 urban / .33 rural	.67 no change / .33 Democrats	.67 no change / .33 shorter	4	3
Montana	1.0 more liberal	1.0 more urban	.67 Democrats / .33 no change	.67 no change / .33 shorter	5	3
Nevada	.50 no change / .50 more liberal	.50 no change / .50 more urban	1.0 Democrats	.50 no change / .50 shorter	4	2
New Hampshire	.50 more liberal / .50 no change	1.0 no change	1.0 Democrats	1.0 no change	4	2
New Jersey	1.0 more liberal	1.0 more urban	1.0 Democrats	1.0 no change	1	1
New Mexico	.50 more liberal / .50 more conservative	.75 more urban / .25 more rural	.50 Democrats / .25 Republican / .25 no change	1.0 no change	4	4
New York	.50 more liberal / .50 no change	1.0 more urban	.75 no change / .25 Democrats	.75 shorter / .25 no change	12	5[b]
North Carolina	.67 more liberal / .33 no change	.67 urban / .33 no change	.67 no change / .33 Democrats	1.0 no change	5	3
North Dakota	.55 more liberal / .45 no change	.77 more urban / .23 no change	.44 Republicans / .33 no change / .23 Democrats	.77 no change / .23 shorter	9	9
Ohio	1.0 more liberal	1.0 more urban	1.0 Democrats	1.0 no change	4	2
Oklahoma	.57 no change / .43 more liberal	1.0 more urban	.85 Republicans / .15 no change	.57 no change / .43 shorter	11	7
Oregon	.67 no change / .33 more liberal	.67 more urban / .33 no change	.67 Democrats / .33 no change	.67 no change / .33 shorter	4	3
Pennsylvania	.33 more liberal / .50 more liberal / .50 no change	.33 no change / .50 more urban / .50 no change	.33 no change / 1.0 Democrats	.33 shorter / .50 no change / .50 shorter	6	4
Rhode Island	.67 more liberal / .33 no change	.67 no change / .33 more urban	.67 no change / .33 Democrats	.67 no change / .33 shorter	5	3

Table 19-1 *(continued)*

State	Difference in Policy: More Liberal or More Conservative	Urban-Rural Benefits	Democratic or Republican Gains	Effects on Tenure	Number of Senators in office, 1967-1979	Number of Respondents
South Carolina	.75 more liberal .25 more conservative	.67 more urban .33 no change	.50 Republicans .25 no change .25 Democrats	.50 shorter .50 no change	10	4
South Dakota	1.0 no change	1.0 more urban	1.0 no change	1.0 no change	2	1
Tennessee	.50 no change .50 more liberal	.50 no change .50 more urban	.50 no change .50 Republicans	1.0 no change	5	2
Texas	.60 more liberal .40 no change	1.0 more urban	.60 Republicans .40 no change	.60 no change .40 shorter	5	5
Utah	1.0 no change	.75 no change .25 more urban	.75 Republicans .25 Democrats	1.0 no change	4	3
Vermont	1.0 more liberal	1.0 more urban	1.0 no change	1.0 no change	1	1
Virginia	1.0 more liberal	.67 more urban .33 more rural	.67 no change .33 Republican	1.0 no change	5	3
Washington	.50 more liberal .50 no change	1.0 more urban	.50 Republicans .50 Democrats	1.0 no change	5	2
West Virginia	1.0 no change	1.0 no change	.50 Democrats .50 no change	1.0 no change	5	4
Wisconsin	.50 more liberal .50 no change	.50 more urban .50 no change	1.0 Democrats	.67 no change .33 shorter	5	4
Wyoming	1.0 no change	.50 more urban .50 no change	.50 no change .50 Democrats	1.0 no change	2	2
Total					222	145

Note: The author wishes to thank Paul D. Saffell for his research assistance.

[a]One senator said it was his policy never to respond to surveys.

[b]One senator was ill at time of survey.

influence of organized labor in agriculture. Urban areas have been more conservative in fiscal matters and they gained representatives after reapportionment. Thus the effect of reapportionment was to push state policy in a conservative direction.

Bicker (1971) suggests a four-step effect of reapportionment. Step one is a change in legislator-constituency relations that occurs almost automatically in all reapportioned states. Step two is a change in the partisan balance and a change in urban-rural conflict. Step three is a change in legislative procedure, including the operation of committees. Step four is a change in policy outcomes. Thus for policy outcomes to change, they must be preceeded by changes in steps one, two, and three. While this study did not examine changes in legislative procedure, the areas that follow do give a picture of changes regarding legislator-constituent relations, gains or losses by Democrats and Republicans, and urban-rural benefits.

Urban-Rural Benefits

State responses were as follows:

More aid to urban areas	65.3 percent of the states
More aid to rural areas	8.4 percent of the states
No difference	26.3 percent of the states

Only in Alaska and Vermont were senators in agreement that rural areas had received more state aid after reapportionment. Some senators in six other states believed that rural areas had received an increase in state aid. In contrast, senators in twenty states agreed that urban areas had received more aid. Some senators in twenty other states responded that aid to urban areas had increased.

O'Rourke (1971) found that aid to urban areas had increased in New Jersey, Delaware, and Kansas, but there was little change in Oregon, South Dakota, and Tennessee. However, he believed that only in Kansas had reapportionment led directly to an increase in urban assistance.

In this survey a Kansas legislator noted: "it has taken some time for urban legislators to realize they must forget their hatred and distrust of other urban areas and unite to fleece the 'Cowboys,' as rural legislators are called here. The last couple of years they have altered state aid distribution formulas in various ways that make rural areas . . . help support urban services . . ."

In New York, a senator noted that the state's "Big Five" (New York City, Buffalo, Rochester, Syracuse, and Yonkers) now get "overburden" aid and New York City gets a variety of extra payments. A California senator believed that there was a neglect of rural areas in his state.

In each of the two states reporting less aid to urban areas, only one seantor responded. In Alaska, the respondent noted that aid had "perhaps slightly tilted to rural."

Democratic or Republican Gains

Here the state responses were the most evenly divided of any category:

Democratic gains	41.3 percent of the states
Republican gains	19.6 percent of the states
No change	39.1 percent of the states

Senators in sixteen states reported Republican gains. Seven of those states (Florida, Georgia, Mississippi, South Carolina, Tennessee, Texas, and Virginia) were in the South. The other states were in the Southwest (Arizona, Oklahoma, and New Mexico), West (Hawaii, Idaho, Utah, and Washington), and North Central (Minnesota and North Dakota). Democratic gains came primarily in the East and Midwest.

These findings are consistent with those of Robert Erickson, referred to earlier in this chapter. They also conform to predictions made by Malcolm Jewell (1962:28-29) that the urban-based Republican party would gain seats in the South and Southwest. O'Rourke found the most obvious change was in Tennessee, where Republican gains were made. In this study, one Tennessee senator reported Republican gains and one saw no change. O'Rourke reported some Republican increases in Delaware and New Jersey and a Democratic increase in Kansas—those findings are generally supported in this survey. In Ohio, it was noted that both the House and Senate went from two-thirds Republican to two-thirds Democratic after reapportionment.

Caution should be exercised here because senators often reported an early shift to one party and then a return to the other party by the state's voters. For example, one senator noted that: "Since 1963 the Delaware legislative political alignment has swung from one party to the other. Both political parties draw district lines to give them an edge—and the voters vote their choice and upset the best conceived political plans."

Length of Tenure

This area showed only modest effects from reapportionment:

Shorter tenure	23.9 percent of the states
Longer tenure	2.5 percent of the states
No change	73.6 percent of the states

Longer tenure was reported only in California, Georgia, and Massachusetts. However, shorter tenure also was reported in California. Only in Colorado, Hawaii, Minnesota, Mississippi, and Nevada were senators agreed that tenure had been shortened.

While Minnesota and Mississippi legislators believed that tenure had been shortened, they attributed the change to factors other than reapportionment. The change to single-member districts in Mississippi was mentioned by one senator as a cause of shorter tenure. The change from four-year terms to two-year terms in Minnesota was cited as a reason for shorter terms.

Still, many senators saw a direct cause-and-effect relationship. A Mississippi senator noted: "There has been more turnover—I was defeated for reelection in 1979 as a result of current reapportionment." In Idaho, one senator pointed out that reapportionment had had the effect of overturning three-fourths of the legislature. Only two of thirty-five Idaho senators had survived since the 1965 reapportionment and only ten of thirty-five were left since the 1970 reapportionment. In Colorado, it was suggested that new urban legislators cannot devote as many years to public service as could retired or rural farmers who had served in the senate. A California senator noted that: "Reapportionment appears to have had an impact on length of tenure in the Senate . . . . The average tenure in the Senate is 5.7 years. The average tenure prior to 1966 was probably 8 years or more."

A Tennessee senator found no change in length of tenure, commenting that "new districts most always have the approval of the incumbent Senator it affects, thus there is no threat to them." A cynical (or realistic) Texas legislator noted little change in length of tenure. It was his opinion that: "We did get rid of a few fossils on the first go around and now we are fossilizing new ones." Another Texan noted that some state legislators had left to serve on the Houston city council. In Houston, a court-ordered plan created single-member council districts and the salary of $20,000 per year was more attractive than $7,200 per year in the state legislature.

O'Rourke reports that there was more turnover in five of the six states he studied. He reported little change in Tennessee. In this survey, all senators in Delaware, New Jersey, and South Dakota agreed that there had not been a change in length of tenure following reapportionment. No change in length of tenure would appear to indicate little change in the rate of turnover among legislators.

Summary

Relatively few of the respondents answered the last question regarding a possible delay after reapportionment before policy changes occurred. As a result, that information is not reported.

Table 19-2
Changes in Worst-Apportioned State Senates

State	More Liberal Policy	More Urban Aid	Partisan Change	Shorter Tenure
Nevada	.50	no change	Dem. 1.00	.50
California	1.00	1.00	Dem. .33	.67
Florida	1.00	1.00	Rep. 1.00	1.00
Maryland	no response			
Montana	1.00	1.00	Dem. 67	.33
Idaho	.50	1.00	Rep. .50	.33
Rhode Island	.67	.33	Dem. .33	.33
New Jersey	1.00	1.00	Dem. 1.00	.00

In general, these data support the contentions of the reformers that more liberal policy would result from reapportionment and aid to urban areas would increase. Clearly, state senators believe that reapportionment has made a substantial impact on their states. In the seven states identified as having the worst apportioned senates in 1962, the changes as shown in table 19-2 were identified.

In the seven best apportioned state senates, the pattern was as shown in table 19-3.

The most significant difference between well- and poorly apportioned states is the very limited change in length of tenure among senators in well-apportioned states. In contrast to well-apportioned states, poorly apportioned states showed a higher degree of liberalization, including a greater likelihood of increased aid to urban areas. The Democratic party gained seats in both groups of states.

State senators are more willing than most political scientists to connect policy changes in their states to reapportionment. It is clear that the general trend of their responses supports the position of the counterskeptics as well as the findings of most case studies of individual states. Although it is difficult to separate impact of reapportionment from other economic and political factors, our survey data indicate that many state senators believe that reapportionment has had a direct impact on state legislative policy.

Table 19-3
Changes in Best-Apportioned State Senates

State	More Liberal Policy	More Urban Aid	Partisan Change	Shorter Tenure
Oregon	.33	.67	Dem. .67	.33
Missouri	.67	.67	Dem. .33	.33
Vermont	1.00	.67	Dem. 1.00	.00
Maine	.50	.50	Dem. .50	.00
West Virginia	.00	.00	Dem. .50	.00
New Hampshire	.50	.00	Dem. 1.00	.00
Wisconsin	.50	.50	Dem. 1.00	.33

Notes

1. For an extensive bibliography of the apportionment literature see Cho and Frederickson (1976:122-139).

2. The terms *reformers* and *skeptics* are used by Bicker (1971).

3. Nebraska was excluded because its unicameral legislature makes comparison with other states difficult.

4. Reynolds v. Sims (1964) 377 U.S. 533.

5. Baker v. Carr (1962) 369 U.S. 186.

6. One text, Adrian (1960) and (1967), made a major shift from a reformer position in the first edition to a skeptic position in the second edition. In the fourth edition (1976), Adrian continues to support the position that reapportionment has had little impact on policy. Citing Dye (1965:319) he adds the sentence, "Research to date indicates that reapportionment may not greatly affect policy outputs."

7. Also see Firestine, 1971, which is noted in Cho and Frederickson (1976:95-98). Firestine found that state aid in reapportioned states increased to both central-city and suburban county areas in the period 1962-1968.

Appendix 19A:
State Reapportionment
Study

Name:

State:

Year first elected to the Senate:

1. Have you perceived any differences in the nature of state policy following reapportionment? For example, has legislation in areas such as welfare, education, and taxation become more conservative or more liberal?

2. Have urban areas received more or less state aid, as compared to rural areas, since reapportionment?

3. Have Republicans or Democrats gained seats since reapportionment?

4. Has reapportionment affected the length of tenure for state senators?

5. If changes have occurred, was there a delay after the first reapportionment before this happened?

Note: The questionnaire was mailed to all state senators on September 16, 1979. It was mailed again on October 29, 1979, to all those who had not responded. A third questionnaire was sent on December 10, 1979, only to senators in those states where there had not been a response or there was only a very limited response.

20 The Impact of Reapportionment on Party Representation in the State of New York

Howard A. Scarrow

Because the malapportionment of state legislatures was for many years the subject of comment by political scientists, it was to be expected that once court-ordered reapportionment occurred, analysts would set about trying to measure its impact. It soon became apparent, however, that the question was not easily to be answered, and reviews of the early literature are surely correct in observing that in their initial rush to judgment political scientists were unduly negative in their conclusions.[1] In particular, by expecting to find measurable policy differences without first inquiring into the more immediate, first-order differences of interest and party representation, they chose a sure formula for finding negative results. Indeed, as two critics have noted, if these early studies found that there *had* been a change in public policy after reapportionment, yet found that there had been *no* change in patterns of interest and/or party representation, the discovered relationships between reapportionment and policy change would probably have been spurious (Uslaner and Weber, 1977).

Benefiting from the lessons of these early inquiries, this chapter focuses exclusively on the impact of reapportionment on political party representation. For years the subjects of malapportionment and unequal party representation were virtually synonomous, either when discussed by political scientists, such as V.O. Key, Jr., or by reformers, such as Governor Al Smith, often quoted for his remark that New York was "constitutionally Republican." It is entirely fitting, therefore, that studies of the impact of reapportionment begin with this aspect of the representation process. The topic of this chapter is a single state, New York, a state that often was cited as one of the most conspicuous examples of malapportionment and provided one of the companion cases before the Supreme Court when it rendered its verdict in *Reynolds* v. *Sims*.[2] We shall look for differences in patterns of party representation before and after reapportionment—that is, before 1966 and after. Among the advantages to be derived from focusing on a single state is avoidance of the problems that are inherent in cross-sectional analysis. Equally important, a one-state focus allows us to go be-

The author wishes to acknowledge the support of National Science Foundation Grant #SOC 77-24474, Program in Political Science, and the computer assistance of Jean Scarrow.

yond the limited sample of election outcomes—usually one election before reapportionment and one immediately after—that has characterized other before-and-after studies. Altogether, we present the outcome of fourteen elections: seven elections prior to reapportionment (1952-1964), and seven elections after (1966-1978). Although there is probably no such thing as a typical election result, a variety of election outcomes will allow us to "smooth out" the effects of the many idiosyncratic factors that are present in any one particular election—the Goldwater candidacy in 1964 is an obvious example—and thereby to achieve a perspective on the apportionment-districting system itself. Also, a variety of elections *within* each of the two apportionment periods will allow us to note differences in outcomes with the apportionment system held constant and thus to see the limitations of this one factor as an explanation of these outcomes.

We shall approach the subject of party representation from three perspectives: (1) legislative balance; (2) proportionality of seats and votes; (3) responsiveness to shifts in voter preferences.

Party Balance within the Legislature

Some studies of the impact of reapportionment on party representation have focused on the balance of partisan division within the state legislature (O'Rourke, 1980; Brady and Murray, 1972), while others have focused on the balance of partisan division within the individual legislative districts (Tufte, 1973). We shall begin our analysis with the former perspective.

Before proceeding, however, it is necessary to clarify what we mean when we speak of "the impact of reapportionment." New York state had a constitution that (a) carefully spelled out the formula by which each legislative house was to be reapportioned—the formula having been adopted in 1894 and faithfully adhered to thereafter; and (b) mandated that reapportionment should take place after each decennial census—this provision having been added in 1931 and also faithfully adhered to thereafter. For New York, then, there is no doubt that reapportionment would have taken place after the 1960 census, and there is no doubt what, absent *Reynolds* v. *Sims*, the resulting map would have looked like. The question of what impact *Reynolds* has had on New York state, therefore, must be answered in terms of a comparison between the maps that would have appeared after the 1960 census and the 1970 census, and the equal-population maps that did appear as the result of Supreme Court intervention.

Unfortunately this comparative methodology has not always been followed, with at least one serious consequence. The National Municipal League-sponsored publication on the impact of reapportionment in New York seemed to confirm the often-stated generalization that the big winners of reapportionment were the suburbs, not the central cities. The study pointed out that representation in the State Assembly from the suburbs surrounding New York City increased after reapportionment from sixteen seats (1964) to twenty-six seats (1966), a healthy gain of ten seats. In contrast, New York City increased its representation by a modest three seats, from sixty-five to sixty-eight (Lehne, 1972:5). When we pose the question that should have been asked, which is, how many seats each region gained or lost as a result of the change from the 1894 formula to equal-population districts, the answer is entirely different (see table 20-1). Because of population movement, the suburbs were slated to gain six seats even under the old formula. Thus only four of their ten-seat gain could be attributed to the Court's ruling. On the other hand, New York City had lost population, so that its share of assembly seats was slated, under the old formula, to decrease from sixty-five to fifty-seven, rather than increase, as it did to sixty-eight. It was New York City, therefore, that was the big winner from the Court's ruling—just as political scientists of the 1940s and 1950s had predicted. After the 1970 census the city's gain was even more impressive, a full thirteen seats.[3]

With this perspective in mind, we are now in a position to inquire into the impact of the Court-ordered formula on party representation in the state legislature. Since party strength is highly correlated with geographical region, we can offer a reasonably accurate estimate of what party representation would have been like after each election had the 1894 formula been used. Table 20-2 compares these estimates for the assembly[4] with the actual election outcomes during the 1970s. It will be seen that the Democrats were clearly the beneficiaries of the new formula, consistently winning about ten more seats than they probably would have won under the old formula. These ten seats had profound impact. From 1920 until the Democratic landslide of 1964 the Democrats had won majority control of the assembly only once (in 1934). Beginning with 1966, however, the Democrats won control of the assembly in four of the next seven elections. On two of those four occasions, 1966 and 1978 (only the latter shown in table 20-2), the result almost certainly stemmed directly from the change in the apportionment formula. The contribution of that change to legislative party balance—the senate has remained Republican—is thus apparent. As table 20-2 also makes clear, however, even under the old formula the Democrats apparently would have won control of the assembly in both 1974 and 1976. A better perspective on Democratic performance, therefore, is provided by looking at seat-vote ratios.

Seat-Vote Ratios

The most revealing method for assessing the impact of reapportionment on party representation is to look at its impact on seat-vote ratios. Although

Table 20-1
The Impact of Change of Apportionment Formula on Regional Representation in New York State Assembly

Region[a]	1950 Census	1960 Census			1970 Census		
	Actual 1894 Formula	Projected 1894 Formula	Actual Equal Population	Difference	Projected 1894 Formula	Actual Equal Population	Difference
New York City	65	57	68	+11	52	65	+13
Four New York City suburban counties[b]	16	22	26	+ 4	26	30	+ 4
Fourteen populous upstate counties[c]	31	33	34	+ 1	34	37	+ 3
Thirty-nine rural upstate counties	38	38	22	−16	38	18	−20

Source: 1960 figures are taken from Ruth Silva "Apportionment of the New York State Legislature," *American Political Science Review* 55 (1961):880. The 1970 figures are calculated on the basis of 1970 census figures, using the formula laid down in the New York State Constitution, and the so-called Brown formula (see National Municipal League 1962. Compendium on Legislative Apportionment, New York).

[a]The four-fold classification does not exactly fit the post-1966 equal-population apportionment maps. Accordingly, where several counties or parts of counties are now included in a single district, classification of the district is based on the nature of the predominant county or counties within that district.

[b]Nassau, Suffolk, Rockland, Westchester.

[c]Albany, Broome, Chautauqua, Dutchess, Erie, Monroe, Niagara, Oneida, Onondaga, Orange, Rensselaer, St. Lawrence, Schenectady, Ulster. These are counties that had population of 100,000 or more in 1960. By the 1970 census, three additional counties had reached this size (Chemung, Oswego, and Saratoga); however, these are shown in the table as part of the thirty-nine rural upstate counties for both census years.

Table 20-2
Estimated Impact of Change of Apportionment Formula on Party Representation in New York State Assembly

Region		1972 Actual	1972 Projected	1972 Difference	1974 Actual	1974 Projected	1974 Difference	1976 Actual	1976 Projected	1976 Difference	1978 Actual	1978 Projected	1978 Difference
New York City	D	53	42		56	45		58	46		58	46	
	R	12	10		9	7		7	6		7	6	
Four New York City suburbs	D	4	3		9	8		12	10		9	8	
	R	26	23		21	18		18	16		21	18	
Fourteen populous upstate counties	D	10	9		23	21		20	18		19	17	
	R	27	25		14	13		17	16		18	17	
Thirty-nine rural upstate counties	D	0	4		0	5		0	6		0	3	
	R	18	34		18	33		18	32		18	35	
Total	D	67	58	+9	88	79	+9	90	80	+10	86	74	+12
	R	83	92	−9	62	71	−9	60	70	−10	64	76	−12

Note: For the thirty-nine rural upstate counties, the projected results are based on the outcomes of the assembly elections within each county. For the other three regions (where reapportionment resulted in an increase in the number of legislative districts), the projected results are derived by applying the actual party seat proportions to the smaller number of districts that would have existed under the 1894 apportionment formula. The figures in boxes represent the party winning majority control.

Americans are not as accustomed as those who live under parliamentary systems to focus on seat-vote relationships, in a state like New York it is entirely appropriate to do so. In New York relatively cohesive political parties square off each year in legislative battle, party leaders in the legislature exercise great power and influence, and the party labels on election day usually correctly signal distinctive orientations and policy preferences. As a result, there are important policy implications stemming from whether one party or the other party wins majority control of one (or both) of the legislative houses. Even when a party fails to gain majority control, its proportion of seats may still be important; the outcome of many legislative votes is not certain, either because party discipline breaks down or because discipline is not imposed, and thus it matters whether Democratic-oriented or Republican-oriented legislators answer the roll call.

The focus on seat-vote relationships pertains to what one author has usefully labeled *collective representation* as contrasted with one-district or *dyadic representation* (Weissberg, 1978). In single-member-plurality systems of election a citizen's vote is liable to be wasted, either because he lives in a district in which his party is on the long end of a 90 percent-10 percent margin, or one in which his party is on the short end of a 49 percent-51 percent margin. Thus it is necessary that we examine the preferences of Democrats and Republicans as respective collectivities and be concerned that those preferences are appropriately reflected in the number of legislative seats won. Terms such as *collective representation* or *seat-vote relationships* were usually not used by critics of malapportionment (such as Key and Governor Smith); nevertheless, it is apparent that such critics clearly had these concepts in mind.

The history of the two-party[5] seat-vote relationships in the pre- and the post-reapportionment periods is shown in table 20-3. It will immediately be seen that there are striking differences in the *direction* and the *size* of the disproportionalities between the two periods. For the assembly, the normally heavily anti-Democratic disproportionalities have been eliminated; today the disproportionalities are more likely to be at the expense of the Republicans than the Democrats. For the senate, the formerly large anti-Democratic disproportionalities have been reduced to ones of modest size.

There are, however, a number of major difficulties with this method of analysis, ones that require that we push our inquiry further. First, the normal clustering of partisan voters makes it extremely unlikely that there ever will be an exact proportionality between seats and votes. It is not at all clear, therefore, at what point we are justified in concluding that seat-vote disproportionalities are reflective of a deliberate *bias* in the apportionment-districting system rather than being simply the product of the chance distribution of partisan strength. Related to this question is the finding of a number of scholars that in single-member-plurality elections the majority

Table 20-3
Proportionality of Seats and Votes: Democratic Proportion of Two-Party Vote and Seats Won, New York State Senate and Assembly Elections, 1952-1978
(percent)

Year	Senate			Assembly		
	Vote	*Seats*	*Difference*	*Vote*	*Seats*	*Difference*
1952	41.9	32.1	− 9.7	42.8	30.7	−12.1
1954	47.5	39.7	− 7.8	47.8	39.3	− 8.5
1956	43.0	27.6	−15.4	43.5	32.0	−11.5
1958	48.0	37.9	−10.1	48.0	38.0	−10.0
1960	50.3	43.1	− 7.2	50.7	43.3	− 7.4
1962	48.4	41.4	− 7.0	48.8	41.3	− 7.5
1964	57.7	53.5	− 4.2	57.6	58.0	+ 0.4
Average difference			− 8.8			− 8.2
1966	49.5	45.6	− 3.9	51.0	54.7	+ 3.6
1968	45.9	45.6	− 0.3	49.5	54.0	+ 4.5
1970	48.2	45.6	− 2.6	49.5	49.3	− 0.2
1972	47.5	43.3	− 4.2	49.6	46.7	− 2.9
1974	53.5	48.3	− 5.2	56.3	61.3	+ 5.0
1976	50.6	46.7	− 3.9	56.3	63.3	+ 7.1
1978	48.2	50.0	+ 1.8	52.5	60.7	+ 8.1
Average difference			− 2.6			+ 3.9

party is systematically advantaged: The greater the margin of victory in terms of votes, the greater will be the party's bonus in terms of seats won. (One version of this generalization is the cube law.[6]) For example, when the Republicans polled 57.3 percent of the two-party vote in 1952, we should not be surprised that they won 70 percent of the seats. (The proportion fits nicely with the cube law prediction. See Grofman, chapter 5, this volume.)

For another reason also, large disproportionalities between vote shares and seat shares do not necessarily reflect a system that is biased. If there are a large number of districts that are closely matched (for example, won by margins of 51 percent-49 percent), the chances are that all of them will alternate each election as party fortunes ebb and flow. The high disproportionalities that would result each year would then stem not from partisan bias in the apportionment-districting system, but from the extreme sensitivity of these districts to changes in voter preferences (that is, their extreme competitiveness).

A fourth problem is that while an apportionment-districting system might be biased against a party given a particular division of the vote, with a different division the bias might be reduced, eliminated, or reversed. The fourteen divisions shown in table 20-3 do not, therefore, provide sufficient basis on which to make a judgment regarding the presence or absence of partisan bias in the apportionment-districting system.

A final limitation of the figures shown in table 20-3 can be seen by noting the wide variations, *within* each of the two periods, in the proportion of seats won with the same (or approximately the same) percentage of votes. From this variation it is clear that seat-vote ratios are influenced by factors that are peculiar to an individual election.[7]

Given these several limitations of interpretation of each election's seat-vote ratios, it is helpful to turn to another method of analysis, one that more nearly illuminates the partisan bias (if any) that is inherent in the apportionment-districting system per se in any one election year. Such a method is presented in table 20-4, which projects what the seat-vote ratios *would have been* in our fourteen elections if in each district a party had increased its vote by one, two, three, and so on percentage points (the other party's vote decreasing by that amount), or if in each district the party had decreased its vote by one, two, three, or more points (the other party's vote increasing by that amount).[8] Rather than project seat-vote ratios under all possible outcomes, the table focuses only on the realistic 40 percent-60 percent range, identifying what the Democrat and Republican seat proportions would have been at five selected levels of statewide support: 40 percent (the other party 60 percent); 45 percent (55 percent); 50 percent (50 percent); 55 percent (45 percent); and 60 percent (40 percent).

On the basis of these data we can pose again the question of what impact reapportionment had on party representation. There is now no doubt that the pre-1966 apportionment-districting system was biased against the Democrats. To return to our example, the high proportion of assembly seats won by the Republicans in 1952 was not simply the result of the systematic advantage that is normally enjoyed by a party that wins a large majority of the vote. Had the Democrats that year won that same high vote total (58.3 percent), they would not have reaped such rewards; indeed, they would not even have won their fair share of the seats. Not only in 1952, but in other years as well, in both the assembly and the senate, the Republicans reaped much greater rewards than the Democrats for the same proportion of the vote. Their advantage was especially conspicuous at the crucial level of around 50 percent. That is, when the electorate was about evenly split between the two parties, the Republicans would win control of both houses by wide margins. In contrast, the Democrats usually needed close to 55 percent of the vote to capture majority control. Even in 1964, when the election resulted in the Democratic portion of the assembly seats slightly exceeding the party's portion of the two-party vote (58 percent), this pro-Democratic disproportionality was misleading. The projection shows that had the Democratic vote fallen to 50 percent, or even several points above that, the Republicans would easily have captured a majority of the seats. During the entire pre-1966 period the only levels where the Democrats held advantage over the Republicans were the unlikely, extreme levels of 40 percent and 60 percent.

Beginning with the first reapportionment election of 1966, the pattern of bias changed dramatically. In the assembly, it is now the Democrats who are usually favored at all points in the 40 percent to 60 percent range. Yet the advantage is much less than that formerly enjoyed by the Republicans. At the crucial 50 percent level, the advantage disappears entirely in three of the seven postreapportionment projections. As in the prereapportionment period, it is only at the extreme levels of 40 percent and 60 percent that the pro-Democratic bias becomes conspicuous.

One key to understanding the post-1966 pattern of bias is provided by the account of knowledgeable observers who have described the district lines drawn for the three elections of 1966, 1968, and 1970 as being the product of a bipartisan gerrymander, and the lines drawn for the elections beginning in 1972 as the product of a one-party, Republican gerrymander (Wells, 1978). Looking at the pattern of bias from this perspective, we can see that the Democratic advantage in the assembly was pronounced during the first three postreapportionment elections, but then disappeared in the first two elections held under the lines drawn by the Republican cartographers. It will be noted, however, that the effect of a one-part gerrymander can be short-lived. Anyone looking at the pattern of bias reflected in the 1976 and 1978 elections would conclude that the Democrats, not the Republicans, had designed the system.

Table 20-4

Projected Percentage of Seats Won by Democrats and Republicans at Various Percentage of Statewide Vote Before Reapportionment and After

Year	Vote[a]	Assembly					Senate					Swing Ratio	
		40±%	45±%	50±%	55±%	60±%	40±%	45±%	50±%	55±%	60±%	%Assembly	Senate
1952	Democrat	26.7%	36.7%	43.3%	52.7%	67.3%	32.1%	39.3%	46.4%	53.6%	67.9%	2.0	1.8
	Republican	32.7	47.3	56.7	63.3	73.3	32.1	46.4	53.6	60.7	67.9		
	Bias[b]	−6.0	−10.6	−13.4	−10.6	−6.0	±0	−7.1	−7.2	−7.1	±0		
1954	Democrat	30.7	36.7	44.0	49.3	62.0	29.3	36.2	41.4	48.3	62.1	1.6	1.6
	Republican	38.0	50.7	56.0	63.3	69.3	37.9	51.7	58.6	63.8	70.7		
	Bias	−7.3	−14.0	−12.0	−14.0	−7.3	−8.6	−15.5	−17.2	−15.5	−8.6		
1956	Democrat	26.7	35.3	40.7	50.0	66.7	24.1	32.8	39.7	48.3	67.2	2.0	2.2
	Republican	33.3	50.0	59.3	64.7	73.3	32.8	51.7	60.3	67.2	75.9		
	Bias	−6.6	−14.7	−18.6	−14.7	−6.6	−8.7	−18.9	−20.6	−18.9	−8.7		
1958	Democrat	32.0	36.7	42.0	58.0	71.3	31.0	32.8	39.7	53.5	74.1	2.0	2.1
	Republican	28.7	42.0	58.0	63.3	68.0	25.9	46.5	60.3	67.2	69.0		
	Bias	+3.3	−5.3	−16.0	−5.3	+3.3	+5.1	−13.7	−20.6	−13.7	+5.1		
1960	Democrat	34.7	38.7	47.3	61.3	76.7	29.3	37.9	43.1	53.5	75.9	2.0	2.1
	Republican	23.3	38.7	52.7	61.3	65.3	24.1	46.5	56.9	62.1	70.7		
	Bias	+11.4	±0	−5.4	±0	+11.4	+5.2	−8.6	−13.8	−8.6	+5.2		
1962	Democrat	32.0	37.3	44.0	52.7	71.3	34.5	37.9	43.1	50.0	74.1	2.1	2.3
	Republican	28.7	47.3	56.0	62.7	68.0	25.9	50.0	56.9	62.1	65.5		
	Bias	+3.3	−10.0	−12.0	−10.0	+3.3	+8.6	−12.1	−13.8	−12.1	+8.6		
1964	Democrat	32.7	39.3	44.7	52.0	65.3	34.5	41.4	44.8	58.6	89.7	2.0	2.0
	Republican	34.7	48.0	55.3	60.7	67.3	10.3	41.4	55.2	58.6	65.6		
	Bias	−2.0	−8.7	−10.6	−8.7	−2.0	+24.2	±0	−10.4	±0	+24.2		
Average bias		−0.6	−9.0	−12.6	−9.0	−4.9	+3.7	−10.8	−14.8	−10.8	+3.7	1.6	2.8
Average Swing												1.9	2.1

Year													
1966	Democrat	38.7	45.3	53.3	60.0	72.7	42.1	43.9	49.6	52.6	70.2		
	Republican	27.3	40.0	46.7	54.7	61.3	29.8	47.4	50.4	56.1	57.9		
	Bias	+11.4	+5.3	+6.6	+5.3	+11.4	+12.3	−3.5	−0.8	−3.5	+12.3	1.7	1.4
1968	Democrat	40.0	45.3	54.7	60.0	71.3	43.9	45.6	49.1	54.4	71.9		
	Republican	28.7	40.0	45.3	54.7	60.0	28.1	45.6	50.9	54.4	56.1		
	Bias	+11.3	+5.3	+9.4	+5.3	+11.3	+15.8	±0	−1.8	±0	+15.8	1.6	1.4
1970	Democrat	40.7	44.7	49.3	59.3	72.7	42.1	45.6	50.9	56.1	63.2		
	Republican	27.3	40.7	50.7	55.3	59.3	36.8	43.9	49.1	54.4	57.9		
	Bias	+13.4	+4.0	−1.4	+4.0	+13.4	+5.3	+1.7	+1.8	+1.7	+5.3	1.6	1.1
1972	Democrat	36.7	40.0	47.3	58.7	69.3	36.7	40.0	45.0	58.3	73.3		
	Republican	30.7	41.3	52.7	60.0	63.3	26.7	41.7	55.0	60.0	63.3		
	Bias	+6.0	−1.3	−5.4	−1.3	+6.0	+10.0	−1.7	−10.0	−1.7	+10.0	1.6	1.8
1974	Democrat	39.3	44.0	50.0	58.7	70.0	38.3	40.0	43.3	53.3	75.0		
	Republican	30.0	41.3	50.0	56.0	60.7	25.0	46.7	56.7	60.0	61.7		
	Bias	+9.3	+2.7	±0	+2.7	+9.3	+13.3	−6.7	−13.4	−6.7	+13.3	1.5	1.8
1976	Democrat	40.7	47.3	55.3	62.7	70.0	40.6	41.1	46.1	61.1	69.4		
	Republican	30.0	37.3	44.7	52.7	59.3	30.6	38.9	53.9	58.9	59.4		
	Bias	+10.7	+10.0	+10.6	+10.0	+10.7	+10.0	+2.2	−7.8	+2.2	+10.0	1.5	1.4
1978	Democrat	46.0	53.3	58.7	63.3	71.3	40.0	46.7	50.0	56.7	63.3		
	Republican	28.7	36.7	41.3	46.7	54.0	36.7	43.3	50.0	53.3	60.0		
	Bias	+17.3	+16.6	+17.4	+16.6	+17.3	+3.3	+3.4	±0	+3.4	+3.3	1.3	1.2
Average bias		−11.3	+6.1	+5.3	+6.1	+11.3	+10.0	−0.7	−4.6	−0.7	+10.0	1.5	1.4
Average Swing													

[a]Because the projections have been calculated beginning with the actual Democratic proportion of the statewide vote carried to one decimal place, the five levels of support for the Democrats are always slightly *above* the level shown, while for the Republicans the support level is always slightly *below* the level shown. For example, if the Democratic vote is 46.4 percent, the five selected Democratic support levels are 40.0 percent, 45.4 percent, 50.4 percent, 55.4 percent, and 60.4 percent; while the Republican support levels are 39.6 percent, 44.6 percent, 49.6 percent, 54.6 percent, and 59.6 percent.

[b]Bias is expressed in terms of the Democrats: a negative sign (−) indicates that the bias is against the Democrats; a positive sign (+) indicates the bias against the Republicans.

The change in the pattern of bias for the senate districts has been as dramatic as the change recorded for the assembly. Gone is the two-digit, pro-Republican bias at most levels of support. During the first three elections after reapportionment the system was nearly perfectly unbiased, not only at the 50 percent level but at the 45 percent and 55 percent levels as well. But then beginning in 1972 a large anti-Democratic bias began to appear at the crucial 50 percent level. The handiwork of the Republican gerrymander now seemed evident. Yet here, too, by 1978 the effectiveness of the gerrymander could no longer be discerned.[9]

The figures in table 20-4 allow us one additional insight into the effect of reapportionment on party representation. By reading from left to right in each projection we can see at what rate seat totals respond to changes in vote totals, thereby gaining insight into the *competitiveness,* and from this the *responsiveness,* of the system. This so-called swing-ratio[10] is shown in the last column of table 20-4 and is obtained by dividing the percentage-point change in seats in the 40 percent-60 percent range by the percentage-point change in vote in that range. It will be seen that, on the average, both the assembly and the senate have become somewhat less responsive since reapportionment. Of course, this means that elections are now less likely to produce high disproportionalities between vote shares and seat shares.

To summarize our conclusions, reapportionment in New York state has had a dramatic impact on party representation: (1) the likelihood of *either* party, not just one party, winning control of one or both houses has increased enormously; (2) seat shares now come closer than before to approximate vote shares; and (3) although inevitably some bias remains (that is, at given levels of vote one party reaps greater rewards than the other), at the crucial level around 50 percent there is much more equity than before. At the same time, the system is now slightly less responsive than before to shifts in voter sentiment.

Notes

1. The best summary of the early literature is Bicker (1971). A more recent perspective is found in O'Rourke (1980).

2. Reynolds v. Sims (1964):377 U.S. 533.

3. It should be noted that the second portion of this chapter, devoted to seat-vote ratios, contrasts the ratios that resulted when the 1894 formula was used during the period 1952-1964 with those that actually resulted beginning in 1966, and not those that would have resulted—following the logic of this first section of the chapter—had the 1894 formula applied to 1960 and 1970 census data. It must be kept in mind, therefore, that what is being compared in that second section are "old" seat-vote ratios that were

the product of the old formula *and* the population distributions (quantities, demographic characteristics) of 1950, and the "new" seat-vote ratios that were the product of the new, equal-population formula *and* the population distributions of 1960 and 1970.

4. The old apportionment formula for the senate was considerably more complex; hence analysis is confined to the one house. There was no constitutional formula for congressional districts.

5. Any attempt to analyze seat-vote relationships in New York is frustrated by the fact that New York is one of only three states in the nation (the others are Vermont and Connecticut) that allow a candidate's name to appear on more than one line on the ballot, once as the nominee of one of the major parties and once more (or twice or thrice more) as the nominee of one of the minor parties (in recent years the Liberal and Conservative parties), which, because of this very possibility, continue to thrive in the state. The strategy followed by these minor parties—one year endorsing a major party's candidate, the next year entering a separate candidate—affects the outcome of elections in closely fought districts. The only way to analyze the effect of the apportionment-districting system on seat-vote relationships, unaffected by the strategies followed by the minor parties, is to focus only on the two-party vote, and to express both vote totals and seat totals as if only two parties were competing. As a result, the proportion of seats won, shown in table 20-3 (and in subsequent tabulations), may sometimes differ from the actual number of seats won by a party. For example, table 20-3 shows the Democrats winning 50 percent of the seats in the senate in the 1978 election, that is, thirty seats. In fact, they won only twenty-five seats, the Conservative line vote for the Republican candidate spelling the difference in five districts.

6. The cube law is elaborated in M.G. Kendall and A. Stuart (1950). Tufte (1973) has offered another formulation of the tendency.

7. For example, a decline or increase in turnout could disproportionately affect the two parties' vote totals.

8. This method is suggested by Tufte (1974) and Tufte (1975). However, the application used here differs from Tufte's in that bias is defined by the percentage of seats won at various percentages of the vote rather than as the excess or deficit percentage of vote required to win 50 percent of the seats. The problem with the latter method is that projections may show that *both* parties are advantaged, or disadvantaged. For example, projections for the New York senate election of 1978 show that the Democrats required only 48.2 percent of the votes to win 50 percent of the seats, while the Republicans required only 47.8 percent to win 50 percent. The reason for this seemingly odd result is that within the range beginning with 48.2 percent Democrat (51.8 percent Republican) and ending with 52.2 percent Democrat and (47.8 percent Republican), no seats change hands. The method used here is that used by Butler (1951:327-33).

9. One explanation for the limited effectiveness of a single-party gerry-mander is that the party is tempted to spread its voting support too thin. See Mayhew (1971).

10. The notion of swing-ratio is discussed by Tufte (1973).

Afterword

If there is little that is conclusive in the preceding chapters, it is as it should be. For there is something immanently inconclusive about legislative districting, apportionment, and representation. The issues involved make for adversary proceedings and simply will not stand still. This has been the case particularly in the last twenty years or so, and I suspect that it will be the case even more so in the next twenty years, when, as I expect, the country's social and cultural proliferation will give rise to an even more pluralistic population than is politically visible today. The battle over appropriate units of representation and commensurate allocation of legislative seats is likely to go on as the states' populations grow or decline unevenly and as old interests yield to new in the wake of social and cultural change. One may consider this good news or bad, depending on one's ideological standpoint, but it will surely not make this book the last word in the matter. Nevertheless, one might hope that the book will stimulate political and other social scientists to subject many of the authors' suggestive theoretical leads to empirical testing. And this, too, is as it should be.

The stakes in the battles over districting and apportionment are high. The issues brought together here make this abundantly clear. Once the partisan composition of our legislative bodies was the primary issue, and it still is to a large extent. Later this issue was joined by the conflict over the representation of urban and rural interests, although this conflict abated with the progressing urbanization of the country. More recently, the representation of women and racial minorities by their own kind has become the primary, unresolved issue. Underlying all of these battles has been the premise that how geographical district lines are drawn and what legislative seats are allocated to whom will make a difference in the political process and in policy outcomes; and there is evidence, at the macro level of the political system, that the premise is warranted.

Whether districting and apportionment make a difference at the individual level—in the conduct and policy positions of the representative as he or she performs legislative and other tasks or as he or she responds to the wants and/or needs of particular constituents—is far from clear. As districts have grown in population and become ever-more heterogeneous, the ability of representatives to reflect some presumed average characteristic or typical policy preference of his or her district may well be doubted, and there is a great deal of empirical evidence for such doubt. That the representative must respond to an ever-increasing variety of single interests, often in conflict with one another, seems to be a logical requirement for electoral survival. This, in turn, increasingly frees the representative from some constraints, only to expose him or her to others. The fairness of a system of representation may well turn, therefore, on the individual representative's or the legislature's sense of fairness vis-à-vis many different segments of the people. However, the relationship between fairness of districting and apportionment, on the one hand, and the representative's or the representative body's sense of fairness in dealing with multiple and diverse constituencies, on the other hand, has yet to be explored. Again, the chapters in this book should serve empirical researchers as valuable points of departure for intensive examination of relevant circumstances and consequences.

What stands out in each chapter is the fact that the terms of reference in the debate over districting and representation have drastically changed in the last twenty years. Only a soothsayer would venture to predict what they are likely to be in the immediate, possibly more conservative, or longer-range future. My impression from some of the chapters is that the one-man, one-vote doctrine, while presently sacrosanct, may not turn out to be the apogee of democratic fulfillment. In a sociological perspective, there is surely something simplistic in the notion that if legislative seats are equally apportioned among artificially created electoral districts, every person is equally represented in the legislative chamber. The U.S. Senate, hardly a model of equal representation, is probably no less a representative, democratic, and responsive body than is the House of Representatives. In fact, viewed in a national perspective, it may be more representative of the nation as a whole than is the House. Much depends, of course, on what one means by representation or what one expects from representatives. Although it appears from some of the chapters that considerations of this sort have come to have some influence on thinking about districting and apportionment, they have barely penetrated the outer shell of the prevailing constitutional doctrine. If they should, it is conceivable that, at some future date, units other than arithmetically defined electoral districts will serve as the building blocks of representation. Or it is conceivable that representatives will give up the silly pretense of representing constituents whose only common property is their having been assigned to an artificially created district. However, only a soothsayer would indulge in such future gazing.

As I write this, the national press reports the outbreak of fisticuffs between representatives in some states where redistricting is on the legislative agenda—evidence of how the issue stirs the passions. Meanwhile it is a pleasant task to recommend careful study of this book.

Heinz Eulau

Appendix:
Additional Conference
Participants

Bruce Adams, Former Director of Issue Development, Common Cause

Samuel A. Alito, Research Director, N.J. Legislature Office of Legislative Services

Charles G. Armstrong, President and Chief Executive Officer, Arnel Management Company, and Vice-President and General Counsel, Arnel Development Company

Michel L. Balinski, Professor of Administrative Sciences and of Organization and Management, Yale University

Kimball W. Brace, President, Election Data Services

Christopher Brewster, Minority Counsel, Subcommittee on Federal Spending Practices and Open Government, Committee on Governmental Affairs, U.S. Senate; and Legislative Assistant, Senator John C. Danforth (R-Missouri)

Carl P. Carlucci, Executive Director, New York State Legislative Advisory Task Force on Reapportionment

Erlinda Cortez, Administrator, Mexican American Legal Defense and Educational Fund, San Antonio, Texas

José Enrique Garriga-Picó, Assistant Professor, Department of Social Science, University of Puerto Rico (Humacao)

Ron Kreiter, Staff Attorney, State Legislative Council, State of Oklahoma

Sheri Lanoff, Director, Government/Voters Service Department, League of Women Voters Education Fund

Elissa C. Lichtenstein, Assistant Director, Public Service Activities Division, American Bar Association

Janet Lund, Administrative Assistant to President of the Senate, State of Minnesota

Guillermo Owen, Professor of Economics, University of Iowa

Dale Read, Jr., Attorney, Vancouver, Washington; and Member, American Bar Association Special Committee on Election Law and Voter Participation

Eric Schnapper, Assistant Counsel, NAACP Legal Defense Fund

Abigail Thernstrom, Author; 9/8/80-9/8/82 on the staff of The Twentieth Century Fund

Marshall L. Turner, Jr., Assistant Division Chief, Data User Services Division, U.S. Census Bureau

Steven J. Uhlfelder, ABA Special Committee on Election Law (Chairman Designate), Attorney (Tallahassee, Florida)

Bibliography

Adams, Bruce. 1977. "A Model State Reapportionment Process: The Continuing Quest for 'Fair and Effective Representation.'" *Harvard Journal on Legislation* 14, no. 4 (June):825-904.

Adrian, C. 1960, 1967, 1976. *State and Local Governments.* New York: McGraw-Hill.

Anderson, Stuart. 1979. *Reapportionment and Redistricting in Other Countries.* Claremont, Calif.: Rose Institute of State and Local Government, Claremont College.

Auerbach, Carl A. 1964. "The Reapportionment Cases: One Person, One Vote—One Vote, One Value." In Philip Kurland (ed.), *Supreme Court Review.* Chicago: Univ. of Chicago Press, 1-87.

Auerbach, Carl A. 1982. "Comments on Criteria for Single-Member Districting." In B. Grofman, A. Lijphart, R. McKay, and H. Scarrow (eds.), *Representation and Redistricting Issues.* Lexington, Mass.: Lexington Books, D.C. Heath and Company.

Backstrom, Charles H. 1982. "Problems of Implementing Redistricting." In B. Grofman, A. Lijphart, R. McKay, and H. Scarrow (eds.), *Representation and Redistricting Issues.* Lexington, Mass.: Lexington Books, D.C. Heath and Company.

Backstrom, Charles H., Leonard Robins, and Scott Eller. 1978. "Issues in Gerrymandering: An Exploratory Measure of Partisan Gerrymandering Applied to Minnesota." *Minnesota Law Review* 62:1121-59.

Baker, Gordon E. 1955. *Rural Versus Urban Political Power.* New York: Random House.

Baker, Gordon E. 1966. *The Reapportionment Revolution.* New York: Random House.

Baker, Gordon E. 1973. "Quantitative and Descriptive Guidelines to Minimize Gerrymandering." In Lee Papayanopoulos (ed.), *Democratic Representation and Apportionment.* Special issue of the Annals of the New York Academy of Sciences 219 (Nov. 9):200-208.

Baker, E. 1982. "Threading the Political Thicket by Tracing the Steps of the Late Robert G. Dixon, Jr.: An Appraisal and Appreciation." In B. Grofman, A. Lijphart, R. McKay, and H. Scarrow (eds.), *Representation and Redistricting Issues.* Lexington, Mass.: Lexington Books, D.C. Heath and Company.

Balinski, M.L. and H.P. Young. 1974. "A New Method for Congressional Apportionment." *Proceedings of the National Academy of Sciences* 71:4602-4606.

Balinski, M.L. and H.P. Young. 1978. "Stability, Coalitions and Schisms in Proportional Representation Systems." *American Political Science Review* 72 (Sept.).

Balinski, M.L. and H.P. Young. 1980. The Webster Method of Apportionment. *Proceedings of the National Academy of Sciences* 77 (Jan.):1-4.

Balitzer, Fred. 1979. *The Commission Experience: Studies of Non-Legislative Approaches to Redistricting.* Claremont, Calif.: Rose Institute of State and Local Government, Claremont College (Nov.).

Banzhaf, John F. III. 1965. "Weighted Voting Doesn't Work: A Mathematical Analysis," *Rutgers Law Review* 19:317-343.

Banzhaf, John F. III. 1966. "Multi-Member Electoral Districts—Do They Violate the 'One-Man, One-Vote' Principle?" *Yale Law Journal* 75:1309-1338.

Banzhaf, John F. III. 1968. "One Man, 3.312 Votes: A Mathematical Analysis of the Electoral College." *Villanova Law Review* 13:314-332.

Bickel, Alexander M. 1968, 1971. *Reform and Continuity: The Electoral College, the Convention, and the Party System* (expanded and revised edition of *The New Age of Political Reform.* New York: Harper and Row.

Bicker, W.E. 1971. "The Effects of Malapportionment in the States: A Mistrial." In N. Polsby, (ed.), *Reapportionment in the 1970s.* Berkeley: Univ. of California Press: 151-201.

Bickerstaff, Steve. 1980. "Reapportionment by State Legislatures: A Guide for the 1980s." *Southwestern Law Journal* (Spring).

Birch, A.H. 1971. *Representation.* London: Macmillan.

Blair, G.S. 1973. "Cumulative Voting: An Effective Electoral Device for Fair and Minority Representation." In Lee Papayanopoulos (ed.), *Democratic Representation and Apportionment.* Special issue of the *Annals of the New York Academy of Sciences* 219 (Nov. 9):20-26.

Blondel, J. 1969. *An Introduction to Comparative Government.* London: Weidenfeld and Nicolson.

Brady, D. and D. Edmonds. 1967. "One Man, One Vote—So What?" *Transaction* (March):41-46.

Brady, David W. and Richard Murray. 1972. "Reformers and Skeptics. Testing for the Effects of Apportionment Patterns on Policy Outputs." In M. Holden, R. Mathew, and D. Dresange (eds.), *What Government Does.* Beverly Hills: Sage Publications, 253-276.

Brams, David and Douglas Edmonds. 1966. *The Effect of Malapportionment on Policy Output in the American States.* Iowa City: Laboratory for Political Research.

Brams, Steven J. 1975. *Game Theory and Politics.* New York: Free Press.

Brams, Steven J. 1976a. *One Man, n Votes.* Module in Applied Mathematics, Mathematical Association of America. Ithaca: Cornell Univ. Press.

Brams, Steven J. 1976b. *Paradoxes in Politics: An Introduction to the Non-obvious in Political Science.* New York: Free Press.

Brams, Steven J. 1977. "When Is It Advantageous to Cast a Negative Vote?" In R. Henn and O. Moeschlin (eds.), *Lecture Notes in Economics and Mathematical Systems, Mathematical Economics and Game Theory: Essays in Honor of Oskar Morgenstern,* 141. Berlin: Springer-Verlag, 564-572.

Brams, Steven J. 1978a. *Comparison Voting.* Innovative Instructional Unit. American Political Science Association. Washington, D.C.: American Political Science Association.

Brams, Steven J. 1978b. *The Presidential Election Game.* New Haven: Yale Univ. Press.

Brams, Steven J. 1979. "Approval Voting: A Practical Reform for Multicandidate Elections." *National Civic Review* 68 (Nov.):549-553, 560.

Brams, Steven J. 1980a. "Approval Voting in Multicandidate Elections." *Policy Studies Journal* (Autumn):102-108.

Brams, Steven J. 1980b. "Approval Voting in New Hampshire." *Concord (N.H.) Monitor* (Jan. 9), Guest Editorial.

Brams, Steven J. 1980c. "Baker Could Have Survived New Hampshire." *Concord (N.H.) Monitor* (March 8).

Brams, Steven J. 1981a. "Approval Voting: One-Candidate, One-Vote." In B. Grofman, A. Lijphart, R. McKay, and H. Scarrow (eds.), *Representation and Redistricting Issues of the 1980s.* Lexington, Mass.: Lexington Books.

Brams, Steven J. 1981b. "One Candidate, One Vote." *Archway: Magazine of the Arts and Sciences at New York University* (Winter):10-14.

Brams, Steven J. and Peter C. Fishburn. 1978, 1979. "Approval Voting." *American Political Science Review* 72, no. 3 (Sept.):831-847; "Reply to 'Comment on Brams and Fishburn,'" *American Political Science Review* 73 (June):552.

Brams, Steven J. and Peter C. Fishburn. 1981. "Reconstructing Preferences and Choices in the 1980 Presidential Election: A Linear-Systems Approach." Mimeographed.

Brams, Steven J. and Peter C. Fishburn. 1982. "Reconstructing Voting Processes: The 1976 House Majority Leader Election under Present and Alternative Rules." *Political Methodology* (in press).

Brams, Steven J. and George Sharrard. 1979. "Analysis of Pilot Study Questions on Preference Rankings and Approval Voting." Mimeographed.

Brooks, Gary H., and William J. Claggett. 1980. "Black Mobilization, White Resistance, and Legislative Behavior: An Exploratory Analysis." Paper read at Midwestern Political Science Association meeting, April 24-26, Chicago.

Browne, Malcolm W. 1980. "Can Voting Become Safer for Democracy?" *New York Times* (June 1).

Bryce, James. 1889. *The American Commonwealth* 1, London: Macmillan.

Bullock, Charles, III. 1975. "Redistricting and Congressional Stability 1962-72." *Journal of Politics* (May):569-575.

Bushnell, Eleanore (ed.) 1970. *Impact of Reapportionment on the Thirteen Western States*. Salt Lake City: Univ. of Utah Press.

Butler, D.E. 1951. Appendix, in H.G. Nicholas, *The British General Election of 1950*. London: Macmillan:306-333.

Campbell, D. and J. Feagin. 1975. "Black Politics in the South." *Journal of Politics* 37 (Feb.):129-139.

Cantrall, William R., and Stuart S. Nagel. 1973. "The Effects of Reapportionment on the Passage of Nonexpenditure Legislation." In Lee Papayanopoulos (ed.), *Democratic Representation and Apportionment*. Special issue of the *Annals of the New York Academy of Sciences* 219:269-79.

Carpenetti, Walter L. 1972. "Legislative Apportionment: Multimember Districts and Fair Representation." *University of Pennsylvania Law Review* 120:666-700.

Carstairs, A.M. 1980. *A Short History of Electoral Systems in Western Europe*. London: Allen and Unwin.

Casper, Gerhard. 1973. "Apportionment and the Right to Vote: Standards of Judicial Scrutiny." *Supreme Court Review,* 1-33.

Cassel, Carol A. 1979. "Change in Electoral Participation in the South." *Journal of Politics* 41:907-917.

Cavala, William. 1974. "Changing the Rules Changes the Game: Party Reform and the 1972 California Delegation to the Democratic National Convention." *American Political Science Review* 68 (March):27-42.

Chartrand, Robert L. 1972. "Redistricting in the 1970's: The Role of the Computer." *Law and Computer Technology* 5 (May/June):58-74.

Cho, Yong Hyo, and H. George Frederickson. 1973. "Apportionment and Legislative Responsiveness to Policy Preferences in the American States." In Lee Papayanopoulos (ed.), *Democratic Representation and Apportionment*. Special issue of the *Annals of the New York Academy of Sciences* 219:248-68.

Cho, Yong Hyo, and H. George Frederickson. 1974. "The Effects of Reapportionment: Subtle, Selective, Limited." *National Civic Review* 63 (June):357-62.

Cho, Yong Hyo and H. George Frederickson. 1976. *Measuring the Effects of Reapportionment in the American States*. New York: National Municipal League.

Clem, Alan L. and W.O. Farber. 1979. "Manipulating Democracy: The Multi-Member District." *National Civic Review* 68 (May):337-43.

Cohan, A.S., R.B. McKinlay, and A. Mughan. 1975. "The Used Vote and Electoral Outcomes: The Irish General Election of 1973." *British Journal of Political Science* 5:363-383.

Cole, Leonard A. 1974. "Electing Blacks to Municipal Office: Structural and Social Determinants." *Urban Affairs Quarterly* 10, no. 1 (Sept.): 17-39.

Comment. 1970. "Effective Representation and Multi-Member Districts." *Michigan Law Review* 68:1577.

Commission on Party Structure and Delegate Selection. 1970. *Mandate for Reform.* Washington, D.C.: Democratic National Committee.

Commission on Party Structure and Delegate Selection. 1972. *The Party Reformed: Final Report of the Commission on Party Structure and Delegate Selection.* Washington, D.C.: Democratic National Committee.

Commission on Party Structure and Delegate Selection. 1974. *Democrats All.* Washington, D.C.: Democratic National Committee.

Commission on Presidential Nomination and Party Structure. 1978. *Openness, Participation, and Party Building: Reforms for a Stronger Democratic Party.* Washington, D.C.: Democratic National Committee.

Committee on Reapportionment of Congress, American Political Science Association. 1951. "The Reapportionment of Congress." *American Political Science Review* 45:153-158.

Common Cause. 1977a. *Reapportionment: A Better Way. A Common Cause Proposal.* Washington, D.C.: Common Cause (Nov.).

Common Cause. 1977b. "Toward a System of Fair and Effective Representation." Report (Nov.).

Congressional Anti-Gerrymandering Act of 1979 (1979). Hearings before the Committee on Governmental Affairs, U.S. Senate: Ninety-Sixth Congress, First Session on S.596 (June 20, 21; July 10).

Cotrell, Charles L. N.D. "Municipal Services Equalization in San Antonio, Texas: Explorations in 'Chinatown.'" Xeroxed monograph, Department of Urban Studies, St. Mary's Univ., San Antonio, Texas.

Cotrell, Charles L. and Arnold Fleischman. 1979. "The Change From At-Large to District Representation and Political Participation of Minority Groups in Fort Worth and San Antonio, Texas." *Urban Affairs Quarterly* 10, no. 1 (Sept.):17-39.

Council of State Governments. 1978. *Book of the States, 1978-79.* Lexington: Council of State Governments.

Cox, Archibald. 1966. "Constitutional Adjudication and the Promotion of Human Rights." *Harvard Law Review* 80.

Craig, W. 1973. "Reapportionment and the Computer." *Law and Computer Technology* 6:50-56.

Crotty, William J. 1978. *Decision for the Democrats: Reforming the Party Structure.* Baltimore: Johns Hopkins Univ. Press.

Dauer, Manning J. and Michael A. Maggiotto. 1979. "The Status of Multi-Member Local Districts in State and Local government." *National Civic Review* 68 (Jan.):24-27.

David, Paul T. and James W. Ceasar. 1980. *Proportional Representation in Presidential Nominating Politics.* Virginia: Univ. Press of Virginia.

Davidson, Chandler. 1979. "At-Large Elections and Minority Representation." *Social Science Quarterly* 60, no. 1 (Sept.):336-337.

Davis, I.R. 1972. *The Effects of Reapportionment on the Connecticut Legislature—Decade of the Sixties.* New York: National Municipal League.

Dawson, R.E. and J.A. Robinson. 1963. "Inter-Party Competition, Economic Variables, and Welfare Policies in the American States." *Journal of Politics* (May):265-289.

DeGrazia, Alfred. 1951. *Public and Republic.* New York: Knopf.

Derfner, Armand. 1982. "Nondiscrimination in Districting." In B. Grofman, A. Lijphart, R. McKay, and H. Scarrow (eds.), *Representation and Redistricting Issues.* Lexington, Mass.: Lexington Books, D.C. Heath and Company.

Dixon, Robert G., Jr. 1968. *Democratic Representation: Reapportionment in Law and Politics.* New York: Oxford Univ. Press.

Dixon, Robert G., Jr. 1969. "The Warren Court Crusade for the Holy Grail of 'One Man-One Vote.'" *Supreme Court Review,* 219-270.

Dixon, Robert G., Jr. 1971. "The Court, The People, and 'One Man, One Vote.'" In Nelson W. Polsby (ed.), *Reapportionment in the 1970s.* Berkeley: Univ. of California Press, 7-45.

Dixon, Robert G., Jr. 1979. "Statement on S. 596, a bill to provide a fair procedure for establishing Congressional districts, before the Committee on Governmental Affairs, U.S. Senate, June 20."

Dixon, Robert G., Jr. 1982. "Fair Criteria and Procedures for Establishing Legislative Districts." In B. Grofman, A. Lijphart, R. McKay, and H. Scarrow (eds.), *Representation and Redistricting Issues.* Lexington, Mass.: Lexington Books, D.C. Heath and Company.

Dixon, Robert G., Jr. and G.W. Hatheway, Jr. 1969. "Seminal issues in State Constitutional Revision: Reapportionment Method and New Standards. *William and Mary Law Review* 10 (Summer).

Dodd, Lawrence. 1976. *Party Coalitions and Parliamentary Government.* Princeton: Univ. of Princeton.

Dolgow, Samuel R. 1977. "Political Representation: The Search for Judicial Standards." *Brooklyn Law Review* 43:431-487.

Douglas, Paul H. 1923. "Occupational Versus Proportional Representation." *American Journal of Sociology* (Sept.).

Duverger, Maurice. 1951. "The Influence of Electoral Systems on Political Life." *International Social Science Bulletin* 3 (Summer):314-352.

Dye, Thomas R. 1965, 1971. "Malapportionment and Public Policy in the States." *Journal of Politics* 27 (Aug.):586-601; reprinted in R.I. Hofferbert and I. Sharkansky (eds.), *State and Urban Politics.* Boston: Little, Brown.

Dye, Thomas R. 1966. *Politics, Economics, and the Public.* Chicago: Rand-McNally.

Dye, Thomas R. 1971. "State Legislative Politics." In H. Jacob and K.N. Vines (eds.), *Politics in the American States,* 2d ed. Boston: Little, Brown.

Dye, Thomas R. 1976. *Policy Analysis.* Birmingham: Univ. of Alabama Press.

Dye, Thomas R. 1978. *Politics in States and Communities.* Englewood Cliffs: Prentice-Hall.

Dye, Thomas R. 1979. "Discriminatory Effects of At-Large Elections." *Florida State University Law Review* 7 (Winter):85-122.

Ely, John H. 1980. *Democracy and Distrust: A Theory of Judicial Review.* Cambridge: Harvard Univ. Press.

Engstrom, Richard L. 1977. "The Supreme Court and Equi-Populous Gerrymandering: A Remaining Obstacle in the Quest for Fair and Effective Representation." *Arizona State Law Journal* 1976, no. 2:277-319.

Engstrom, Richard L. 1978. "Racial Vote Dilution: Supreme Court Interpretations of Section 5 of the Voting Rights Act." *Southern University Law Review* 4, no. 2 (Spring):139-163.

Engstrom, Richard L. 1980. "Racial Discrimination in the Election Process: The Voting Rights Act and the Vote Dilution Issue." In Robert P. Steed, et al. (eds.), *Party Politics in the South.* New York: Praeger.

Engstrom, Richard L. and John K. Wildgen (1977) "Pruning Thorns from the Thicket: An Empirical Test of the Existence of Racial Gerrymandering." *Legislative Studies Quarterly* 2 (Nov.):465-479.

Erikson, Robert S. 1971. "The Partisan Impact of Reapportionment," *Midwest Journal of Political Science* 57:57-71.

Erickson, Robert S. 1972. "Malapportionment, Gerrymandering, and Party Fortunes in Congressional Elections." *American Political Science Review* 66 (Dec.):1234-45.

Eulau, Heinz, 1967. "Changing Views of Representation." In Ithiel de Sola Pool (ed.), *Contemporary Political Science.* New York: McGraw-Hill, 53-85.

Eulau, Heinz, et al. 1959. "The Role of the Representative: Some Empirical Observations on the Theory of Edmund Burke." *American Political Science Review* 53 (Sept.):742-756.

Eulau, Heinz and Paul D. Karps. 1977. "The Puzzle of Representation: Specifying Components of Responsiveness." *Legislative Studies Quarterly* 2 (Aug.):233-254.

Eulau, Heinz and J.C. Wahlke. 1978. *The Politics of Representation: Continuities in Theory and Research.* Beverly Hills: Sage Publications.

Fabricant, S. 1950. *The Trend of Government Activity in the United States.* New York: National Bureau of Economic Research.

The Federalist or, The New Constitution. 1911. London: J.M. Dent and Sons Ltd, Everyman Edition.

Feig, Douglas G. 1978. "Expenditures in the American States: The Impact of Court-Ordered Legislative Reapportionment." *American Politics Quarterly* 6 (July):309-324.

Feller, B. and H.A. Bone. 1948. "Repeal of P.R. in New York City: Ten Years in Retrospect." *American Political Science Review* 12 (Dec.):127-148.

Fenno, Richard R., Jr. 1978. *Home Style.* Boston: Little, Brown.

Ferejohn, John A. 1977. "On the Decline of Competition in Congressional Elections." *American Political Science Review* 71 (March):166-176.

Finer, S.E. (ed.). 1975. *Adversary Politics and Electoral Reform.* London: Anthony Wigram.

Finkelstein, Michael. 1978. *Quantitative Methods in Law.* New York: Free Press.

Fiorina, Morris P. 1977. *Congress: Keystone of the Washington Establishment.* New Haven: Yale Univ. Press.

Firestine, R.E. "Some Effects of Reapportionment on State Government Fiscal Activity." Ph.D. dissertation, Syracuse University.

Fishburn, Peter C. 1978a. "Axioms for Approval Voting: Direct Proof." *Journal of Economic Theory* 19 (Oct.):180-185.

Fishburn, Peter C. 1978b. "A Strategic Analysis of Nonranked Voting Systems." *SIAM Journal on Applied Mathematics* 35 (Nov.):488-495.

Fishburn, Peter C. 1978c. "Symmetric and Consistent Aggregation with Dichotomous Voting." In Jean-Jacques Laffont (ed.), *Aggregation and Revelation of Preferences.* Amsterdam: North-Holland, 201-218.

Fishburn, Peter C. 1980. "Deducing Majority Candidates from Election Data." *Social Science Research* 9, no. 3 (Sept.):216-224.

Fishburn, Peter C. 1982. "An Analysis of Simple Voting Systems for Electing Committees." *SIAM Journal on Applied Mathematics* (in press).

Fishburn, Peter C., and Steven J. Brams. 1981a. "Expected Utility and Approval Voting." *Behavioral Science* 26, no. 2 (April):136-142.

Fishburn, Peter C., and Steven J. Brams. 1981b. "Approval Voting, Condorcet's Principle, and Runoff Elections." *Public Choice* 36, no. 1:89-114.

Fishburn, Peter C., and Steven J. Brams. 1981c. "Efficacy, Power and Equity in Approval Voting." *Public Choice* (in press).

Fishburn, Peter C., and Steven J. Brams. 1981d. "Deducing Simple Majorities from Approval Voting Data." *Social Science Research* 10:256-266.

Fishburn, Peter C., and William V. Gehrlein. 1979. "Majority Efficiencies for Simple Voting Procedures: Summary and Interpretation." Mimeographed.

Flinn, T. 1964. "Party Responsiveness in the States: Some Causal Factors." *American Political Science Review* (March).

Francis, W. 1967. *Legislative Issues in the Fifty States: A Comparative Analysis.* Chicago: Rand-McNally.

Frederickson, G. and Y.H. Cho. 1971. "Sixties Reapportionment: Is it Victory or Delusion?" *National Civic Review* 60 (Feb.):73-85.

Frederickson, G. and Y.H. Cho. 1974. "Legislative Apportionment and Fiscal Policy in the American States." *Western Political Quarterly* (March):18.

Friedrich, Carl J. 1950. *Constitutional Government and Democracy.* Boston: Ginn.

Fry, B.R. and R.F. Winters. 1970. "The Politics of Redistribution." *American Political Science Review* (June):522.

Furness, S.W. 1973. "The Response of the Colorado General Assembly to Proposals for Metropolitan Reform." *Western Political Quarterly* (Dec.):747-765.

Gilbert, Charles E. 1962. "Electoral Competition and Electoral Systems in Large Cities." *Journal of Politics* 24:323-347.

Gordon, Daniel N. 1968. "Immigrants and Urban Governmental Form in American Cities, 1933-1960." *American Journal of Sociology* 74:158-171.

Gosnell, Harold F. 1948. *Democracy, The Threshold of Freedom.* New York: Ronald Press.

Grofman, Bernard N. 1975. "A Review of Macro-Election Systems." In Rudolph Wildenmann (ed.), *German Political Yearbook (Sozialwissenschaftliches Jahrbuch fur Politik)* 4, Munich: Verlag, 303-352.

Grofman, Bernard N. 1976. "Not Necessarily Twelve and Not Necessarily Unanimous: Evaluating the Impact of *Williams* v. *Florida* and *Johnson* v. *Louisiana.*" In Gordon Bermant, Charlan Nemeth, and Neil Vidmar (eds.), *Psychology and the Law: Research Frontiers.* Lexington: D.C. Heath, 149-168.

Grofman, Bernard N. 1981a. "Fair Apportionment and The Banzhaf Index." *American Mathematics Monthly* 88, no. 1:1-5

Grofman, Bernard N. 1981b. "Fair and Equal Representation." *Ethics* 91 (Apr.):477-485.

Grofman, Bernard N. 1982a. "Alternatives to Single-Member Plurality Districts: Legal and Empirical Issues." In B. Grofman, A. Lijphart, R. McKay, and H. Scarrow (eds.), *Representation and Redistricting Issues.* Lexington, Mass.: Lexington Books, D.C. Heath and Company.

Grofman, Bernard N. 1982b. "For Single-Member Districts Random Is Not Equal." In B. Grofman, A. Lijphart, R. McKay, and H. Scarrow (eds.), *Representation and Redistricting Issues.* Lexington, Mass.: Lexington Books, D.C. Heath and Company.

Grofman, Bernard N. 1982c. "Should Representatives Be Typical of Their Constituents?" In B. Grofman, A. Lijphart, R. McKay, and H. Scarrow (eds.), *Representation and Redistricting Issues.* Lexington, Mass.: Lexington Books, D.C. Heath and Company.

Grofman, Bernard N. and Howard Scarrow. 1978. "Game Theory and the U.S. Courts: One Man, One Vote, One Value." School of Social Sciences Research Report, Univ. of California, Irvine (Dec.).

Grofman, Bernard N. and Howard Scarrow. 1979. "*Iannucci* and Its Aftermath: Game Theory and Weighted Voting in the State of New York." In S. Brams, A. Schotter, and G. Schwodiauer (eds.), *Applied Game Theory*. Vienna: Springer-Verlag.

Grofman, Bernard N. and Howard Scarrow. 1980. "Mathematics, Social Science and the Courts: Two Case Studies." In Michael Saks and Charles Baron (eds.), *The Use/Nonuse/Misuse of Applied Social Research in the Courts*. Cambridge: Abt Associates, 117-127.

Grofman, Bernard N. and Howard Scarrow. 1981a. "The Riddle of Apportionment—Equality of What?" *National Civic Review* 70, no. 5 (May):242-254.

Grofman, Bernard N. and Howard Scarrow. 1981b. "Weighted Voting in New York County Government." *Legislative Studies Quarterly* 6, no. 2 (May):287-304.

Grove, S.K. 1973. "Policy Implications of Legislative Reorganization in Illinois." In J.A. Robinson (ed.), *State Legislative Innovation*. New York: Praeger.

Grumm, J.G. 1971. The Effects of Legislative Structure on Legislative Performance." In R.I. Hofferbert and I. Sharkansky (eds.), *State and Urban Politics: Readings in Comparative Public Policy*. Boston: Little, Brown.

Gudgin, Graham, and Peter J. Taylor. 1974. "Electoral Bias and the Distribution of Party Voters." *Transactions, Institute of British Geographers* 63 (Nov.):53-74.

Hallett, G.H., Jr. 1937, 1940. *Proportional Representation*. New York: Macmillan.

Halpin, Stanley A., Jr., and Richard L. Engstrom. 1973. "Racial Gerrymandering and Southern State Legislative Redistricting: Attorney General Determinations Under the Voting Rights Act." *Journal of Public Law* 22:37-66.

Hamilton, Charles V. 1974. "Streets and Courts." *The New York Times* (July 11).

Hamilton, Howard D. 1967. "Legislative Constituencies: Single Member Districts, Multi-Member Districts, and Floterial Districts." *Western Political Quarterly* 20:321-340.

Hamilton, Howard D. 1966. *Reapportioning Legislatures: A Consideration of Criteria and Computers*. Columbus, Ohio: Charles Merrill.

Hamm, K.E., R. Harmel, and R.J. Thompson. 1979. "The Impact of Districting on County Delegation Cohesion in Southern State Legislatures:

A Comparative Analysis of Texas and South Carolina." Paper read at the Southern Political Science Association Annual Meeting in Gatlinburg, Tenn.

Hand, G., J. Georgel, and C. Sasse (eds.) 1979. *European Electoral Systems Handbook*. London: Butterworths.

Hansard Society Commission. 1976. *The Report of the Hansard Society Commission on Electoral Reform*. London: Hansard Society for Parliamentary Government.

Hanson, Roger A. and Robert E. Crew. 1973. "The Policy Impact of Reapportionment." *Law and Society Review* 8 (Feb.):69-93.

Hardy, Leroy C. 1977. "Considering the Gerrymander." *Pepperdine Law Review* 4 (Spring):243-284.

Hardy, Leroy C., Alan Heslop, and Stuart Anderson (eds.). 1981. *Reapportionment Politics: The History of Redistricting in the 50 States*. Beverly Hills: Sage.

Hardy, Richard J. and Kathryn N. Harmon. 1979. "The Impact of Reapportionment on Policy Expenditures: A Quasi-Experimental Time-Series Analysis, 1957-1977." Paper read at Midwest Political Science Association Annual Meeting, Chicago. April.

Havard, W.C. and L.P. Beth. 1962. *The Politics of Misrepresentation*. Baton Rouge: Louisiana State Univ. Press.

Hawkins, Brett W. 1971. "Consequences of Reapportionment in Georgia." In R.I. Hofferbert and I. Sharkansky (eds.), *State and Urban Politics*. Boston: Little, Brown.

Heath, Robert and Joseph H. Melrose, Jr. 1972. *Pennsylvania Reapportionment: A Study in Legislative Behavior*. New York: National Municipal League.

Heilig, Peggy. 1978. "The Abandonment of 'Reform' in a Southern City: Outcomes of a Return to District Politics." Paper read at Midwest Political Science Association Annual Meeting. April, Chicago.

Heilig, Peggy and Robert J. Mundt. 1980. "Urban Racial Mix and Demands for District Representation." Paper read at Southern Political Science Association Annual Meeting, November, Atlanta.

Heilig, Peggy and Robert J. Mundt. 1981. "Do Districts Make a Difference?" *Urban Interest* (April).

Heslop, Alan. 1978. *Redistricting: Key to the Politics of the 1980s*. Claremont, Calif.: Rose Institute of State and Local Government, Claremont College.

Heslop, Alan. 1979. *Redistricting: Shaping Government for a Decade*. Claremont, Calif.: Rose Institute of State and Local Government, Claremont College.

Hinich, Melvin and Peter Ordeshook. 1974. "The Electoral College: A Spatial Analysis." *Political Methodology* 1, no. 3 (Summer):1-30.

Hoag, Clarence G. and George H. Hallett, Jr. 1926. *Proportional Representation*. New York: Macmillan (Reprinted in 1969.).

Hofeller, Thomas Brooks. 1979. *Redistricting: Shaping Government for a Decade*. Claremont, Calif.: Rose Institute of State and Local Government, Claremont College.

Hofeller, Thomas Brooks. 1980. *Redistricting Technology: An Overview*. Claremont, Calif.: Rose Institute of State and Local Government, Claremont College.

Hofferbert, R. 1966. The Relation Between Public Policy and Some Structural and Environmental Variables in the American States." *American Political Science Review* (March):73-82.

Hoffman, Dale T. 1979a. "Mathematics and Voting: Approval Voting is Better." Mimeographed.

Hoffman, Dale T. 1979b. "Relative Efficiency of Voting Systems: The Cost of Sincere Behavior." Mimeographed.

Hoffman, Dale T. 1982. "A Model for Strategic Voting." *SIAM Journal on Applied Mathematics* (in press).

Hogan, J. 1945. *Election and Representation*. Cork: Cork Univ. Press.

Huber, C.H. 1979. "Legislation for European Elections in the Nine." In G. Hand, J. Georgel, and C. Sasse (eds.), *European Electoral Systems Handbook*. London: Butterworths, 234-252.

Huntington, E.V. 1931. "Methods of Apportionment in Congress." *American Political Science Review* 25 (Nov.):961-965.

Imrie, R.W. 1973. "The Impact of the Weighted Vote on Representation in Municipal Governing Bodies of New York State." In Lee Papaganopoulos (ed.), *Democratic Representation and Apportionment*. A special issue of the *Annals of the New York Academy of Science* 219 (Nov.9):192-199.

Jacob, H. 1964 "The Consequences of Malapportionment: A Note of Caution." *Social Forces* (Dec.):260.

Jacob, H. and K.N. Vines (eds.). 1965. *Politics in the American States, a Comparative Analysis*. Boston: Little, Brown.

Jewell, Malcolm (ed.). 1962. *The Politics of Reapportionment*. New York: Atherton Press.

Jewell, Malcolm. 1962. *The State Legislature: Politics and Practice*. New York: Random House.

Jewell, Malcolm. 1966. "The Political Setting." In A. Heard (ed.), *State Legislatures in American Politics*. Englewood Cliffs, N.J.: Prentice-Hall.

Jewell, Malcolm. 1969. *Metropolitan Representation: State Legislative Districting in Urban Counties*. New York: National Municipal League.

Jewell, Malcolm. 1970. "Commentary on 'The Court, The People, and

'One-Man, One-Vote.' " In Nelson Polsby (ed.), *Reapportionment in the 1970s*. Berkeley: Univ. of California Press, 46-52.

Jewell, Malcolm. 1979. "Toward a New Model of Legislative Representation." *Legislative Studies Quarterly* 4, no. 4 (Nov.): 485-500.

Jewell, Malcolm. 1980. "The Consequences of Legislative Districting in Four Southern States." Paper read at Citadel Symposium on Southern Politics, Charleston.

Jewell, Malcolm. 1982. "The Consequences of Single- and Multimember Districting." In B. Grofman, A. Lijphart, B. McKay, and H. Scarrow (eds.), *Representation and Redistricting Issues*. Lexington, Mass.: Lexington Books, D.C. Heath and Company.

Johnston, Ronald J. 1976. Spatial Structure, Plurality Systems and Electoral Bias." *Canadian Geographer* 20, no. 3:310-325.

Johnston, Ronald J. 1976. "Parliamentary Seat Redistribution: More Opinions on the Theme." *Area* 8:30-34.

Johnston, Ronald J. 1981. *Political, Electoral, and Spatial Systems*. Oxford: Oxford Univ. Press.

Jones, Bryan D. 1976. "Distributional Considerations in Models of Government Service Provision." Paper read at Southwest Political Science Association Meeting, April, Dallas.

Jones, Clinton. 1968. "The Impact of Local Election Systems on Black Political Apportionment." *American Political Science Review* 62 (March):205-207.

Kaiser, Henry R. 1966. "An Objective Method for Establishing Legislative Districts." *Midwest Journal of Political Science* 10:200-213.

Kaiser, Henry R. 1968. "A Measure of the Population Equality of Legislative Apportionment." *American Political Science Review* 62 (March):205-207.

Karnig, Albert K. 1976. "Black Representation on City Councils: The Impact of District Elections and Socioeconomic Factors." *Urban Affairs Quarterly* 12, no. 2 (Dec.):223-241.

Karnig, Albert K. 1979. "Black Resources and City Council Representation." *Journal of Politics* 41, 2 (Feb.):134-149.

Karnig, Albert K. and Susan Welch. 1978. "Electoral Structure and Black Representation on City Councils. An Updated Examination." Paper read at Midwest Political Science Association Annual Meeting, April, Chicago.

Karnig, Albert K. and Susan Welch. 1979. "Sex and Ethnicity in Municipal Representation." *Social Science Quarterly* 69, no. 3 (Dec.).

Katz, R.S. 1980. *A Theory of Parties and Electoral Systems*. Baltimore: Johns Hopkins Univ. Press.

Keech, W.R. 1968. *The Impact of Negro Voting: The Role of the Vote in the Quest for Equality*. Chicago: Rand McNally.

Keefe, W.J. and M.S. Ogul. 1964. *The American Legislative Process*. Englewood Cliffs, New Jersey: Prentice-Hall.

Kellett, John, and Kenneth Mott. 1977. "Presidential Primaries: Measuring Popular Choice." *Polity* 9 (Summer):528-537.

Kelley, S., Jr., R.E. Ayres, and W.G. Bowen. 1967. "Registration and Voting: Putting First Things First." *American Political Science Review* 61:359-375.

Kendall, M.G. and A. Stuart. 1950. "The Law of Cubic Proportions in Electoral Results." *British Journal of Sociology* 1 (September):183-197.

Key, V.O. 1932. "Procedures in State Legislative Apportionment." *American Political Science Review* 26:1050-1058.

Key, V.O. 1956. *American State Politics: An Introduction*. New York: Knopf.

Kiewiet, D. Roderick. 1979. "Approval Voting: The Case of the 1968 Election." *Polity* 12 (Fall):170-181.

Kirkpatrick, J.J. 1974. "Representation in National Political Conventions: The Case of 1972." Paper read at American Political Science Association Annual Meeting.

Kirkpatrick, J.J. 1975. "Representation in American National Conventions: The Case of 1972." *British Journal of Political Science* 5 (July):265-322.

Klain, Maurice. 1955. "A New Look at the Constituencies: A Recount and a Reappraisal." *American Political Science Review* 49:1105-1119.

Koury, E.M. 1976. *The Crisis in the Lebanese System: Confessionalism and Chaos*. Washington, D.C.: American Enterprise Institute for Public Policy Research.

Kuklinski, James H. 1973. "Cumulative and Plurality Voting: An Analysis of Illinois's Unique Electoral System." *Western Political Quarterly* 26 (Dec.):726-746.

Kuklinski, James H. 1978. "Representativeness and Elections: A Policy Analysis." *American Political Science Review* 72 (March):165-177.

Kuklinski, James, H. 1979. "Representative-Constituency Linkages, A Review Article." *Legislative Studies Quarterly* 4, no. 1. (Feb.)

Lakeman, Enid. 1974. *How Democracies Vote, A Study of Electoral Systems*. 4th ed. London: Faber and Faber.

LaPonce, J.A. 1957. "The Protection of Minorities by the Electoral System." *Western Political Quarterly* 10 (July):318-339.

Latimer, Margaret. 1979. "Black Political Representation in Southern Cities." *Urban Affairs Quarterly* 15 (Sept.):65-86.

Lee, Eugene C. 1960. *The Politics of Nonpartisanship*. Berkeley: Univ. of California Press.

Lehne, Richard. 1972. *Reapportionment of the New York Legislature: Impact and Issues*. New York: National Municipal League.

Lembke, Bud. 1979. "A Proposal for Ballot-Box 'Stuffing,' " *Los Angeles Times*, (May 12).

Lengle, James I. 1981. *Representation and Presidential Primaries: The Democratic Party in the Post-Reform Era*. Westport, Conn: Greenwood.

Lengle, James I. 1982. "Participation, Representation, and Democratic Party Reform." In B. Grofman, A. Lijphart, R. McKay, and H. Scarrow (eds.) *Representation and Redistricting Issues*. Lexington, Mass.: Lexington Books, D.C. Heath and Company.

Lieske, Joel and Jan Hillard. 1979. "The Racial Factor in Urban Elections." Paper read at Southern Political Science Association Annual Meeting, November 1-3, Gatlinburg, Tenn.

Lijphart, Arend. 1969. *Politics in Europe: Comparisons and Interpretations* (ed.), Englewood Cliffs, N.J.: Prentice-Hall.

Lijphart, Arend. 1975. *The Politics of Accommodation: Pluralism and Democracy in the Netherlands*. Berkeley: Univ. of California Press, 2d ed.; Japanese translation, Tokyo: Iwanami Shoten.

Lijphart, Arend. 1977. *Democracy in Plural Societies: A Comparative Exploration*. New Haven: Yale Univ. Press; German translation, Wiesbaden: Westdeutscher Verlag; and Japanese translation, Tokyo: Sanichi Syoboo.

Lijphart, Arend. 1980. "Federal, Confederal, and Consociational Options for the South African Plural Society. In R.I. Rotberg and J. Barratt (eds.), *Conflict and Compromise in South Africa.*. Lexington, Mass.: Lexington Books, D.C. Heath and Company.

Lijphart, Arend. 1982. "Comparative Perspectives on Fair Representation: The Plurality-Majority Rule, Geographical Districting, and Alternative Electoral Arrangements." In B. Grofman, A. Lijphart, R. McKay, and H. Scarrow (eds.), *Representation and Redistricting Issues*. Lexington, Mass.: Lexington Books, D.C. Heath and Company.

Lijphart, Arend and R.W. Gibberd. 1977. "Thresholds and Payoffs in List Systems of Proportional Representation." *European Journal of Political Research* 5 (Sept.):219-244.

Lineberry, Robert L. and Edmund P. Fowler. 1967. "Reformism and Public Policies in American Cities." *American Political Science Review,* 61 no. 3 (Sept.):701-716.

Lockard, D. 1959. *New England State Politics*. Princeton: Princeton Univ. Press.

Lockard, D. 1969. *The Politics of State and Local Government*, 2d ed. New York: Macmillan.

Longley, Lawrence D. and Alan G. Braun. 1972. *The Politics of Electoral College Reform*. New Haven: Yale Univ. Press.

Loosemore, John and Victor J. Hanby. 1971. "The Theoretical Limits of Maximum Distortion: Some Analytic Expressions for Electoral System." *British Journal of Political Science* 1 (Oct.).

Lowell, A. Lawrence. 1921. *Public Opinion and Popular Government*. New York: Longmans, Green.

Lucas, William F. 1974, 1976. "Measuring Power in Weighted Voting Systems." Case Studies in Applied Mathematics. Mathematics Association of America, Module in Applied Mathematics, 1976. (Originally published as *Technical Report No. 227*, Department of Operations Research, College of Engineering, Cornell Univ., Ithaca (Sept.).

MacKenzie, W.J.M. 1958. *Free Elections: An Elementary Textbook*. London: Allen and Unwin.

Mackie, T.T. and R. Rose. 1974. *The International Almanac of Electoral History*. London: Macmillan.

MacManus, Susan A. 1976. "Determinants of the Equality of Female Representation on 243 City Councils." Paper read at American Political Science Association Annual Meeting, Sept., Chicago.

MacManus, Susan A. 1978. "City Council Election Procedures and Minority Representation: Are They Related?" *Social Science Quarterly 59,* no. 1 (June):153-161.

MacManus, Susan. 1979. "At-Large Elections and Minority Representation: An Adversarial Critique." *Social Science Quarterly* 60 (Sept.): 338-340.

March, James. 1957-59. "Party Legislative Representation as a Function of Election Results." *Public Opinion Quarterly* 21 (Winter):521-542.

Markowitz, Joseph C. 1978. "Constitutional Challenges to Gerrymanders." *University of Chicago Law Review* 45 (Summer):845-81.

Marshall, T.R. 1976. "Delegate Selection in Non-Primary States: The Question of Representation." *National Civic Review* (Sept.):390-393.

Mason, Alpheus T. 1965. *Free Government in the Making*, 3d ed. New York: Oxford Univ. Press.

Mayhew, David R. 1971. "Congressional Representation: Theory and Practice in Drawing the Districts." In Nelson Polsby (ed.), *Reapportionment in the 1970s*. Berkeley: Univ. of California Press.

Mayhew, David R. 1974. *Congress: The Electoral Connection*. New Haven: Yale Univ. Press.

Mayhew, David R. 1974. "Congressional Elections: The Case of the Vanishing Marginals." *Polity* 6, no. 3:295-317.

McGehee, John Michael 1979. "Reapportionment Commissions: The Reform We Don't Need." *State Legislatures* (Dec.):11-15.

McKay, Robert B. 1965. *Reapportionment: The Law and Politics of Equal Representation*. New York: Simon and Schuster.

McKay, Robert B. 1968. "Reapportionment: Success Story of the Warren Court." *Michigan Law Review* 67:223-36.

McKay, Robert B. 1982. "Affirmative Gerrymandering." In B. Grofman, A. Lijphart, R. McKay, and H. Scarrow (eds.), *Representation and Redistricting Issues*. Lexington, Mass.: Lexington Books, D.C. Heath and Company.

McRobie, A.D. 1978. "Ethnic Representation: The New Zealand Experience." In S. Levine (ed.), *Politics in New Zealand: A Reader*. Sydney: Allen and Unwin, 270-283.

Merrill, Samuel, III. 1979a. "Approval Voting." *New York Times* (July 20), Op-Ed Essay.

Merrill, Samuel, III. 1979b. "For Approval Voting." *New York Times* (July 20), Op-Ed Essay.

Merrill, Samuel, III. 1981. "Strategic Decisions under One-Stage Multi-Candidate Voting Systems." *Public Choice* 36, no. 1:115-134.

Mill, John Stuart. 1890, 1961, 1969. *Considerations on Representative Government*. London: Longmans, Green; reprint Bobbs-Merrill.

Miller, W.E. and D.E. Stokes. 1963. "Constituency Influence in Congress." *American Political Science Review* 57 (March):45-56.

Milnor, Andrew J. 1970. *Stability and Representation: Legislative Electoral Systems*. New York: Little, Brown.

Morrill, Richard L. 1973. "Ideal and Reality in Reapportionment." *Annals of the Association of American Geographers* 63, no. 4 (Dec.):463-477.

Mundt, Robert J. 1979. "Referenda in Charlotte and Raleigh, and Court Action in Richmond: Comparative Studies on the Revival of District Representation." Paper read at the American Political Science Association Annual Meeting. Sept., Chicago.

Murray, W. Richard and Donald S. Lutz. 1974. "Redistricting Decisions in the American States: A Test of the Minimal Winning Coalition Hypothesis." *American Journal of Political Science* (May):233-256.

Musgrove, Philip. 1977. *The General Theory of Gerrymandering*. Sage Professional Papers in American Politics 3:04-034. Beverly Hills and London: Sage Publications.

Nagel, Stuart S. 1965. "Simplified Bipartisan Computer Redistricting." *Stanford Law Review* 17:863-899.

Nagel, Stuart S. 1972. "Computers and the Law and Politics of Redistricting." *Policy* 5.

Navasky, Victor S. 1977. *Kennedy Justice*. New York: Atheneum.

Neels, L. 1979. "Preparations for Direct Elections in Belgium, Part II." *Common Market Law Review* 16 (May):243-249.

Neighbor, Howard D. 1980. *City Council Districting in the 1980s*. New York: National Municipal League.

A New Government for Atlantic City: A Strong Mayor—Strong Council Plan. 1979. Philadelphia: Government Study Group, Department of Political Science, Univ. of Pennsylvania.

Niemi, Richard G. 1982. "The Effects of Districting on Trade-Offs Among Party Competition, Electoral Responsiveness, and Seats-Votes Relationships." In B. Grofman, A. Lijphart, R. McKay, and H. Scarrow (eds.), *Representation and Redistricting Issues.* Lexington, Mass.: Lexington Books, D.C. Heath and Company.

Niemi, Richard G. and John Deegan, Jr. 1978. "A Theory of Political Districting." *American Political Science Review* 72 (Dec.):1304-1323.

Nohlen, D. 1978. *Wahlsysteme der Welt: Daten und Analysen.* Munich: Piper.

Note: 1976. "Proportional Representation By Race: The Constitutionality of Benign Racial Redistrictions," *Michigan Law Review* 74:820-841.

Note: 1978. "Group Representation and Race-Conscious Apportionment: The Roles of the States and the Federal Courts." *Harvard Law Review* 91.

O'Loughlin, John. 1979. "Black Representation Growth and the Seat-Vote Relationship." *Social Science Quarterly* 60 (June):72-86.

O'Rourke, Terry, B. 1972. *Reapportionment: Law, Politics, Computers.* American Enterprise Institute, Washington, D.C.

O'Rourke, Timothy. 1980. *The Impact of Reapportionment.* New Brunswick, New Jersey: Transaction Books.

Orren, G. 1976. "The 1976 Presidential Primaries." Unpublished paper.

Papayanopoulos, Lee (ed.). 1973. *Democratic Representation and Apportionment.* Special issue of *Annals of the New York Academy of Sciences* 219 (Nov. 9).

Papayanopoulos, Lee 1973. "Quantitative Principals Underlying Apportionment Methods." In Lee Papayanopoulos (ed.), *Democratic Representation and Apportionment.* Special issue of the *Annals of the New York Academy of Sciences* 219:181-191.

Papayanopoulos, Lee. 1982. "Compromise Districting." In B. Grofman, A. Lijphart, R. McKay, and H. Scarrow (eds.), *Representation and Redistricting Issues.* Lexington, Mass.: Lexington Books, D.C. Heath and Company.

Parker, F. 1973. "County Redistricting in Mississippi: Case Studies in Racial Gerrymandering." *Mississippi Law Journal* 44:391.

Patterson, S.C. 1976. "American State Legislatures and Public Policy." In H. Jacob and K.N. Vines (eds.), *Politics in the American States,* 3d ed. Boston: Little, Brown.

Pennock, J.R. 1979. *Democratic Political Theory.* Princeton: Princeton Univ. Press.

Pennock, J.R. and J.W. Chapman (eds.). 1970. *Representation.* New York: Atherton Press.

Pitkin, Hannah F. 1967. *The Concept of Representation.* Berkeley: Univ. of California Press.

Polsby, Nelson W. (ed.). 1971. *Reapportionment in the 1970s.* Berkeley: Univ. of California Press.

Polsby, Nelson W. and R.B. McKay. 1973. "Reapportionment in the 1970s." *Columbia Law Review* 73, no. 1:170-175.

Pulsipher, A.G. and J.L. Weatherby. 1968. "Malapportionment, Party Competition, and the Functional Distribution of Government Expenditures." *American Political Science Review* (Dec.):1218.

Quandt, Richard. 1974. "A Stochastic Model of Elections in Two-Party Systems." *Journal of the American Statistical Association* (June): 315-324.

Quinn, T. Anthony. 1979. *Still Unequal—The Failure of the One Man-One Vote to Achieve Fair Representation,* Claremont, Calif.: Rose Institute of State and Local Government, Claremont College.

Rae, Douglas W. (1967, 1971) *The Political Consequences of Electoral Laws.* New Haven: Yale Univ. Press.

Rae, Douglas W. 1971. "Reapportionment and Political Democracy." In N. Polsby, (ed.), *Reapportionment in the 1970s.* Berkeley: Univ. of California Press.

Rae, Douglas, W., V. Hanby, and J. Loosemore (1971) "Thresholds of Representation and Thresholds of Exclusion: An Analytic Note on Electoral Systems." *Comparative Political Studies* 3 (Jan.):479-488.

Ranney, Austin. 1972. "Turnout and Representation in Presidential Primary Elections." *American Political Science Review* 66 (March):21-37.

Ranney, Austin. 1975. *Curing the Mischief of Faction: Party Reform in America.* Berkeley: Univ. of California Press.

Ranney, Austin. 1977a. *Participation in American Presidential Nominations, 1976.* Washington, D.C.: American Enterprise Institute.

Ranney, Austin. 1977b. "The Democratic Party's Delegate Selection Reforms, 1968-1976." In A.P. Sindler (ed.), *America in the Seventies.* Boston: Little, Brown.

Ranney, Austin. 1982. "Comments on Representation Within the Political Party System." In B. Grofman, A. Lijphart, R. McKay, and H. Scarrow (eds.), *Representation and Redistricting Issues of the 1980s.* Lexington, Mass.: Lexington Books, D.C. Heath and Company.

Rehfuss, John. 1972. "Are At-Large Elections Best for Council-Manager Cities?" *National Civic Review* 61 (May):236-241.

Rice, Stuart. 1928. *Quantitative Methods in Politics.* New York: Russell and Russell.

Robeck, Bruce W. 1970. "Urban-Rural and Regional Voting Patterns in the California Senate Before and After Reapportionment." *Western Political Quarterly* 23 (Dec.):785-794.

Robeck, Bruce W. 1972. "Legislative Partisanship, Constituencies, and Malapportionment: The Case of California." *American Political Science Review* 66:1246-1255.

Robeck, Bruce W. 1978. *Legislators and Party Loyalty: The Impact of Reapportionment in California.* Washington, D.C.: Univ. Press of America.

Roberts, G.K. 1977. "Point of Departure? The Blake Report on Electoral Reform." *Government and Opposition* 12 (Winter):42-59.

Robinson, Theodore P. and Thomas R. Dye. 1978. "Reformism and Black Representation on City Councils." *Social Science Quarterly* 59, no. 1 (June):133-141.

Rogowski, Ronald. 1981. "Representation in Political Theory and in Law: A Formal Analysis." *Ethics* 91, no. 3 (April):395-431.

Rokkan, Stein. 1968. "Elections: Electoral Systems." *International Encyclopedia of the Social Sciences.* New York: Crowell-Collier, Macmillan.

Rokkan, Stein. 1970. *Citizens, Elections, Parties: Approaches to the Comparative Study of the Processes of Development.* Oslo: Universitetsforlaget.

Rose Institute Staff. 1979. *California Redistricting.* Claremont, Calif.: Rose Institute of State and Local Government, Claremont College.

Rose Institute Staff. 1979. *1978 General Election: Analysis by Legislative District.* Claremont, Calif.: Rose Institute of State and Local Government, Claremont College.

Rose Institute Staff. 1979. *1980 Census and the "One Man-One Vote": Do We Yet Know What Fair Representation Is?* Claremont, Calif.: Rose Institute of State and Local Government, Claremont College.

Rose Institute Staff. 1979. *Redistricting in Illinois.* Claremont, Calif.: Rose Institute of State and Local Government, Claremont College.

Rose, R., and D. Urwin. 1969. "Social Cohesion, Political Parties and Strains and Regimes." *Comparative Political Studies* (Jan.):7-67.

Saffell, David C. 1982. "Reapportionment and Public Policy: State Legislators' Perspectives." In B. Grofman, A. Lijphart, R. McKay, and H. Scarrow (eds.), *Representation and Redistricting Issues.* Lexington, Mass.: Lexington Books, D.C. Heath and Company.

Salisbury, Robert H. and Gordon Black. 1963. "Class and Party in Partisan and Non-Partisan Elections." *American Political Science Review* 57 (Sept.):584-592.

Sankoff, David and Koulla Mellos. 1973. "La Regionalisation Electoral et l'Amplification des Proportions." *Canadian Journal of Political Science* 6 (Sept.): 380-398.

Sartori, Giovanni. 1968. "Political Development and Political Engineering."
In J.D. Montgomery and A.O. Hirschman (eds.), *Public Policy*
17:261-298. Cambridge: Harvard Univ. Press.

Sawyer, Jack and Duncan Macrae, Jr. 1962. "Game Theory and Cumulative Voting in Illinois 1902-1954." *American Political Science Review*
56:936-946.

Scarrow, Howard A. 1982. "The Impact of Reapportionment on Party
Representation in the State of New York." In B. Grofman, A. Lijphart, R. McKay, and H. Scarrow (eds.), *Representation and Redistricting Issues.* Lexington, Mass.: Lexington Books, D.C. Heath and
Company.

Schubert, Glendon A. (ed.). 1965. *Reapportionment.* New York: Scribner.

Schubert, Glendon and Charles Press, 1964. "Measuring Malapportionment." *American Political Science Review* (June):302-327.

Sickels, R.J. 1966. "Dragons, Bacon Strips, and Dumbbells: Who's Afraid
of Reapportionment." *Yale Law Journal* 75 (July):1300-1308.

Silva, Ruth C. 1964. "Compared Values of the Single and the Multi-
Member Legislative District." *Western Political Quarterly* 17
(Sept.):504-516.

Silva, Ruth C. 1964. "Relation of Representation and the Party System to
the Number of Seats Apportioned to a Legislative District." *Western
Political Quarterly* 17:742-769.

Sloan, Lee. 1969. "'Good Government' and the Politics of Race." *Social
Problems* 17, no. 2 (Fall):161-167.

Sloan, Lee and R.M. French. 1971. "Black Rule in the Urban South."
Transaction/Society 9 (Nov./Dec.).

Sokolow, A.D. 1976. "Legislative Pluralism, Committee Assignments, and
Internal Norms: The Delayed Impact of Reapportionment in Califor-
nia." In Y.H. Cho and H.G. Frederickson, *Measuring the Effects of
Reapportionment in the American States* 26. New York: National
Municipal League.

Soper, C.S. and Joan Rydon. 1958. "Underrepresentation and Electoral
Prediction." *Australian Journal of Politics and History* 4, no. 1
(Aug.).

Sorauf, F. 1962. *Party and Representation.* New York: Atherton.

Sperlich, Peter W. and Martin L. Jaspovice. 1979. "Methods for the
Analysis of Jury Panel Selections: Testing for Discrimination in a
Series of Panels." *Hastings Constitutional Law Quarterly* 6, no. 3 (Spr-
ing):787:852.

Still, Jonathan. 1981. "Political Equality and Election Systems."*Ethics*
91, (April).

Taagepera, Rein. 1973. "Seats and Votes: A Generalization of the Cube
Law of Elections." *Social Science Research* 2, (Sept.):257-275.

Taagepera, Rein and B. Grofman. 1981. "Effective Size and Number of Components." *Sociological Methods and Research* 10, no. 1 (August):63-81.

Taagepera, Rein and Markku Laakso. 1980. "Proportionality Profiles of West European Electoral Systems." *European Journal of Political Research* 8:423-446.

Taagepera, Rein and Markku Laakso. 1979. " 'Effective' Number of Parties: A Measure with Application to West Europe." *Comparative Political Studies* 12, no. 1 (April):3-27.

Taagepera Rein and J.L. Ray. 1977. "A Generalized Index of Concentration." *Sociological Methods and Research* 5:367-384.

Taebel, Delbert. 1978. "Minority Representation on City Councils: The Impact of Electoral Structure on Blacks and Hispanics." *Social Science Quarterly* 59 (June):142-152.

Taylor, Peter J. 1973. "A New Shape Measure for Evaluating Electoral Districts Patterns." *American Political Science Review* 67:947-950.

Taylor, Peter J. and Graham Gudgin. 1975. "A Fresh Look at the Parliamentary Boundary Commissions." *Parliamentary Affairs* 28:405-415.

Taylor, Peter J. and Graham Gudgin. 1976. "The Myth of Non-Partisan Cartography: A Study of the Electoral Biases in the English Boundary Commissions Redistribution for 1955-1970." *Urban Studies* 13 (Feb.):1325.

Taylor, Peter J. and Graham Gudgin. 1976. "The Statistical Basis of Decision-making in Electoral Districting." *Environment and Planning A* 8:43-58.

Taylor, Peter J. and Graham Gudgin. 1980. *Seats, Votes, and the Spatial Organization of Elections.* London: Pion.

Taylor, Peter J. and R.J. Johnston. 1978. "Population Distributions and Political Power in the European Parliament." *Regional Studies* 12:61-68.

Taylor, Peter J. and R.J. Johnston. 1979. *Geography of Elections.* Harmondsworth: Penguin Books.

Theil, H. 1969. "The Desire for Political Entropy." *American Political Science Review* 63.

Theil, H. 1970. "The Cube Law Revisited." *Journal of American Statistical Association* 65:1213.

Thernstrom, Abigail M. 1979. "The Odd Evolution of the Voting Rights Act." *The Public Interest* (Spring):49-76.

Toward Equality of Public Service. 1974. Report of the Conference on Public Service Equalization Litigation, May 16-17, 1974. Trinity Grants Program, New York.

Tribe, Lawrence. 1978. *American Constitutional Law.* Minneola, N.Y.: Foundation Press.

Tufte, Edward R. 1973. "The Relationship Between Seats and Votes in Two-Party Systems." *American Political Science Review* 67:540-554.

Tufte, Edward R. 1974. "Communication." *American Political Science Review* 68:211-213.

Tufte, Edward R. 1975. "Determinants of Midterm Congressional Elections." *American Political Science Review* 69:812-826.

Tyler, Gus and David I. Wells. 1962. "New York, Constitutionally Republican." In *The Politics of Reapportionment*. New York: Atherton, 221-248.

U.S. Commission on Civil Rights. 1975. *The Voting Rights Act: Ten Years After*. U.S. Government Printing Office.

Urwin, D.W. 1974. "Germany: Continuity and Change in Electoral Politics." In R. Rose (ed.), *Electoral Behavior: A Comparative Handbook*. New York: Free Press, 109-170.

Uslaner, Eric M. 1978. "Comparative State Policy Formation, Intraparty Competition, and Malapportionment: A New Look at V.O. Key's Hypothesis." *Journal of Politics* 40:409-432.

Uslaner, Eric M. and Ronald E. Weber. 1977. "Reapportionment, Gerrymandering, and Change in the Partisan Balance of Power in the American States." Paper read at American Political Science Association Annual Meeting, (Sept.), Chicago.

Van den Bergh, G. 1955. *Unity in Diversity: A Systematic Critical Analysis of All Electoral Systems*. London: Batsford.

Verba, S. and N.H. Nie. 1972. *Participation in America: Political Democracy and Social Equality*. New York: Harper and Row.

Wahlke, John C. 1982. "Logic and Politics in Electoral Engineering." In B. Grofman, A. Lijphart, R. McKay, and H. Scarrow (eds.), *Representation and Redistricting Issues*. Lexington, Mass.: Lexington Books, D.C. Heath and Company.

Walker, J. 1969. "The Diffusion of Innovations among American States." *American Political Science Review* (Sept.):886.

Washington, Robert B. 1971. "Does the Constitution Guarantee Fair and Effective Representation to All Interests Groups Making Up the Electorate?" *Harvard Law Journal* 17:91-130.

Weaver, James B. 1970. *Fair and Equal Districts: A How-To-Do-It Manual on Computer Use*. New York: National Municipal League.

Weaver, Leon and Carol A. Cassel. *Nonpartisanship in Local Elections*. National Municipal League, forthcoming.

Weaver, Warren, Jr. 1979. "New System Urged in Presidential Primary Voting." *New York Times* (April 13).

Weber, Robert J. 1978a. "Comparison of Voting Systems." Mimeographed.

Weber, Robert J. 1978b "Multiply-Weighted Voting Sytems." Mimeographed.

Weber, Robert J. 1978c "Reproducing Voting Systems." Mimeographed.

Weissberg, Robert. 1978. "Collective versus Dyadic Representation in Congress." *American Political Science Review* 72:535-547.

Weissberg, Robert. 1979. "Assessing Legislator-Constituency Policy Agreement." *Legislative Studies Quarterly* 4, no. 4 (Nov):605-622.

Welch, Susan. 1978. "Recruitment of Women to Public Office: A Discriminant, Analysis." *Western Political Quarterly* 31 (Sept.):372-380.

Welch, Susan and Albert Karnig. 1978. "Representation of Blacks on Big City School Boards." *Social Science Quarterly* 59:162-171.

Welch, Susan and Albert Karnig. 1979. "Correlates of Female Officeholding in City Politics." *Journal of Politics* 41, no. 2:478-491.

Wells, David I. 1972. "The Impact of Gerrymandering: The 1972 Elections." *American Federationist* 79 (Feb.):14-20.

Wells, David I. 1978a. "Affirmative Gerrymandering Compounds Districting Problems." *National Civic Review* (Jan.):10-17.

Wells, David I. 1978b. "Redistricting in New York State: It's a Question of Slicing the Salami." *Empire* (Oct./Nov.):9-13.

Wells, David I. 1979a. "The Reapportionment Game." *Empire* 5, no. 1 (Feb.):8-14.

Wells, David I. 1979b. Testimony at the Hearings before the Committee on Governmental Affairs of the U.S. Senate on S.596, Ninety-Sixth Congress, First Session, 529.

Wells, David I. 1982. "Against Affirmative Gerrymandering." In B. Grofman, A. Lijphart, R. McKay, and H. Scarrow (eds.), *Representation and Redistricting Issues*. Lexington, Mass.: Lexington Books, D.C. Heath and Company.

Wildavsky, Aaron. 1979. "Oh, Bring Back My Party To Me!" *The Public Interest* 57 (Fall):94-98.

Wildgen, John K. and Richard L. Engstrom. 1980. "Spatial Distribution of Partisan Support and the Seats/Votes Relationship." *Legislative Studies Quarterly* 5, no. 3 (Aug.):423-435.

Wolfinger, Raymond and John Osgood Field. 1966. "Political Ethos and the Structure of City Government." *The American Political Science Review* 60 (June):306-326.

Wollock, Andrea J. (ed.). 1980. *Reapportionment: Law and Technology*. Denver: National Conference of State Legislatures, June.

Young, Roy E. 1965. *The Place System in Texas Elections*. Austin: Institute of Public Affairs, University of Texas.

Zimmerman, Joseph F. 1978. "The Federal Voting Rights Act and Alternative Election Systems." *William and Mary Law Review* 19 (Summer): 621-660.

Court Cases

Arlington Heights v. *Metropolitan Housing Development Corporation* (1977) 429 U.S. 252

Baker v. *Carr* (1962) 369 U.S. 186

Beer v. *United States* (1976) S. Ct. 1357

Brown v. *Board of Education* (1954) 347 U.S. 483

Burns, Kilgarlin et al. v. *Hill* (1964) 386 U.S. 120

Burns v. *Richardson* (1966) 384 U.S. 73

Castaneda v. *Partida* (1977) 430 U.S. 482

Chapman v. *Meier* (1975) 420 U.S. 1

City of Mobile, Alabama v. *Bolden* (1980) 48 L.W. 4436

City of Petersburg, Virginia v. *United States* (1973) 410 U.S. 926

City of Richmond, Virginia v. *United States* (1975) 422 U.S. 358

City of Rome, Georgia v. *United States* (1979) 472 F. Supp. 221

Colegrove v. *Green* (1946) 328 U.S. 549

Connor v. *Johnson* (1971) 402 U.S. 690

David v. *Gamson* (1977) 553 F.2d 923

Dayton Board of Education v. *Brinkman* (1979) 61 L. Ed. 2d 720

East Carroll Parish School Board v. *Marshall* (1976) 424 U.S. 636

Fortson v. *Dorsey* (1965) 379 U.S. 433

Gaffney v. *Cummings* (1973) 412 U.S. 735

Gomillion v. *Lightfoot* (1960) 364 U.S. 339

Graham v. *Board of Supervisors of Erie County, New York* (1967) 267
     N.Y.S. 2d 383

Graves v. *Barnes* (1972) 343 F. Supp. 704

Graves v. *Barnes* (1974) 378 F. Supp. 640 W.D.

Gray v. *Sanders* (1963) 372 U.S. 368

Griggs v. *Duke Power Company* (1971) 401 U.S. 424

Guinn v. *United States* (1915) 238 U.S. 347

Hazelwood School District v. *United States* (1977) 433 U.S. 299

Hendrix v. *Joseph* (1977) 559 F.2d 1265

Iannucci v. *Board of Supervisors of Washington County, New York*
     (1967) 282 N.Y. 2d 502

Kirkpatrick v. *Preisler* (1969) 394 U.S. 526

Kirksey v. *Board of Supervisors of Hinds County, Mississippi* (1977) 554
     F.2d 139, 5th Cir.

Klahr v. *Williams* (1972) 339 F. Supp. 922 (D. Arizona)

Kruidenir v. *McCulloch* (1966) 142 N.W. 2d 355

Lucas v. *44th General Assembly of the State of Colorado* (1964) 377 U.S.
     713

Mahan v. *Howell* (1973) 410 U.S. 315

Myers v. *Anderson* (1915) 238 U.S. 368

Nevitt v. *Sides* (1978) 571 F.2d 209

Regents of the University of California v. *Bakke* (1978) 438 U.S. 365

Reynolds v. *Sims* (1964) 377 U.S. 533.

Robinson v. *Commissioners Court* (1974) 505 F.2d 674, 5th Cir.

Swann v. *Adams* (1967) 385 U.S. 440

United Jewish Organizations of Williamsburg v. *Carey* (1977) 430 U.S. 144

United Steelworkers of America v. *Weber* (1979) 61 L. Ed. 2d 480
Wallace v. *House* (1975) 515 F.2d 619, 5th Cir.
Washington v. *Davis* (1976) 426 U.S. 229
Wells v. *Rockefeller* (1969) 394 U.S. 542
Wesberry v. *Sanders* (1964) 376 U.S. 1
Whitcomb v. *Chavis* (1971) 403 U.S. 124
White v. *Regester* (1973) 412 U.S. 755
White v. *Weiser* (1973) 412 U.S. 783
Wright v. *Rockefeller (1964) 376 U.S. 52*
Zimmer v. *McKeithen (1973) 485 F.2d 1297*

Indexes

Index of Names

Index of Subjects

Index of Court Cases

About the Contributors

Carl A. Auerbach is professor of law at the University of Minnesota. He is the author of numerous articles in legal journals, including "The Reapportionment Cases—One Person, One Vote–One Vote, One Value," and "The Supreme Court and Reapportionment." He was a member of the Minnesota Governor's Reapportionment Commission from 1964 to 1966; a member of the Rules Commission of the Democratic National Committee from 1969 to 1972; and a member of the Minnesota State Constitutional Commission from 1971 to 1973, at which time he drafted a proposed constitutional amendment to create a bipartisan commission for legislative and congressional redistricting.

Charles H. Backstrom is professor of political science at the University of Minnesota. He is coauthor of "Issues in Gerrymandering: An Exploratory Measure of Partisan Gerrymandering Applied to Minnesota," which appeared in the *Minnesota Law Review*. He was a member of the Minnesota Governor's Bipartisan Commission on Reapportionment in 1964-1965. In 1972 he prepared data for the plaintiff's case in *Beens* v. *Erdahl* that resulted in court-drawn districts in Minnesota.

Gordon E. Baker is professor of political science at the University of California at Santa Barbara. His major research interests have centered on reapportionment and representation. He is author of three books (*Rural versus Urban Political Power, State Constitutions: Reapportionment, and The Reapportionment Revolution*) plus various articles and chapters in books. In 1975 he served as consultant to court-appointed masters charged by the California Supreme Court with the redistricting of the state's legislative and congressional districts.

Steven J. Brams is professor of politics at New York University. His major research is on voting systems, particularly approval voting. He is the author of three books (*Game Theory and Politics, Paradoxes in Politics: An Introduction to the Non-Obvious in Political Science,* and *The Presidential Election Game*) and many articles that have appeared in leading social-science journals. Articles, editorials, and news stories on approval voting and his efforts to get it implemented in New Hampshire and other states have appeared in newspapers such as *The New York Times* and *Los Angeles Times.*

Armand Derfner is a partner in the law firm of McClain and Derfner in Charleston, South Carolina. He is coauthor of the book, *Federal Review of Voting Changes: How To Use Section 5 of the Voting Rights Act,* and author of two articles in law journals on racial effects on voting. He has appeared before the federal bench and the U.S. Supreme Court in numerous reapportionment and voting cases and has testified before congressional committees on reapportionment and the Voting Rights Act.

Robert Dixon (1920–1980) was, until his untimely death, a Daniel Noyes Kirby Professor of Law at Washington University. His brief for the state of Connecticut in *Gaffney* v. *Cummings* formed the basis for the U.S. Supreme Court's ruling in that landmark case. His earlier articles on reapportionment, most notably "The Warren Court Crusade for the Holy Grail of One Man, One Vote" in the 1969 *Supreme Court Review,* have become classics—displaying remarkable prescience as to the reapportionment problems that would rise to haunt the courts in the 1970s and 1980s. His 1968 book, *Democratic Representation,* remains the basic source book for the complex issues and tangled history of reapportionment doctrine. Because of his involvement and intellectual leadership in redistricting and representation questions as lawyer, political scientist, and citizen activist, Robert Dixon became known as "Mr. Reapportionment." The editors of this book are proud to dedicate it to his memory.

Heinz Eulau is William Bennet Munro Professor and chair of the Department of Political Science at Stanford University. A former president of the American Political Science Association, he now chairs the Board of Overseers, National Election Studies, Center for Political Studies at the University of Michigan, and he serves as an associate director of the Inter-University Consortium for Political and Social Research. A member of the American Academy of Arts and Sciences, he is the author or coauthor of many books and articles, including *The Legislative System* (1962), *The Behavioral Persuasion in Politics* (1963), *Micro-Macro Political Analysis* (1969), *Labyrinths of Democracy* (1973), *Technology and Civility* (1977), and *The Politics of Representation* (1978). Since 1980 he has been editor of the journal *Political Behavior.*

Malcolm E. Jewell is professor of political science at the University of Kentucky. He edited *The Politics of Reapportionment* and has written articles and papers on topics such as problems of minority representation in the United States and other countries, legislative politics, and the consequences of reapportionment. He has worked on the development of district plans on the state and local level in Kentucky and has been working on a nine-state study of state legislative representation and how various districting arrangements affect actual representation of districts by legislators.

James I. Lengle is assistant professor of political science at Georgetown University. He is the author of *Representation and Presidential Primaries: The Democratic Party in the Post-Reform Era* and coeditor of *Presidential Politics: Readings on Nominations and Elections,* which includes his article "Demographic Representation in California's 1968 and 1972 Democratic Presidential Primaries."

Richard G. Niemi is professor of political science at the University of Rochester. His theoretical research has centered on the relationship between the percentage of votes won by a given party and the percentage of seats won by that party and on criteria for fair and effective representation. Among the articles he has written or coauthored are "A Theory of Political Districting" and "Competition, Responsiveness and the Swing Ratio."

Lee Papayanopoulous is a professor in the Rutgers Graduate School of Business Administration. He is active in voting and districting research. Since the late 1960s he has drawn up computerized reapportionment plans for about half of New York's county legislatures and appeared in court to explain and validate the plans. In 1972 he organized a conference entitled "Democratic Representation and Apportionment: Quantitative Methods, Measures, and Criteria," and he subsequently edited the proceedings for the special issue of the *Annals of the New York Academy of Science.* He serves as a consultant in combinatorial voting and districting.

Austin Ranney is a Resident Scholar of the American Enterprise Institute and author of numerous books and articles on American political parties and political institutions. Mr. Ranny has been involved with procedures to change the composition and modes of delegate selection for the parties' national nominating conventions and has published a book (*Curing the Mischiefs of Faction*) and several articles on the subject. He was a member of the Democratic Party's McGovern-Fraser Commission (1969-1972) and Winograd Commission (1975-1978). He is a past president of the American Political Science Association.

David C. Saffell is professor of political science at Ohio Northern University. He is the author of *State and Local Governments: Politics and Public Policy.* He participated in a summer seminar at the University of California, Santa Barbara, on the subject of direct democracy in 1979 and presented a paper on reapportionment at the Midwest Political Science Association in 1980.

John C. Wahlke is professor of political science at the University of Arizona. He has long been concerned with problems of representation, especially in legislative bodies. He is author of *The Politics of Representation* and coauthor of *The Legislative System* and several other articles on American politics in leading political-science journals. He is a past president of the American Political Science Association.

David Wells is associate director of the Political Science Department of the International Ladies Garment Workers Union. He is the author of numerous articles and essays on redistricting and malapportionment in publications such as *New Republic, Empire, National Civic Review,* and the AFL-CIO's *Federationist.* He was the plaintiff in *Wells* v. *Rockefeller* (1966–1970) and was advisor to the plaintiffs in *WMCA* v. *Lomenzo* (1964) and in several New York State court cases. He has been advisor to AFL-CIO COPE on redistricting and lectures frequently to academic, political, and trade-union groups on the subject of representation and apportionment.

About the Editors

Bernard Grofman is professor of political science and social psychology, School of Social Sciences, University of California at Irvine. His principal research is on mathematical models of collective decision making. He has written numerous articles that have appeared in leading social-science journals on subjects such as jury decision making, voter turnout, the political consequences of electoral laws, and law and social-science issues. He is also interested in political propaganda and political cartooning and satire.

Arend Lijphart is professor of political science at the University of California at San Diego. His fields of specialization are comparative politics (in particular, Western democratic states) and international relations, with a special interest in proportional representation. He is the author of three books—*The Trauma of Decolonization: The Dutch and West New Guinea, The Politics of Accommodation: Pluralism and Democracy in The Netherlands*, and *Democracy in Plural Societies: A Comparative Exploration*—and numerous articles in leading international journals on democratic theory and comparative electoral politics and election systems.

Robert B. McKay is a Senior Fellow at the Aspen Institute for Humanistic Studies and director of the Institute of Judicial Administration. He is the author of *Reapportionment: The Law and Politics of Equal Representation* and several monographs and articles in major law reviews on this topic and other legal and social-science topics. In 1966 he was the chair of the New York State Advisory Council on Reapportionment to the Legislature of the State of New York, and in 1969 he appeared before the Supreme Court in *Wells* v. *Rockefeller* to argue against a New York congressional districting plan.

Howard A. Scarrow is professor of political science at the State University of New York at Stony Brook, where he has taught since 1963. He is a specialist on comparative electoral politics and public administration at both the local and federal level and is author or coauthor of four books (including *Canada Votes* and *European Society and Politics*) and numerous articles in major political-science journals, including *Journal of Politics, World Politics,* and *Comparative Politics.*